D0821496

What people are saying . . .
about **50 - 50 at 50:**

"When most people are climbing into camper-vans or migrating to Florida, Robert Graham wants to burn brightly and selflessly. I love his view of life . . . as a flaming torch, lighting the way for future generations."

> –*Anita Roddick, OBE, founder of* The Body Shop

"A wonderful, inspirational and educational book, serious yet crafted with humor . . . destined to impact its readers in powerful -- even shamanic -- ways!"

> –*John Perkins, author of* The World Is As You Dream It, *and of* Psychonavigation

"50 - 50 at 50 sets a new benchmark for ethics, spirituality, and the old-fashioned idea of service to others in the business life. It is also a beautiful human story. I hope its message will inspire others to the same path."

> –*Riane Eisler, author of* The Chalice and the Blade, *and of* Sacred Pleasure

"Both in person and in his autobiography, Robert Graham embodies the three yogas of the Bhagavadgita -- thinking, action and love. An inspiring account of an admirable life."

> –*Robert McDermott, author of* The Essential Aurobindo *and President, California Institute of Integral Studies*

"50 - 50 at 50 is one of the most compelling personal accounts of life I have read . . . He is a master storyteller, a man of great wisdom, and a solid businessman with such an active and exciting spiritual life that it breaks open one's thinking into new realms of possibility and magic."

> –*Lynne Twist, co-founder of* The Hunger Project

"Most people will not cram so much into life as Robert Graham. Or, they will fill lives with wrong things. In *50 - 50*, read how a modern life can be richly lived."

> –*John O'Neil, author,* Paradox of Success, *and President of the Center for Leadership Renewal*

"An inspiring story . . . and a heart warming tale not only of the valuing of family, but also of the importance of involving one's family in the building of a better future."

> –*David Loye, author of* The Healing of a Nation, *and of* Darwin's Lost Theory

"*50 - 50 at 50* is evidence...that both women and men are stepping up to new levels of creative entrepreneurship, generosity, spiritual depth and inspired living..."

> –*Tracy Gary, founder, Resourceful Women, and donor-activist*

*W*as it the unusual events he experienced that caused Robert Graham, at age fifty, to devote 50% of his money, time and energy to helping others, or was it his turn toward a life of service that accelerated the unusual events? And of these unusual events, how does a typical businessman react to circumstances that might be described as...flights of fancy, hallucinations, chimera, clairvoyance and–dare we say it–even miracles?

This is the true story of a highly successful, conservative accountant/businessman who is increasingly drawn from the world of logic and linear thinking into the world of spirit. Yet in this brave new world, symbols, ritual and ancient wisdom do not replace the "bottom line" but become a complementary part of it.

At first confused and resistant, Robert Graham's initial steps into nonordinary reality are timid and halting. Then, gradually, he learns to listen to the song of life being sung to him. His steps carry him into a myriad of adventures, beautiful and profound, from headhunters in a tropical rain forest to the child-incarnation of a high Tibetan Lama.

The author discovers, to his great joy, that life truly begins in the Golden Years. Then, in living it to the fullest, he voluntarily takes upon himself the most solemn of vows: to devote his life in service to all inhabitants of the Creation, and never to accept heaven (or paradise or *nirvana*) for himself until all other sentient beings achieve it.

Drawing on his unusually broad and varied experiences, Robert Graham offers the reader, especially businesspersons like himself, insights and suggestions that are as practical as they are profound. He invites the reader to enter a world...or is it an attitude... by "going just beyond."

Warning! Once entered, the world described and experienced by Robert Graham is highly addictive. You will never want to leave it.

To Jamie + Frank

Many blessings,

Robert Graham

About the Author

Robert E. Graham has had careers as a Certified Public Accountant, as co-founder of a large California food processing company, and in philanthropy and volunteer work. He is the founder of the Katalysis North/South Development Partnership which assists over ten thousand women's community banking members in Central America, and of Namaste, a family foundation.

Graham is a frequent speaker on the transformative potential of volunteerism, philanthropy, and family foundations, and on the possibility of ending poverty in the world through microcredit. He is also working towards a Master's degree in Philosophy, Cosmology and Consciousness at the California Institute of Integral Studies.

He lives with his wife, Wendy, in Carmel, California: their six children are scattered throughout the United States.

50-50 at 50

...Going Just Beyond!

by

Robert E. Graham

Library of Congress Catalog Card Number: 97-73568

ISBN 0-9660347-0-8

Dedication

To Barbara and Wendy
The two loves of my life

To you I have said my love little enough; and
yet all the heart requires. How the world gives
and takes away, and brings sweethearts near,
sometimes only to separate them again into
distant lands; but to love is the great amulet
which makes the world a garden; and hope,
which comes to all, outwears the accidents of
life.

(Paraphrased from Robert Louis Stevenson,
Travels With a Donkey in the Cévennes.)

Acknowledgments

I would like to acknowledge the assistance that David Loye and Colin Ingram provided me in writing this book. David, an accomplished author, provided me with early encouragement and followed my progress with great interest and continuing counsel. (Busy Bob, my alter ego, was created at David's suggestion.) Colin also played a very special role in the book. He first served as my writing coach, critiquing my efforts, and delivering numerous teachings and instructions along the way. He helped bring Busy Bob to life. Finally, he served as the editor of the book. My deepest appreciation goes to both David and Colin.

And there was my family, patiently reading my drafts or listening to me read them, offering encouragement and support, convinced that I was indeed working on a book of great import. Wendy, Carin, Merede, Lara, Sarah, Laura and Michael, and my mother, Margy Graham; you all have my thanks and love!

Several people read sections of the book, and I appreciate their willingness to contribute a part of themselves to my undertaking. They include, in addition to my family, Dino Cortopassi, Roy Williams, Dr. Roger Mills, Syd Banks, Fr. Charlie Moore, Ram Dass, Richard Weingarten, Jeremy Tarcher, Ramona Nason, John Perkins, Carlos Santos, Dr. Hector Prestera, Dr. Jerry Wycker, Stuart Miller and Little Bear Nason.

Any my thanks go to Robert Willett for providing the beautiful cabin in Big Sur, where the most creative parts of the book writing took place.

CONTENTS

PREFACE

What dictates the major episodes and changes in our lives? Are they preordained? Sometimes, so much seems to hang on a simple decision. Like the one I made back in 1983. It was a spring morning and I was sitting in my office reading the Wall Street Journal. The sun drifted in a sort of yellowish haze onto the patio next to my office. From my desk I could see golden Japanese carp swimming in a small pool. Things were peaceful; my phone was silent and nothing demanded my immediate attention. I noted a story about a successful businessman working with poor people in his community. I was fascinated by the account of his exposure to people living in deplorable conditions, and how he had taken up their cause, spending substantial time and money in helping them acquire better housing. His friends had mixed feelings about his activities, some of them wondering if the fellow was "losing it." To many others, though, he was something of a hero.

When I finished the article I put down the paper and stared out at the patio. I saw the sun play on the water and the fish. My mind seemed to stop. Suddenly, an idea came over me: "I want to be my own hero!" I repeated the thought to myself, slowly: "I—want—to—be—my—own—hero!" I didn't know exactly what that meant, but was I excited! I felt like I had been shown a map of buried treasure.

I kept the idea to myself for several months and, although unspoken, it became more firmly lodged in my psyche. Sometime that fall, Dino Cortopassi, my business partner, stuck his head in my door. "Hey Bob! Ready for a break?"

"Sure, come on in." We chatted about business matters until he said, "How are things in your life?"

"They're going pretty well. Wendy is a marvel and the kids are doing okay. We have our ups and downs, but mostly ups. You know, Dino, I've been thinking about things a little further down the road." I paused, considering what I wanted to say. It was about change, big change, and I felt tense. Finding no way to sugar coat it, I blurted, "I want to get involved in some sort of service project— you know, helping other people. I want to spend real time at it, like half my time. But I don't want to completely give up my work. I would still be here half time. I don't know if that would work out..." My voice trailed off. I anxiously studied Dino's face, which had seemed to darken.

"When?" he asked.

"Beginning in '86. I'll be fifty then. That feels right to me." Dino lapsed into silence. Then I saw his face lighten and his chin came up.

"So, it's 50-50 at 50, eh?" He couldn't suppress a chuckle over his clever turn of phrase. Greatly relieved, I echoed his words, delighted with the image they created. "Yes, it's 50-50 at 50!"

• • • • • • • • • • • •

It was probably no coincidence, although it was surely unexpected, that when my focus started to shift towards the plight of the rest of humanity, I began having unusual experiences. Soon I, a conservative, straight-laced businessman, now turned social entrepreneur[1] was receiving messages and teachings through my intuition. More came through meditation. And then they came through visions, spontaneous regressions and especially in dreams.

How should I deal with them? The value of these experiences became so apparent, so profound, I could not dismiss them. As I gained more confidence in them, I consciously chose to integrate them into my everyday life, into the world of business, logic and linear thought.

The result has been a marvelous fit and, I believe, has produced some benefits to myself, to those near me and to the world.

• • • • • • • • • • • •

I did not always see it this way. When I was a young man, a Certified Public Accountant and junior partner in a prestigious CPA firm, with a new bride and a new house, I thought "personal growth" was a term of the past, not of the future. After all, personal growth, like physical growth, is usually thought to belong only to the young. How often is it said about an attractive, energetic, inquisitive twenty-some year old, "What a fine person they've become! Their parents should be proud of their good work."

We hear these remarks made as if the young woman or man had become a fixed being, grown intellectually, psychologically and physically to full maturity, or nearly so. Oh sure, there is some professional growth expected and, yes, there are some psychologically expanding experiences to come, mostly through marriage and parenting. But essentially these young people are seen as fully formed, with just a few rough edges to be knocked off here and some polishing required there.

That was my belief at age twenty-seven, but it wasn't true! The most wonderful surprise of my life has been to learn how wrong I was. My Golden Age of personal development began after I made the decision to devote half my time and resources to service and giving at the age of fifty, while continuing to work and maintain my present life in the remainder.

I believe that in my decision to begin a life of service—and giving far more of myself and my resources than I or my contemporaries would have ever believed to be prudent, or even possible—I became personally whole. This newfound sense of completeness became the bedrock of my existence.

From my present vantage point of sixty years, I now surmise that my personal development and the richness of my life in the last ten years has been greater than in any other ten year period of my life! I suspect this fulfillment is available to everyone else who is open to it. So I want to shout out to everyone in their forties, fifties, sixties, seventies and beyond—"Your Golden Age has yet to come! It's waiting for you!"

This book is my attempt to help you find it.

1. Social entrepreneurs are people who have had successful business careers, built profitable enterprises, and who decide, at some point, to transfer their business expertise to the charitable sector. So they're still doing business, it's just for the benefit of others rather than themselves. For example, they might have an idea of an initiative that will help their community, and they start something. Or they get hooked up with an existing cause that can really use their

entrepreneurial drive. Either way they give of themselves...and contribute money as well.

I've been fortunate to meet quite a number of social entrepreneurs, some of whom also use descriptive phrases like my 50-50 at 50. One, Bob Buford, started the Social Entrepreneurs Initiative. He wrote a book called *Half-Time*, in which he asserts that mid-way through one's life is an opportunity point for business and professional people to begin devoting substantial amounts of their time and talent to making the world a better place.

Another friend, Dave Ellis, uses a great metaphor for his vision, as well. He determined that he wanted to "be able to pay the rent by noon," meaning that he could cover his material needs by working until noon each day, and then have the afternoons free for service projects. He accomplished that goal, and more.

Note the congruence of my 50-50, Bob's Half-Time, and Dave's splitting his day in two. There's something magical in sharing half of ourselves with the world!

1

MEMORIES

My mother's face flashed before me. I imagined her as I had seen her last Sunday. Her skin was weathered and deeply-lined, but the lines were those of kindness and understanding. At eighty, Margy's memory was a bit rusty, but I decided to try it out. In my mind I could hear her reminiscing.

"Max Graham and I were married in 1935, when we were students at the University of Nebraska. Bobby, I've always called him, was born in Omaha in 1936. That was during what everybody called the Great Depression. He was the oldest of our three children. His brother, Dick, came two years later and their sister, Mary, seven years after that.

"I've noticed he's always been interested in money and saving, and I suppose it had something to do with the Depression. The war came along and times got better in 1942, but our family—parents, grandparents, aunts and uncles—carried on with something called the 'depression mentality' for decades after that. I guess we passed on to him the virtues of 'hard work,' 'saving for a rainy day,' 'frugality,' that sort of thing. So he began working and saving at a very young age.

"For years he delivered The Des Moines Register every day in our small hometown of Red Oak, Iowa. Iowa has some very ornery weather in the winter, and his remembrances of delivering papers on his bike in rain, sleet and snow have now reached mythic proportions, I can tell you. He's completely forgotten about the times I took him in the car when it was cold and snowing at 6 a.m.

"When Bobby got older, he was an apprentice—what they called a 'printer's devil' back then—at The Sun. He made lead 'pigs' to feed the Linotype machine, worked on the printing presses, wrote stories covering high school athletics and generally made himself useful. It must have been interesting down there at The Sun. It was an old-fashioned weekly newspaper that hadn't changed much since the turn of the century.

"He seemed to like the feel of newspaper work. I remember him talking about the rhythmic sound of the printing press, the melody made by the keys dropping down through the Linotype machine, the smell of new paper and the look of fresh black ink. He said he even liked the times when molten lead spit on him from its cauldron. He said the sight of burn marks on his arms and the silvery lead embedded in his jeans made him feel good, like a man with a real job. I sure didn't appreciate trying to wash that lead out of his jeans! For a while he considered a career in journalism, no doubt influenced by his dad having majored in that subject during his two years of college.

"During the summers, Bobby worked for my brother on the wheat ranch I grew up on in southwestern Nebraska. He loved those five summers with his Uncle Windy and Aunt June, said they were like his 'second parents.' He would come home in the fall with stories of learning how to drive an army surplus jeep, of being responsible for the grain elevator, of gorging on fried chicken, and of home made ice cream with strawberries that he had gathered. And he once talked of feeling 'the lovely solitude' of driving a diesel tractor and one-way plow down half-mile rows for days at a time, and the satisfaction that came with sweat and exhaustion from a day's hard work. Bobby seemed to think it was all great fun, and I reckon some of it was. Myself, I was glad to get away from that country and all that work, though. I can sure tell you that!"

● ● ● ● ● ● ● ● ● ● ●

I've begun to explore my family tree in the past few years, having had little interest before that. Previously I'd been a captive of the American Dream, where all things of value lie in the future, just awaiting the actions of an endless stream of todays for realization. When my children began asking me questions about their grandparents and great grandparents, I could see that I had failed to deliver to them the stories, legends and inspiration of their roots. My childhood preceded television and back then families entertained themselves with stories of ancestral memories.

While my exploration is not yet complete, I do know that my Graham blood came to the U.S. about 150 years ago when a newly-married, male Graham and female Campbell from two of the principal clans of Scotland arrived in New York City. It was undoubtedly a migration the like of which is portrayed in romantic novels, given that the Grahams and the Campbells had been warring fiercely since the 1600s. On my mother's side, the Skeltons sailed from Sweden to the U.S. over 300 years ago to "Charles Towne" in what is now South Carolina.

Like so many immigrants, successive generations of both the Grahams and Skeltons gradually made their way West, with my ancestors' restlessness finally satisfied in what is now Nebraska. There is speculation that the arrival in Nebraska sparked the introduction of Lakota Sioux blood into my lineage, and, if so, I proudly claim it.

My male ancestors were pioneers, bull-whackers, farmers and small town merchants. They were all moderately successful (oh, I'm sure there must have been a black sheep or two), but only after many struggles. There have been few public figures of note. There was a turn-of-the-century great uncle Robert Graham, who was a successful grain mill operator and Mayor of Lincoln, Nebraska's capital. More famous was a shirt-tail great-great aunt, Florence Nightingale, whom many recall of when they think of pioneer nurses. Further down the shirt tail is the comic Red Skelton—famous in my time, but completely out of my children's sphere of recognition.

While there were a few farms that passed from generation to generation, the cycles of crop failures and commodity busts usually prevented any significant accumulation of capital in my ancestry. What did accumulate was a succession of Grahams and Skeltons farming in their respective areas of East and West Nebraska—stretching back for the last 120 years for the Grahams and 110 years for the Skeltons.

Few of my ancestors had steady incomes. The family upkeep was done from a system of allowances doled out from a stash of working capital. Whenever the working capital hoard had more than several months allowance needs, something was acquired. A few more acres, a piece of equipment, or if it was absolutely necessary, something for the house. As one might surmise, the men in my ancestry ruled in money matters, and in miserly fashion, no doubt.

My male relatives were generally non-verbal, and sometimes I've been called "taciturn." A strong Scotch influence and the rigors of prairie homesteading created a culture of frugality that extended to speech, to movement and, especially, to emotions. My female ancestors had a difficult time in striving for equality with their men. I imagine this was true in most families in the times they lived. The women would sometimes have to resort to extreme measures to get their way, employing religion, mental derangement or the withholding of sex—all dangerous maneuvers.

I can't vouch for the accuracy of the sex withholding tactic as sex was never, never openly discussed where I come from. Ignorance and guilt were the orders of the day. No, what I know is innuendo, hints and rumor. On the other hand, I did witness the use of religion as a club, backed up by the church-supplied gospels of original sin, guilt, Hell and damnation.

And clinical depression—regular and manic-depressive—runs its fist through my mother's family, just as alcoholism slithers down through my father's. While I've personally avoided significant problems with depression, it has, by extension through several family members, had an effect on me.

• • • • • • • • • • •

The scene is prairie wheat land—southwestern Nebraska hard by the Colorado and Kansas borders.

"Earl?" The soft melodious voice of plump Grandmother Alice wafted across the warm spring Nebraska evening in the 1930s. It sought the attention of the man sitting on the porch steps, peering out towards the fields and sizing up the plowing work for the next day.

"Earl?"

"Yes?"

The faint acknowledgment came without his turning towards her. It irritated Alice that he treated her with such distance, but she let the steady creaking of her porch swing comfort her. Now was not the time to become angry, not when she was steeling her courage to ask for money.

"Earl, I want to buy a piano!" She got it out, and firmly, too.

The magnitude of such a purchase and the absurdity of a house-wife on the prairie buying a piano during the Depression caused Earl to quickly steal a glance at Alice over his shoulder.

Was she going crazy? Some of her actions made him suspicious. He had to be careful for if she really got her dander up, the soft voice of the large, stout woman could turn into a shrill stridence that could set the house to shaking.

"My God," he whispered, "how much would a piano cost?"

Alice's heart jumped and she calculated how much she could ask for without the spare, hard man wordlessly standing and walking away, walking away to the barn where he sometimes spent the night.

Music became an important part of Grandmother's life and she went on to write several songs which were published by a music company in Lincoln. But she could use her budding obsession in more ways than one.

"Earl?" Grandmother Alice's voice had a dangerous tone which signaled she wanted something that he wouldn't like.

"Earl, I want some money to send away for sheet music."

"You've already got a box of that stuff! Why don't you just use what you've got? It's too damn expensive!"

Her voice rose as if she were reading an opera score. "Earl, just give me the ten dollars and don't argue with me. I need more music so I can learn things."

"No, we can't spend any more money until after harvest." Earl's voice was sharp. He was determined to resist this petty whim.

"Earl, are you going to prevent me from learning how to write music? Are you going to get in the way of God's gift to me?" Alice was shouting now; she knew she was going to have to pull out all the stops to overcome Earl's opposition. "Don't you know I'm doing this because God is telling me to?"

He looked at her large figure, her face now dark red where it had previously been so white you'd never know she lived on a farm. He said nothing, but his stomach began to hurt.

"I want to write a song about Virgil!" she was hysterically crying now. Their son, Virgil Emmanuel, had died at nine months of age, and Earl had been embarrassed and frightened when Alice insisted two weeks later that Virgil's grave be opened and the coffin transferred to a cement vault. Alice made the two teen-age girls in the family, Carolyn and Margy, go with her to the cemetery.

Later they told their father that what Mother had in mind all along was raising Virgil from the dead. They prayed on the way to God's Acre and more fervently still while the grave was being dug up. When the coffin was exposed, Alice made the workmen open it, "for just for a minute." When that was done, everyone could see "a small spot of green mold on his nose," according to the shaken Margy. And that's when they all went to praying in shouts, "Rise up, Virgil. Rise up, beloved sweet baby!"

They were unsuccessful. Alice was so distraught that Earl had to go clear across the state and bring his father-in-law back to help calm her down.

Alice's out-of-control voice cut through his black memories, "And now you're going against God, and against Virgil! I'm going to.."

"All right...all right." He could hold up against his wife and even against God, but not when she threw in Virgil's memory, too. Setting her off that way just wasn't worth the misery. "All right."

Alice only dimly understood that he had acquiesced, but enough that she slowly began her descent away from the towering brain chemical imbalance she was experiencing. Later she would rejoice that she had won again. It was her winning formula. But it was a little scary, this going further into the darkness each time.

Grandmother Alice was in the state mental hospital in Lincoln, had been there for two days. The attending physician looked at her charts once again.

"Family reports that patient periodically 'goes crazy' and is possessed by intense emotions, is completely unpredictable, uses uncharacteristically profane language, believes that God is telling her what to do, doesn't know the difference between night and day, temporarily possesses incredible strength and energy, and is dangerous to anyone who won't do as she wants. The family is terrified."

He continued reading, "Family reports that one time they were driving and patient tried to get out of the car in heavy traffic at forty miles per hour, prevented only by a dramatic rescue."

The doctor flipped through all the examination charts that had been created during her stay, and shook his head. No doubt, the woman was a menace to herself and others. He sighed, wrote his conclusions into the files and scheduled her operation for the day after next. The surgeons would bore through the fifty-five year old woman's skull and sever selected brain pathways. They would have to be exceedingly careful. Too much cutting and she'd never be able to live outside an institution again.

There was only one member of the family, daughter Margy, able to be there during the operation. She waited patiently until a doctor opened a door into the visitor's room. "Mrs. Graham," he said. "We've finished with your mother. We think she'll be okay now." He seemed bewildered at Margy's horrified expression. Then he noticed with chagrin that she was staring at the forgotten probe in his hand, bearing Alice Skelton's warm blood and damp hair still alive in the slow summer air.

I vaguely remember my Grandmother before the lobotomy, and very well afterwards. I believe the doctors called the operation a success, as she was able to go home, and she did become much more docile. We grandchildren, taking our cues from the older generation, no longer called her crazy; we called her "strange," or said she "wasn't all there." The last part was true, because she was no longer whole. And although they were probably unaware of it, each member of the family had lost a bit of themselves along with her.

●●●●●●●●●●●

My mother said I've always been interested in work and money. It's easy for me to remember why this came about. I can still remember Dad giving me my first lesson about work—as I sat on the toilet.

One day when I was very, very young, Dad took me into the bathroom, put me on the toilet, and said, "Okay, now you must get the habit of having a bowel movement the first thing in the morning. That way you wouldn't have to do it on your bosses' time. It'll help you get ahead in this world."

Crude? Yes. Money oriented? Yes. But the teaching was superbly practical.

I'm sure my father was greatly influenced in the subject of money and work by his male ancestors, just as he's influenced me. For Dad, the experience of growing up in the Great Depression compounded the message of his lineage for the need for fiscal frugality. While his small-farm family never lost its "home place" or went hungry for days as many people did, the Depression must have been a scary experience for the Grahams. Their normal, hard existence must have taken on an edge tinged with fear of foreclosure and eviction into the stream of homeless families that was generated by the most severe depression in U.S. history.

Dad had lots of ideas about money and he didn't miss many chances to pass them on. I remember some of his opinions. "You can learn everything you need to know in life by making money. In order to make money and get ahead, you'll need to get to work early and be the last one to leave the job at night. You can learn what other people are like by the way they treat money. If they treat money with respect, if they save for a rainy day rather than spending, they're good people. If they throw their money around trying to impress people or just blow it without saving for the future, they're not. Don't fool around with them.

"No one will give you something for nothing. Remember that. That's why you'll work for your allowance. I'm not going to give you kids something for nothing. As soon as you're old enough, you'll need to get a job. And, if you have any ideas about having a car someday or of going to college, you'll be the one to pay for it. So you better start saving now."

It was so ironic to me that Dad later drank up everything he saved! However, after hitting bottom in a San Jose jail, he had 16 years of sobriety before he died. During those years he spent most of his waking time in Alcoholics Anonymous activities, becoming a saver of souls. I'm really proud of the way he pulled himself together and made his life a success in the fullest sense of the word, on the soul level. And, although he had only small amounts of income in his last years, somehow there was also $120,000 in his estate when he passed on. Old habits have a hard time dying out.

• • • • • • • • • • •

"Nigger." My Dad used that ugly term a lot when I was young. In addition, several of the common sayings that I was taught revolved around race.

"Gee, that's white of you," indicated that you had just performed a noble service, presumably just the way white people acted by nature. "Indian giver" were fighting words, used frequently by my friends and me. "Niggardly" was heard now and then, with the fact that it appeared in the dictionary giving it legitimacy. By and large, in my early years I was socialized to see people in groups; essentially, whites on one side and everyone else on the other. And I was given to understand that we whites were superior.

My first experience with the fallout of that training came around the age of seven, in the early 1940s. My family had driven in from the countryside to visit friends of Mom and Dad's in Omaha. World War II was on and that family had moved into the city, where the man of the house got a job in a defense plant. Housing was in short supply and they lived right on the edge of a black neighborhood. As we neared their home my Dad supplied a running commentary on "niggers," how they lived, how inferior they were in intelligence and cleanliness, and how they were taking jobs from decent white people.

The friends had a young son about my age and after a while we became bored with being cooped up in the small bungalow. We went outside to play at a park about a block away. After a time I spotted a black youth cutting across the edge of the park. My heart sped up as this was the first time I had actually been in close proximity to the object of my father's hate. I summoned up my courage and my breath and hollered out.

"Hey, nigger! Hey, nigger!"

The black youth stopped dead in his tracks and wheeled to see who was doing the hollering. Although at a distance, our eyes locked into each other's and we stood for a moment, frozen in recognition that we were two kids suddenly cast into the same fearsome and unwanted roles that had been played out by millions of people before us.

"Yeaaah!" He screamed and set after me. With his first step I saw that he was bigger than I, and I lit out for the house, terrified. My little friend was already halfway there as he had had enough experience to see what was coming.

"Yeaaah!"

Twice more the black youth let out that terrible cry of generations of pain, and each time he was closer to me. Even the fear of the beating I would receive at his hands could not propel me faster than he was running. As I reached the bottom of the porch steps, Dad and the other man stormed out the door, alerted by the little boy who had run crying before me.

The black boy stopped and hightailed it back down the street when he saw the reception committee. As I reached the porch and the safety of the men, they yelled, "Go home, nigger! Go home!"

I didn't yell a thing, and not just because I was out of breath and thoroughly terrified at my experience. Deep inside, I had learned a lesson. I never called anyone a "nigger" again. In those moments of tapping into the fear (mine) and the pain (his) of hatred and prejudice, I had tasted the bitter fruit of ignorance. I knew I was wrong, dead wrong. I sensed that the situation could easily have been reversed, by the fate of birth or otherwise.

Ultimately I would have to deal with my personal prejudices about religion, politics, sexual preferences and several other less intense issues, small step by small step. But the race matter was pretty well settled in a hurry for me that Sunday afternoon in Omaha.

● ● ● ● ● ● ● ● ● ● ●

A few years after my escape from the black kid who had chased me, my father was fit to be tied. In March, 1947, a black man, Jackie Robinson, was in the spring training camp of the Brooklyn Dodgers National League baseball team. The camp was being held in Havana, Cuba, to avoid the segregationist "Jim Crow" laws of the South where the Dodgers normally trained. The word out of Havana was that Jackie Robinson had enormous talent and that the Dodgers' owner, Branch Rickey, was determined to see him become the first black man to play major league baseball. At the same time there were rumors that some of Robinson's potential teammates might strike to keep him off the club.

Blacks and baseball were an explosive combination for my father. They combined the two great passions of his life: his hatred of blacks and his love of baseball. Dad was a pretty fair baseball player himself, first as a youth and then as the first baseman for the University of Nebraska Cornhuskers in his two years at college. After that he played semi-pro ball well into his twenties. Now at thirty-two, he avidly coached me, eleven, and my younger, nine-year-old brother in the "Great American Pastime." He was also a part-time scout for the St. Louis Cardinals, fierce rivals of the Dodgers

Dad's rage knew no bounds as the spring wore on and it became a stronger likelihood that Jackie Robinson would actually be asked to sign a Dodger contract and break the color barrier. To top it off, the Dodgers and the Cardinals had several scores to settle from the previous year. It was just too much for Dad; not only were blacks perceived economic and social threats to him, now they would be invading the holy ground of major league baseball! This space was sacred for Dad whose major fantasy in life had been to play big league ball.

This combination of blacks and baseball proved explosive for me as well. Brooklyn was the team I rooted for, as I played shortstop and the Dodgers had a great one, Peewee Reese. I was a peewee myself, so you see the connection. Robinson was a superb second baseman and the linkage of Reese and Robinson as the Keystone Kops, double-play-makers par excellence, fueled my fantasies. Since Reese was my alter ego, it was really Jackie and me performing defensive miracles around second base on April 10, 1947, when Robinson made history by playing in the season opener at Ebbets Field in Brooklyn, New York!

Two months later I excitedly put down the newspaper and ran to find Dad. "Did you see what Robinson did? A homer and two singles, five RBIs! He's tearing up the league!"

"Luck, pure luck. Just wait until the pitchers get used to him.

That nigger will be out of there, fast!"

"But, Dad, he and Reese made three double plays! The paper said he could be Rookie of the Year!" (The season was less than half over, but the paper's prediction later proved correct.)

"He's a bum! A bum!" Dad was shouting now and I hightailed it. After the adrenaline rush of our confrontation subsided, I jumped as I ran and laughed loudly. "You're right, Dad. He's a Bum!" The Dodgers were sometimes called, "Dem Bums" in Brooklyn by their faithful fans who had suffered many a losing season. However their fans didn't cotton to anyone else calling them "Bums." Those would have been fighting words if only I were big enough!

In the next four or five years, most of my conflicts and the first stirrings of my inevitable breakaway from my father (also known as growing up) got played out on the stage of the Dodgers versus the Cardinals. We argued, taunted and teased each other at every opportunity. During the summer a ball game was always on the radio at our house. We listened to play-by-play recreations when the real thing wasn't available. My mother thought we were nuts, and couldn't see why we were so consumed by a game. But she didn't see, and we weren't aware, that we were carrying out the classic father/son struggle. Dad was teaching me to endure the inevitable slings and arrows of life by his continual wounding and healing of me—all through baseball.

Some of our struggles became legendary in the neighborhood, especially the day we were listening to a Dodgers-Cardinals game on the radio and we were in our normal fighting mode. Robinson, who had led the Dodgers to the World Series in his rookie year and would later be inducted into The Baseball Hall of Fame, was pounding the Cardinals' pitching for one hit after another. I think it was the year that Robinson would lead the National League in batting and each of his hits that day was like a right-cross to Dad's jaw.

Late in the game, Robinson made an error on a potential double-play ball with the bases loaded, allowing the Cardinals to score two runs and go ahead. Dad was immediately in my face, taunting and razzing me! I ran screaming from the room, slamming the door behind me.

Too late, I realized that I had shut myself in the bathroom!

Dad turned up the radio full blast and I had to listen in rage as the Cardinals closed out the game, beating the Dodgers by a run. I cried, even though I had been told a hundred thousand times that men don't cry. After the game was over, I held my hands over my ears as the radio blared the post game interviews, comments and the wrap-up. At last it was finished.

But wait, Dad was still in the living room! The bastard wouldn't leave. He was going to make me walk out of there, enduring his taunts once again! I couldn't, I just couldn't. Realizing the only way out was through the window, I went for it. Unfortunately it was small and screened. I stood on the edge of the tub, butted my head through the screen and hoisted myself up and out, falling headfirst into a scratchy bush. I picked myself up, my head bleeding, and ran to a friend's home.

When I came home that night, at least we didn't talk about the game. No, we talked about what an idiot I was for breaking the screen, how much it would cost to fix and how I was going to pay for every cent of it! My father did show a certain amount of mercy though, and didn't take the strap to me. He knew I had suffered enough. He knew how to take me to the edge, but he never pushed me over.

Dad's "certain quality of mercy" also showed itself when each summer we left our lily-white Iowa racial environment and went to St. Louis to see some games. He always scheduled it so that we saw the Dodgers. He did it for me, God bless him—he could have picked games when an all-white team was in town and avoided the indignity of watching blacks compete on even turf.

Traveling to St. Louis continued my education in race relations, as it was said to be the most segregated city in the Major Leagues. Each time, Dad drove us through East St. Louis, an impoverished black slum across the river. Thankfully, Dad didn't rant and rave about the "niggers." I guess he thought that what I saw did his talking for him. Similarly, the "White Only" and the "Colored" drinking fountains at the ball park spoke to me.

But what I "heard" most was the sight of the right field bleachers occupied solely by black people, while every other section of the park, from home base all the way down the right field line, from home base down the left field line, and the left field and center field bleachers, was completely occupied by white people. The black people were allocated a small percentage of the worst seats in the stadium, and it seemed that their every move was monitored or policed in some way to keep them separate and from "defiling" white people. That sight is emblazoned on my mind to this day, bringing with it a sickening awe. What a metaphor for the state of much of the U.S. in the late 1940's!

The fallout of what I was seeing, and my interaction with Dad about the issue of race, albeit largely expressed through the world of baseball, was that I came to identify with the underdog. I almost always rooted against the favorite in sporting events. In later life, I gradually extended this metaphor of sports to other of life's activities and came to have a bias in favor of those out of power, out of position, out of a decent standard of living, or just plain out. Ironically, I have my father to thank for these particular beliefs that I so cherish; my persuasions around the issues of race are opposite of the beliefs he attempted to give me as a youth, which shows that we learn best from our own comparing and contrasting, and not by listening to someone else.

My dad never talked to me about race after I left home. In his last fifteen or so years he became quite interested in metaphysics and my hunch is that his racial prejudices fell away as his consciousness expanded. Now that he is "in heaven," I'll bet he relishes watching video reruns of Bob Gibson, an absolutely awesome black pitcher for the Cardinals in the late 1960s and 1970s, flailing the Dodgers he despised with strikeouts and shutouts, winning again and again!

●●●●●●●●●●●

On a bleak winter day in 1952, I stopped in at my dad's insurance office on my way to my after-school job at The Sun. Dad wanted to give me instructions about something, and, when he finished, I asked him about the stranger working in the spare office.

"Who's the man in the office, Dad?"

"He's a CPA from Omaha. He'll be here for two weeks doing

income tax returns for local businesses. He's doing my taxes in exchange for using that office," Dad explained, peering over his glasses. His tilt showed that he was balding before his 40th birthday.

"A CPA. That's a Certified Public Accountant. I've heard about them in my bookkeeping class. I don't think there are many of them around."

"That's probably right, son." He leaned towards me, running a hand through his thinning hair, and whispered, "I think he takes in $40 a day." I stared at him in total amazement. I was making 40 cents an hour at the newspaper. $40 a day was an unbelievable amount!

"Can I meet him?" I begged. "Sure, his name is Mr. Parsons. But don't take up much of his time. Remember, time is money to him!" Dad took me to the next office to meet a man grown to gigantic proportions in my imagination.

We shook hands and arranged to meet the following afternoon at his coffee break time. We went to the Green Parrot restaurant and found a booth. Mr. Parsons relaxed his lanky frame and seemed pleased to tell me about his profession. I told him about my high marks in school and my particular interest in numbers.

"You say you like numbers a lot. Why?" He seemed genuinely interested.

"Mr. Parsons, I think it's because they make sense to me. Once you know the rules and how numbers work, how they relate to each other, they never change. And yet there's something kind of magic about them, too. I mean, you can do all sorts of things with them, tricks really, but you can do a lot more than that. So many things are measured—how many eggs the family needs, or how many yards there are to go for a first down. I think you can just about plan your life with numbers. And besides, I'm good at numbers. All those math classes are a breeze for me."

He seemed to like my answer and settled in to recruit me as a future CPA. Everything he said sounded wonderful to me, a well-paid profession where one worked closely with a variety of clients on very confidential, and often exciting, matters. I didn't have the nerve to ask him how much money he made each day, but I learned that he had quite a few expenses and that income tax time, or his "busy season," only lasted about three months. The rest of the year was not nearly as profitable. But I didn't care. I had already made up my mind to major in accounting in college and become a CPA just as soon as I could!

But, as it seems to be with things of knowledge and personal growth, there was first a price to be paid.

2

INITIATION

The traditional people of Africa say that the initiatory process of transforming a boy into adult manhood is not complete unless it includes putting the lad's life at risk; and that the only proof of having done that is if, from time to time, a few fatal casualties occur.

I refused to look at the twenty other young marines crouched along either side of the bay of our amphibious tractor, which sat in a line of brother tractors on a sandy beach waiting for the 9 p.m. launch into the Pacific. It had to be dark outside, as the operation was supposed to be guided by flares fired from the LSDs, the large mother ships, floating offshore. It would be my first ride to sea in an iron tractor—the others had been through this before.

I couldn't understand why there was such a strong smell of fear coming from their armpits, but I took momentary comfort in it, as its putridness masked mine. But my terror went up a notch when it came to me that they must know something I didn't. The sounds of the twin diesel engines at idle and the pounding of the surf drowned out any chance of my asking why the hell they were so afraid.

Without warning, the amtrack driver jammed the engines full throttle and our iron horse shuttered, gathered steam, and accelerated down the beach slope into the surf. The driver timed our plunge and we entered the sea between waves. We hit the water with a jolt and the tractor churned forward. Suddenly, we felt the amtrack being lifted by an incoming wave, and the water, which sought every tiny chink in our armor, found some holes at the hatches and showered in on us. The nose of the tractor went down and the engine propellers temporarily lost traction in the sea, causing them to race. Momentarily we were suspended in a dark, splashing purgatory between the sea and the air.

The wave crested under us and the propellers bit again, gaining hard-won yardage against the surf. My head pounded and bile rose in my mouth as I reached behind me to grip the tractor's metal with one hand, while the other wedged a M-1 rifle between my legs.

The next wave was a repeat of the first, but as we came out of the crest, the rear of the tractor swung partially forward and we skidded on the water. The driver throttled down the left engine to correct our direction and had but partially succeeded when the next wave hit, throwing increasing amounts of water into our hull and down over our helmets. This time the wave left us sideways at its crest and I hollered up a supplication to God and Jesus as the driver fought to regain position. Even I, an initiate, knew that we were in extreme danger of taking the next wave sideways and being rolled over. If that happened, the amtrack would drown like a rat going down a rapids, and we would join the death process in our iron coffin.

The driver fought to regain our original direction, and then the sea was upon us expressing its fury in massive fourteen-foot waves. For the first time, the screams of the marines were louder than the unmuffled diesels at our sides and the pounding of the waves, which poured new volumes of water in on us, sloshing around our boots. I abandoned my petitions to God and screamed along with everyone else, screamed at the injustice of dying at eighteen without knowing what it was like to be a man, to be with a woman, to have children.

The toll from our one week training mission was three amtracks swamped and nine men drowned in the surf, one land-based fighter and its pilot lost when the plane clipped the reconnaissance tower of a destroyer, and two infantry men killed when a tank lost traction on a hill-side of our invasion target and rolled down over their foxholes. An even dozen dead out of a couple of thousand participants. According to traditional African standards, our initiation rites had properly qualified.

I lived through it, but beyond that saw little value in the exercise. Oh, yes, I did get something out of it. Later, when I was discharged, I was informed that the exercise had taken place in international waters off California's coast, and in accordance with the illogic of military regulations, I received an extra $300 mustering out pay for "overseas duty."

● ● ● ● ● ● ● ● ● ● ●

Actually, getting into the U.S. Marine Corps was touch and go. I recall standing on a scale, soaking wet from an anxiety as intense as that in the amphibious landing exercise. I tried to stand straight in spite of my stomach cramps and gas from stuffing myself with nine large candy bars during the previous hours. My discomfort was multiplied by the fact that I had not allowed myself to pee for fear of losing weight. A staff-sergeant with "white-walls" (short hair, no side burns) ran the balance beam while I looked ahead, afraid to watch. He seemed to be taking an awfully long time.

Why was I here? I tried to remember.

As I approached my senior year in high school, I saw only one thing standing between me and college—money. I had "invested" much of my savings in the purchase of a 1942 Ford Coupe a year earlier, only to find out the car didn't appreciate in value as I used it! At the same time it was obvious that my parents were not going to be a funding source.

The whole process of attending college was actually a mystery around my school; out of a graduating class of seventy-seven, only a hand-full were planning to continue with academic studies, and a few others were looking for athletic scholarships. The majority immediately entered the work force in town, on the farm, or at home.

When a Marine Corps recruiter came to our school that winter and offered to trade me two years in the Marines for four college years of the GI Bill at $110 a month, I was all ears. The year was 1954 and the Korean War was headed toward a truce, so I disregarded the recruiting poster of Marines planting a bloody flag at Iwo Jima, and signed up. When I went for my physical exam in Omaha, none of the humiliating scenes of standing nude in long lines of pimply, teenage boys waiting to have various orifices probed, right there in front of God and everybody, produced as much anxiety for me as the did the weigh-in. I had to make a 140-pound minimum and had been eating mightily for weeks in an attempt to gain weight. But my last trip to our bathroom scales at home said I was still two pounds short of my goal.

I felt the sergeant's intense stare heating my face. I refused to budge and looked directly at the sign on the wall. It said, "Once a Marine, always a Marine!" Finally, I felt his eyes withdraw and he wrote something on my chart. "Next," he said brusquely.

They say that scales never lie. But I came down from the platform with the distinct impression that those did. Or did the Marines at that little sub-station have a quota to fill that day? The truth will never be known, but three weeks after my graduation from high school, I was on a train headed from Omaha to the Marine Corps Recruit Depot at San Diego, California. At the end of the tracks awaited twelve weeks of organized hell, commonly called "boot camp."

•••••••••••

"Fall out, shit-heads!" Our drill sergeant stood outside his office, his blood-curdling voice carrying into our two squad bays. Sixty teenagers made a mad dash for the front of our barracks, fighting each other for running room. Sergeant Gibson walked to the assembly area, counting loudly, "five...six..." A clumsy farm boy from Ohio fell in the rush, and those behind made no attempt to avoid trampling him.

"Twelve...thirteen...fourteen..." Now that we were breaking clear, many of us tried desperately to tuck in our shirts as we ran.

"Nineteen...twenty! Freeze!" Everyone stopped in their tracks. About half of us had made it to our positions. The sergeant yelled to those who hadn't, "You fat-assed molasses-slow shit-heads, get in the barracks, get into combat gear and report outside in four minutes!" He looked at his watch. "Get going—RUN!"

"Now, I'll inspect the rest of you sorry looking shit-heads!" Everything he said was a yell. He passed through our ragged ranks, yelling obscenities at each recruit who had something wrong with their uniform. One by one he yelled them back into the barracks to get into their combat gear as well. As he approached me, I trembled and sweat rolled down my back. Even if it hadn't been 99°, I would have been sweating from fear.

Luckily I hadn't taken off any of my uniform when we were told we could have a twenty-minute Sunday afternoon break to write letters. I didn't trust the two bastards who were our drill instructors. It had been good thinking on my part, as the call to fall out had come only ten minutes into the break.

The sergeant looked at me contemptuously. "Where are you from, shit-head?"

"Sir, Iowa, sir!"

"Well, you're a shit-headed runt if I've ever seen one! We'll bust your ass at the rifle range!"

"Sir, yes sir!" I shouted, believing that they would, indeed.

He eyed me suspiciously. "What were you doing when I called for 'fall out?' Writing your mummy and daddy?" He made the "mummy and daddy" sound like baby talk.

"Sir, no sir! I was shining my shoes, sir!"

"Oh, a smart-ass, huh! Lying to me! You'll pay for this, you brown-nosing shit-head! Show me your hands!"

"Sir, yes sir!" I shouted and stuck my hands out, palms up, trying to control their shaking.

He scowled with surprise at the brown shoe shine polish on my hands. "Well...if you like to shine shoes so goddamn much, get your ass to my quarters and start shining my shoes, right NOW!"

"Sir, yes sir!" I ran back into the barracks, barely suppressing my new-found glee. I would escape the grueling, blazing-sun run on The Grinder. Twenty minutes earlier I had decided that shiny shoes were more important to the DIs (Drill Instructors) than how many letters I wrote home. Now I would benefit from having done the right thing at the right time. The DI might well own my ass, as he often proclaimed, but he didn't own my brain.

Confrontations like that one were served up daily, sometimes hourly. Crusty, cocky, obscene drill sergeants—perhaps modern day equivalents of brutal, initiating elders in our ancestors' time—piled verbal abuse on top of verbal abuse, their battle-lined faces smack up against my own. Or, as we say now, real up front and personal. Given their vigilant efforts, there seemed to be no end to all the bad things that could happen to me. Fear was constant. Their continual confrontation forced me to confront myself. The question was not when would I stand up and fight; that would have been a form of instant suicide. Rather, it was if I could learn to control my own emotions and fear, and be unaffected by their ravings. I gradually acquired, though never quite perfected, this skill.

Soon I was forced to confront another of my emotional hang-ups—guns. I had disliked firing them since I was a kid. My dad would take my younger brother, Dick, and I hunting—rabbits initially—but after going through a few desultory motions I would find my way back to the car and wait for the two warriors to return with the spoils. I could see it was only a game for us, but it was life and death to the animal. I could never reconcile this difference as being fair, although I did participate in the eating of their kills. Now here I was, firing machine guns in mock fire-fights and handling a brutal .45 pistol.

But it was the M-1 rifle that really forced me to deal with my personal baggage. We each had our own rifle, and its serial number was emblazoned on my brain, just underneath my Marine identification number. We spent a great deal of time disassembling, cleaning, oiling and reassembling our M-1s, often under a DI's time clock, with severe punishment meted out for the losers. Intimate relationships were necessarily formed with these weapons, as a failure to recognize a rifle's individual foibles, a failure to manipulate it just right, could result in disaster for the owner.

Freudian implications were rampant, both explicit and implied. For example, all of the military services have a phobia against calling a small-arms weapon a "gun." And whenever a recruit forgot and made the mistake of calling an M-1 a "gun" within hearing of a DI, he would be forced to go before the platoon, hold the rifle overhead with one hand and place his other hand on his crotch, chanting:

"This is my rifle, this is my gun;
This one's for shooting, this one's for fun!"

That was the explicit side. On the implicit side, it was said that when you dreamed of your rifle and shooting it, you were really dreaming about having sex with a girl from back home. It was the first time I heard of dream analysis, something I would revisit years later.

The real challenge for me in this rifle business was to acquire enough skill to "qualify." That meant achieving the minimum grade of "Marksman" at the rifle range. (I had no illusions about making "Sharpshooter," let alone "Expert.") Our DIs ragged us the whole two weeks at the rifle range about qualifying. They let it be known that "all you assholes *will* qualify." It seemed there was intense competition among the various DI teams to have platoons with 100% qualification, huge bets and all, and our team was not going to be allowed to lose. The promised punishment for failure to qualify included a threat to "run your ass out of boot camp." In other words, you would be a marked man, and your life a twenty-four-hour-a-day hell until you broke and washed out as "unsuitable."

As I remember it, we had fifty shots to take with a bulls-eye worth five points, and a threshold score of 190 points required for Marksman. We shot ten rounds slow fire, standing, from 200 yards; 10 rounds rapid fire, both sitting and prone, from 300 yards; and ten rounds slow fire, both sitting and prone, from 500 yards. 500 yards! That's five football fields, laid out end-to-end. This seemed to me to be a hell of a challenge for anybody but a country-bred hunter.

The day our platoon was to qualify dawned cold, with high fog. My stomach was in too much of a turmoil to eat the SOS served for breakfast ("shit on a shingle," the military's version of creamed, chipped beef on toast), and I dumped it when no one was looking. My anxiety was sky-high. Two nights before, a recruit had blown his brains out in his tent one row over from us because he had failed to qualify that day. Our DIs didn't say much about it, one way or another, adding to my confusion. Did they actually approve of the guy killing himself out of disgrace? I knew that it was bad not to qualify, but...that bad?

We had to wait at the 100-yard station as the fog was still too thick for clear sight. The waiting intensified my nervousness, as the 100-yard offhand was my weakest position. I felt I had to do something, anything! I wished I could disappear, just dig a hole in the ground and merge into the earth. In desperation, I picked up a handful of dirt, spat into it, and rubbed it on my face. It felt good, cool to my feverish face. I kept adding more dirt and spit and when my face was covered, commenced rubbing great quantities of dirt into my hair. I worked diligently, and in silence except for rhythmic grunts. My mates eyed me warily, all of them a little jumpy from that goon in Baker Company splashing his blood tent-side.

When I got good and dirty, unrecognizable I'm sure, I sat and tried to breath in the dirt and spit through my every pore. The overall effect was soothing, and I couldn't wait to do the prone position shots, where I would be able to burrow in the dirt like a gopher. In retrospect I can only think that it was some primordial hunting preparation that came over me.

The fog lifted and the loud speaker said, "Commence firing!" My first two slow-fire offhands were 4s. Confidence rose up from my gut. By the time we had finished, my score was 206, only four points away from "Sharpshooter!" The Marines had taught me how to shoot an M-1, and they had taught all of my mates as well. Our platoon qualified 100%, and our DIs actually let up on us—just a hair—the last month of boot camp.

After a few weeks of boot camp, I could see that the Marines' primary teaching tool was fear. They were masters at manufacturing and manipulating it, but I supplied plenty on my own! Which brings me to swimming. I was never taught how to swim as a kid, and there were few opportunities to learn. When I was older and some of my friends were learning how, I was working on my uncle's ranch in Western Nebraska—and not a swimming hole in sight. I did take a few lessons in the two weeks before I went to the Marines, because I knew that swimming would be part of the testing process.

And so one hot Southern California morning I found myself trying to qualify for the lowest rank in swimming. Nothing fancy; just four laps across the short side of the pool. But I got a stomach cramp and went down in the middle of the last lap.

As I went down I could still see the outlines of the two sergeants crouching down towards the pool's edge, their faces contorted with screamed instructions. But their words were blocked from my hearing by the water which received me as I went down, down, for the second, or was it the third time? I flailed, my hands and feet churning madly, except I was dropping vertically rather than moving horizontally. My chest was on fire; I had swallowed water going down as I fought for air, and my lungs were failing me. I was terrified that I would hit bottom and a swimming instructor would jump in and pull me out. But I was even more terrified that one wouldn't, or at least not until it was too late.

I thought I had passed out because it was suddenly getting lighter, rather than darker as before. Now I could see the skylight of the indoor pool closing down on me and I was amazed to feel my body rising rather than sinking. I struggled with new-found strength and broke through the water's surface only to see the edge of the pool 100 feet away. I'd never make it!

Then the screams from the deck to my right found me, and I turned my head and saw the Sergeants again. I had been looking down the long side of the pool and not the short side! I surged the remaining six feet and let the hands of a swimming instructor haul me up and over the edge. My limp body was dragged back like a small, beached marlin and flopped onto the wet concrete. I was crying, but no one could tell my tears from the pool water, and my heaving contributed a half-digested breakfast of SOS to the wetness I laid in. When the SOS finished clearing from my system, my tears stopped and my breath returned. I opened my eyes and looked across the concrete at Sergeant Gibson's highly polished shoes, noting more than a few flecks of SOS.

I rolled on my side and looked up at him. He motioned to a pail and mop someone had bought over. "Clean this mess up, Pvt. Graham!" He looked down at his shoes. "And you owe me a shoeshine tonight, you shit-head!"

Then a slight smile—or was it a smirk—came to his face. "Oh yeah, you qualified...asshole!" There was a certain softness to the "asshole" that I'd never heard from Sgt. Gibson before.

Truth is, I've never lost my distaste for swimming, or guns, or confrontations in general. But I can handle them all, if I have to. I learned that in Marines Corps boot camp.

It's logical to me that I divide my life into two periods: before boot camp, when I was a boy, and afterwards, when I have been a man. As I see it, the Marine Corps contained the Continental Divide of my life, and in crossing it I crossed the line between childhood and adulthood. In a way, my crossing was like those in traditional initiations, where at some point the neophyte is ceremoniously pulled by the elders across a symbolic line, although no single event sticks in my mind as "The Line."

But by the cumulative effect of night-time forced marches under heavy pack, hand-to-hand bayonet combat practice, the ever-present guns, my brushes with death and near-death, and the repetitive demonstration of the value of discipline and teamwork in a multiracial/socio/economic setting, I discovered that I could do just about anything I set myself out to do, be it physical, psychological or mental. The discovery, or perhaps the development, of my inner resources was the Marine Corps' greatest gift to me. I call it a gift because I hadn't bargained for it, the way I did the GI Bill and the monthly pay.

I've often said I hated the Marine Corps, but it set me up for life.

•••••••••••

I reported for duty with the Third Amphibious Tractor Battalion of the First Marine Division at Camp Del Mar, California, in September, 1954. I had gone home to Red Oak for leave between boot camp and my first duty assignment, and found everything the same and yet everything different. It was nice to see my family again, but beyond that, Red Oak no longer held any attraction for me, and I was anxious to get on with my life. And that life included getting out of the Marine Corps and through college as fast as I could. I knew damn well I wanted a better kind of life than my Marine Corps mates seemed destined for.

Near our base, our liberty town of Oceanside had a community college; Oceanside J.C., and the opening of the fall semester coincided with my arrival at Camp Del Mar. Within days I had enrolled in two classes, and was going to school four nights a week. It seemed a futile gesture on my part as my outfit expected to ship out to Korea anytime.

"Dumb. A waste of time and a waste of money on those books!" an "old salt" marine told me. I didn't contradict him. No use stirring people up if it wasn't necessary.

About a month later our Company Commander, Major Warren, stood before Able Company and yelled out the news to the 240 or so of us. About 210 men, under Executive Officer Captain Delaney's command, would ship out in two weeks for Korea and merge into various outfits as replacements. Major Warren would stay behind with one captain, several tired non-coms and various other staff types to handle the influx of returning Korean vets rotating home and a batch of newly graduated recruits.

I wasn't too happy with the news, given that the Korean Peace Talks hadn't yet produced a firm truce, and people were still getting shot at from time to time. Korea was said to be lousy duty even when there wasn't any shooting; and the winters were absolutely miserable. As we were dismissed from formation I heard my name and two others called out with orders to stay behind and report front-side. Our little group huddled near the major and Captain Delaney. Major Warren asked for Pfc. Graham and I stepped towards him with high anxiety to learn what I had done wrong.

"It says here that you are enrolled at Oceanside J.C. and are going to school four nights a week. Is that true? What are you taking?" He looked up from his clipboard.

"Yes sir, that's correct. I'm taking a math class and a science class. They'll be worth six units of college credit when I transfer them," I said, thinking I should have said they would have been worth six units if I wasn't going to Korea.

"Well, I've never had a soldier go to college during my command. Pretty unusual in the Marines, I'd say. I'll be damned if I'll let this opportunity pass me by. You'll stay here for now, and you can go over with the next unit that leaves after your semester ends. Dismissed."

Because I wasn't going to Korea with the others, I was held back from the tractor park and given odd jobs. A couple of days later I was assigned to go to the Company supply shed for menial labor. An old gunnery-sergeant, Technical Sergeant Tenny, ran the place and he showed me a big pile of equipment and supplies that needed stowing.

Satisfied that I knew what to do, he climbed a ladder that took him to a loft and shouted back for me to "keep my eyes open for anyone coming." If I spotted anyone important, I was to yell at him. With that he disappeared into a pile of mattresses.

About three hours later he climbed down the stairs. It was time to go for chow. Yawning, he asked me what I wanted to do when I got out.

"I'm going to college and then I'll be a Certified Public Accountant."

He looked startled and then ruminated, "An accountant. I'll be. Say, we need a clerk here to keep our records, do the paperwork. It's a mess." He looked at me questioningly.

"I'm your man, Sarge. This looks like good duty to me!" The place was blissfully quiet and there hadn't been anybody come by all morning. Judging by the Sergeant's habits, the work didn't look at all stressful.

"Well, what's the answer, Corporal Graham?" A year later, Supply Officer Lt. Coffin snapped at me, his gray eyes cold, contrasting with his wavy black hair.

"Here's a list of the differences. I priced them out and they add up to about $18,000."

"$18,000! No way! Major Warren will skin all of us alive. I think you better recheck your work, Corporal!" He threw the papers back on my desk and stalked out.

"Geez, Sarge, I've triple checked my numbers. They're right! What am I supposed to do? Is it my fault that no one kept track of anything for three years? It's a wonder it's not worse than this." I stopped short of proclaiming that the problem of the shortage lay not only with years of sloppy record keeping, but also with the sergeant's poor management and his not doing anything about the scores of Marines who had been stealing everything that wasn't nailed down.

"Well, look at the problem this way." He rubbed his stubbled chin reflectively. He was a "short-timer," close to retirement, and his attention to appearance was declining. "Major Warren is being promoted to Colonel and transferred to battalion headquarters. So now there will be an official inventory taken which the new

Commanding Officer will have to sign for. No way around it. Major Warren will be responsible to make up the difference between what we've got and what he signed for when he came on, from his own money. Now, we can't let that happen. We'll just have to work around it. Let me have the list." He called Sgt. Hess, his number two in command, into the office and they began reviewing the items.

After a long discussion that seemed to me to only underline how far-gone the situation was, Sarge brightened. "OK, we've got three weeks. Graham, call the motor pool and order a truck for every day between now and the inventory day. And get some grease-heads over here for temporary assignment. We've got to make room for another $18,000 worth of stuff," he smiled and chuckled with an energy that I'd never seen from him.

It was an amazing three weeks. Sarge played every trick he knew, and after twenty-two years in Supply, he knew a lot. He had favors coming from everywhere: other Company Supply officers, Battalion Supply, Division Supply and the Survey Depot up on the hill at Camp Pendleton that took worn-out and ruined equipment. Soon items were coming out of the woodwork. He was gathering scrap from all over the place, barely recognizable scrap that somehow could be turned in for new units. He was even getting soldiers who had stashed stolen stuff to return it in exchange for future favors.

I knew we had a real chance to make up the shortage the first time Sarge took a truckload of worn out maintenance equipment to the Survey Depot and came back not only with a credit for everything I had written down, but the worn out stuff he had gotten credit for as well. He must have taken that same load of junk up there five times! God, a single, dilapidated floor-jack generated credits for five jacks for me to post to the books, plus we still had the original!

Our biggest shortage was blankets, a very popular item for pilferage. No problem. New blankets were torn into strips of four and five and taken to the Survey Depot and exchanged for four and five new blankets!

Each night I tallied our net gain for the day and our little group prepared for our next maneuvers. We enthusiastically conjured up new ways to vanquish the only-said-in-whispers "shortage." If I thought about the morality of what we were doing and my part in the project—dare I say fraud?—I sure don't remember it. Once the Lt. walked in as we were tearing up brand new blankets, and just as quickly turned on his heels and wordlessly departed. We never saw him at the shed again until the official inventory, when he stood by, smiling smugly as count after count tallied perfectly to what was supposed to be there.

Aside from the occasional combat training exercise, life at Camp Del Mar was pretty routine. The Korean Peace Talks went well and there were no more threats of overseas duty. "Keep your nose clean and you've got nothing to worry about," the brass would say. I had week-end leave most of the time and went to Los Angeles to visit my Aunt Merna and her husband, John—and Betty, the high school senior two doors down from them. The intensity of boot camp contrasted with my peaceful life as a supply clerk, and I was thankful. Of course, all the Marines who went from boot camp to combat or other tough overseas duty assignments received no such relief.

About ten days before my discharge in June, 1956, each marine in our Battalion was given a survey form to complete. It came from Marine Corps Headquarters at the Pentagon, and contained several potentially explosive questions.

A couple of months before, eight recruits had died during a forced night march in the swamps at Paris Island, South Carolina, Marine Corps Recruit Depot. There had been a big hue and cry in the newspapers about the "Ribbon Creek incident," and calls for an investigation into the brutality of boot camp, but the Corps had successfully stone-walled the affair. Now for some unfathomable reason, the Corps had decided to ask some of its soldiers what they thought about boot camp. It was the first time in anyone's memory, from the Commanding Officer on down, that the big brass had been interested in the rank-and-file's opinion about anything.

Everyone in the Company was told to complete the form and then fall out in front with it for collection. Two buddies, Don Biesack and Don True, and I sequestered ourselves in the clerks' office to do ours. We were soon in a raging debate as to how to answer the questions. On the one hand we wanted to get into writing for the first time just how lousy we thought boot camp was. On the other hand, there was the danger that the Corps might initiate reform and those who came behind us would have an easier time than we. We were on the horns of a dilemma. We constantly changed answers, and grew more uproarious by the moment.

Finally, in a fit of frustration, and giddy with my impending discharge, I dramatically said, "I'm sick of everything to do with this chicken-shit outfit!" and haughtily tore up the form, tossing it into the waste basket. Biesack and True laughed and laughed, but proceeded to finish theirs.

I had torn up a form. Okay, get another one and fill it out. Right? Wrong! A major uproar occurred in the executive offices when I didn't have my form to turn in. The Top Sergeant acted like I had committed a treasonous offense. We headed back to the office and my buddies and I taped the form together, then poured coffee on it. I swore to the Top that I had accidentally spilled coffee on the survey as I worked on it, and the tears in the paper occurred when I tried to wipe up the mess.

"That's the best you can do? That's the best goddamn story you can make up? Don't you know we have to account for every last one of these goddamn forms? What do think would happen if the New York Times got hold of the goddamn survey and found out that maybe the Corps was rethinking basic training? The Pentagon would go berserk, and everybody within ten miles of your sorry ass would be hung, Graham!" His face, dangerously red, turned and disappeared, showing the sweat coming through the back of the sergeant's khaki shirt.

I didn't sleep for two nights, didn't go to chow, and laid low at the supply shed trying to stay out of the sight of everybody sergeant and above. I wondered, was I going to receive some heavy discipline just as I was ready to get out? I tossed and turned. Everybody was so mad at me. Didn't they have their dumb form, even if it was messed up? I was glad I didn't have another year or so to go. It was the kind of a thing that could cost you a promotion.

No word came from Battalion about my misdeed. After a few days I started breathing again, but I continued my low profile until June 21, 1956. On that day I picked up my discharge papers at the Battalion Office, and strode down its long polished linoleum hallway towards the door.

"Corporal Graham!" an authoritative voice came from the office marked S-4. I looked into the frosty blue eyes of Lt. Col. James Warren, Commanding Officer, Intelligence Division. His white bushy eyebrows arched imperially and he turned to go back into his office. I followed him, and stood stiffly at attention.

"Graham, do you know how much trouble you caused us by mucking up that survey form?" His voice was stern and I wondered if the honorable discharge papers tightly grasped in my left hand were official yet, or if I was still at risk.

"Yes, sir...I mean, no sir. I'm sorry sir." I felt like a condemned man pleading for mercy from a sentencing judge.

"Well, Graham, you're pretty lucky...you have...friends in high places." He chuckled, "At ease." I almost fell onto the floor.

He stuck out his large hand and I put mine in his, feeling the deep lines that lived there. I realized he was old enough to be my father.

"I know you're off to college. I'd sure like to see you take ROTC and come back in the Corps as an officer. You'd make a good one...an officer and a gentleman." He said the last softly, reflectively.

I stammered my thanks, backed out of his office, and bolted for the front door and freedom.

• • • • • • • • • • •

Initiation. In some ways, the word smacks of mystery. Remember the clandestine clubs we joined as little kids, the secret handshakes? Or later on, the social organizations, the "one true church?" And how we felt special, different really, after we were initiated? From then on, we defined ourselves in new ways.

Yes, we all have defining experiences in our lives, and the Marine Corps was certainly one for me. But it was more than just a defining experience; it marked my leaving behind childhood and entering adulthood. It was leaving home, and more. In my last months of high school I was still dependent on the financial and emotional support of my parents, my relatives, and my school friends. Once I entered boot camp, that support system became irrelevant. Nothing anyone could have sent me in the way of money or gifts could have made one iota of difference in my life. And the emotional support that could come via the mail was a drop in the bucket compared to the emotional needs I experienced in dealing with the seventeen-hour days of a Marine Corps recruit—no, make that twenty-four hour days because my dreams were filled with nightmares. "Back home" was another world, and I had to discover my own inner resources to make it through.

In the Marine Corps, I believe I underwent a version of the initiation rites that have been integral to the human experience until the last few hundred years. It appears that generalized initiation ceased when we entered the industrial age, and I believe many of the problems of modern-day young people can be traced to the fact that our society has no initiation, or rites of passage, that induct them into adulthood. As a consequence, they are stuck as a man-child, or a woman-child, psychologically incomplete, still unconsciously expecting someone...anyone...to take care of them.

Separation. I think about how boot camp separated me, severed me, from my old life—physically and emotionally. There was no option to take a break, to get away for a few days. Separation is a key element of initiation whether it be in the military or being taken away for a time by the village elders. A successful initiation separates a person from his or her community, then indoctrinates and transforms, and finally returns the person to society in a new status. There must be danger and hardship involved, because the youth is being wrested from childhood, especially from the mother. Normally the instructors are strangers of the same sex who teach great quantities of sacred lore and countless taboos. In the case of males, there's an old saying, "Only women can make babies: and only men can make men."

But for all that, I don't think my Marine initiation was complete. Although it was a mighty testing ground for things physical and psychological, it didn't include a spiritual component. And so my spiritual initiation was to await another, crushingly painful, time.

3

TAKING CARE OF BUSINESS

At last I was freed from the Marines. I headed to San Jose, California, where my parents had moved. I found that San Jose State College had a highly regarded accounting degree program and I looked forward to reuniting with my family. There I would make an all-out assault on obtaining a CPA certificate. I was more than ready to put down the gun and take up the books!

School was a piece of cake after the preceding two years of military life, and the A's and the B's came easily. Through a combination of summer school and carrying a heavy load, I graduated with honors in three years, working twenty-hour-week jobs all the while. Late in 1957, I was able to get a part time job at a local CPA firm and I loved it. The firm offered me a full time job at graduation and I didn't hesitate to accept!

The CPA firm that hired me was called Gottenberg, McDowell, and Krouskup. (It later became McDowell, Krouskup and Graham when I made partner in 1963.) It had been in business for decades and had a fine practice with about a dozen staff people. The older members of the firm, especially Harold McDowell, Wayne Krouskup and Gordon Brooks, quickly took me under their wings and began the mentoring process that is so often found in business. I passed the CPA examination the spring I graduated and a year later, with my experience requirements fulfilled, was awarded a CPA license. The year was 1960, I was twenty-four and one of the youngest CPAs in California. I felt like I wasn't missing a step at anything.

Throughout the 1960s our accounting firm prospered, and I proved to be excellent at bringing in new business, as well as building a reputation as a "can do" CPA. I relished the challenges of educating clients on reading their financial statements and using the information to improve their business, and of minimizing their income taxes. And I loved the fabric of accounting, that everything had to balance, that there was a system for everything. No matter how difficult something might be in my personal life, plunging into the orderliness of accounting was an absorbing antidote.

While I liked the structure of accounting—actually, the science of it—I was alert for opportunities to create art-forms within it, or at least to adapt the art-forms of others into my work. Within a year of my graduation from college, I showed the Graystone Cement Company a draft of their financial statements with all amounts rounded to the nearest dollar. This was not a new concept; large companies were doing it, but it hadn't been done at our firm. The client liked the presentation, as they felt it made their balance sheet look more substantial.

Flushed with success, I did the same thing on my next assignment: Merrill Farms. It was a bit risky as the owner, Russ Merrill, had a reputation for being highly adverse to change unless it was to a new farming method that he believed in. But I felt confident as Mr. Merrill had taken a liking to me, and I approached him with the anticipation of earning a pat on the back. When we met, he looked at the statements and then at me with surprise. I plunged into my pitch as to why this was a more professional approach, that it was the coming thing, and so on. He listened with his unfailing courtesy, and when I finished, leaned across his desk.

"Young man," his weather-beaten face emphasized his sixty years of experience and contrasted it to my twenty-five years of greenness, "What will my bankers think—that we don't keep track of the dollars and the cents around here?" (For years I hated to hear a conversation begin with "young man." It always meant the answer was "no!")

The high-points in the profession for me were the relationships I developed. Money is usually everyone's greatest secret and I was privy to all manner of closely-guarded information. I never violated a confidence, and gained the respect of the old and young alike on that score. It was also a peek into the lives of the well-off and the wealthy. Because I intended to be wealthy as well, I carefully studied their habits. I received a lot of insight into both positive and negative behavior.

Some clients with wealth used it to reward their employees for good work or to help out in the community, and that impressed me. And many of them took a great interest in their children's education, trying to give them a head start. I thought that was quite good, given that my folks had been pretty passive about what I did after high school.

On the other hand, some people seemed subconsciously determined to spend their money loafing around the social clubs, dabbling at whatever they did. Some seemed to be trying to drink it up. And others seemed almost frozen by their wealth, agonizing over what to do in even the most unimportant areas of their lives. They reminded me of the uncomfortable feeling of ice cubes in my hands, their coldness freezing the slight moisture on my fingers, bonding the cubes to my skin. Doing business with them was always sticky and slightly painful.

I'd had a long-standing interest in agriculture, stemming from my boyhood days on my uncle's ranch. And there was my boyhood passion for cars, which had continued, unabated. So I specialized in the particular business and tax problems of agribusiness and auto dealers. When my family and I moved to a small cattle ranch 50 miles south of San Jose, in 1967, I created a long commute to my office but also enhanced my image in the ag community as an accountant who related to cow manure on a man's boots and soil under a man's fingernails.

Fueled by success, by 1971 I was chafing at my perceived restraints of operating in a local accounting firm environment. I was looking for bigger worlds to conquer. That spring I lobbied my two older partners and received their okay to call Ed Bostick at one of the "Big Eight" international accounting firms, Haskins & Sells, about their prior overture to discuss a merger. After a lot of negotiations we merged in September of that year. I immediately set about prospecting for new, and much larger, clients. Over the next five years my efforts were quite successful and included bringing about a merger with another local accounting firm in the area. Haskins and Sells was very generous with me, and in 1975 I was told that I should move back to San Jose, where I would soon take over as Partner In Charge of what had grown to be a good-sized office.

I left public accounting about a year later, in 1976. But accounting still has a strange hold on me. For years I've had nostalgic dreams of being a CPA. Why? Have I missed something in my life that practicing as a CPA gave me? I know it isn't money, because I made my fortune after I left the profession. Maybe it's the satisfaction of helping people solve their business and personal problems. Maybe I miss the many close friendships. Or maybe I regret not having stayed with the firm that now employs about 50,000 people internationally, and seeing how high I could have risen in the hierarchy. More than once I've asked myself, "Should I return to accounting?"

Unable to discern just what the dreams tell me, I usually conclude, "Never come out of the same hole twice." That terminates my day-dreaming, if not the dreams.

•••••••••••

Of course, there were a lot of other things going on in my life while I was practicing accounting. There was a long interval in Europe, getting married, starting a family—and the flame-out of a love affair with cars.

"Well, what do you think?" the stuffy car salesman with a phony English accent asked me.

I found it hard to speak. It was finally here! I had waited months for a new Morgan to come in. This one was a 1959 Plus 4 roadster, black, with white leather seats and wire wheels. It looked like a classic to me, and not just because Morgan hadn't changed the body design or the use of a wooden frame since before World War II. ("Watch out for the termites," jealous detractors would hoot at me.)

No, it was also classic for its sloping front fenders, its prominent hood shroud which I would strap and buckle down, like drawing a cinch on a horse, and its total lack of creature comforts. No heater, no radio, a by-hand top for the rain, an un-synchronized first gear, no glove compartment door and non-absorbing shock absorbers comprised its list of features.

And now this classic would be mine! I got behind the wheel and my hands tingled as I stiff-armed the wooden steering wheel, race-driver style. My mind's eye saw myself drifting through turn seven at

Laguna Seca, my head framed by a black roll bar and my white driving suit topped with a red racing scarf around my neck, its ends beating in the wind.

"Do you want it?" The phony accent was impatient.

"Write up the papers. Let me know when you're ready," I said. I intended to sit right there, sign the papers right there, and when I had, start the engine and drive out the showroom doors onto San Carlos Avenue in San Jose. I wasn't going to get out of the car until I ran out of gas or had to go to the bathroom, whichever came first.

Within a month, the Morgan was outfitted for Class E Production racing. My first outing was at the San Luis Obispo, California airport.

As I waited on the starting grid with a squadron of cars for my first practice session, I noticed a late arrival being pushed out to the end of the pack. It was my hero, Lew Spencer of Los Angeles, and his newest Morgan, Baby Doll III. As if I weren't already nervous enough, I now felt like a teen-age girl at an Elvis concert. That was not a good feeling for someone who would soon to be trying to shoehorn among other cars into the first turn at ninety miles-an-hour.

The flag fell, everyone pushed their accelerators to the floor board, and the black smell of burning rubber and the soupy brown smell of Castrol conspired with the smoke to disorient me. As my Morgan charged forward like its racehorse namesake, I seemed to stop breathing and the lump in my throat cut off my wind.

I shifted up through the gears, giving the horse full rein. Suddenly the cars in front of me started to down-shift and brake for turn one, and my brain came back on, shouting that I had to do the same thing or risk the horse running away with me. Making it through the turn I let out a deep sigh of relief, accelerating once again, but consciously now. I remembered that this was just the practice, not the actual race!

Driving home to San Jose that Sunday night, I relived the race a hundred times. I had driven decently enough, and thought that I could only get better. Now I saw myself as a major character in an adventure novel, and it was exhilarating. As time went on, I stroked that image the best I could.

In the winter of 1961, I participated in a series of practice races at the Cotati Raceway that were a prelude to the start of the official racing season. For the last of the sessions, I installed Frendo brake pads on the car, and made several other improvements. Frendo brakes were becoming popular: they expanded as they got hotter, producing a better braking effect as the race went on.

I felt confident the morning of the race, even thrilled in a controlled sort of way. As the race progressed it was obvious that my improvements to the Morgan were having a positive effect, and I was running near the leaders, going faster each lap. Halfway through, I got a great jump out of turn five and surged down the main straight, picking off another car. I down-shifted smoothly, and when I reached my brake point, hit the brakes.

My foot went directly to the floorboard! Panicking, I tried pumping the breaks—nothing! I crash-shifted from second to first, running the engine way over red-line, expecting it to blow. I was clipping the hay bales lining the outside of the turn with the left side of my front bumper. There were still no brakes, and, at the apex of the turn, I knew I was about to crash.

My brother, Dick, and my friends, the Scotts, were watching with binoculars almost a half-mile away. They saw the Morgan fly up over the hay bales and yelled at each other, "There he goes! He's crashed!"

All I saw through my goggles was hay flying, blue sky, and then, as the car arced back to earth, green grass and a lone tree. The car shuttered as it hit the earth, finally restrained by the tree enfolded in the Morgan's hood.

I sat stunned, feeling the salty warmth of blood running from my nose across my lips and chin. "Get out!" Two course marshals ran my way, each carrying a large fire extinguisher. "Get the hell out!" Their urgency cut through my fog, and I struggled out of my seat belt. Jumping out of the car, I stumbled towards them.

"I'm okay, I'm okay," I yelled as much as for myself as for them. One marshal stopped and sat me down. We both looked to the Morgan where the other marshal watched warily, his extinguisher at the ready. Thankfully, no flames came.

• • • • • • • • • •

Between recovering from my minor scrapes and writing checks all over the place to fix the car, a flame that had burned within me died. I had lost my love of driving fast—although not of fast cars. But I was still only twenty-five and too young to give up my carefree youth. I took a six month leave of absence from my CPA firm, and my brother and I took an ocean-liner for Europe.

To give my sojourn an air of legitimacy, I told people I wanted to learn about the history of Western civilization, and we did study briefly at the University of the Central Mediterranean in Nice, France. And we looked at every church and historical monument we could find. I even took a number of volumes of Will Durant's, "The History of Western Civilization" with me, leaving them behind to an unknown fate at a country inn in Germany after discovering that I wasn't reading them and that they were painfully heavy.

Truth is, we were much more interested in the daily life of Europeans, especially those our age, especially female. We hitch-hiked all over England and the continent, working our way down to Paris, then crossing over to Germany and all the way through the Scandinavian countries to Oslo, Norway. From there we plunged south to Spain. Later we would add a trip through Italy to our adventures.

Hitch-hiking was pretty easy in those days. We taped an American flag to our largest suitcase, stuck out our thumbs and smiled. I think the sight of young Americans hitch-hiking must have been somewhat unusual as we were able to snag one ride after another, meeting dozens of people. However, it seemed that every driver assumed we could speak at least a little of their language, and we spent many miles comically trying to communicate. The easiest method was by using our maps, and the few symbols that constitute universal sign language.

Dick and I liked most everything we came across, the people, the sights, the food, and the beer. But our favorite time on the trip was our two months as bartenders at the Casa Martín in Tossa de Mar, Spain.

Tossa de Mar! My memories are reinforced by a packet of letters I wrote more than thirty years ago to Barbara Drotleff, my future bride. She saved them, and now they bring back the memories of why I liked Spain so much.

Dick and I lived with the Martín family, and we each worked four or five hours a day in the family-run bar and sandwich shop, the "Casa Martín." It was mostly a tourist place, so our English got us by, although we did learn quite a bit of Spanish as we went along. I went to work at the bar around eleven at night and closed the place at four-thirty in the morning, cleaning up and reaching bed at 5 a.m. It was a strange routine, but it gave me the opportunity to go to the rocky Mediterranean beach of the fishing village each afternoon, or to take the bus to Barcelona for the library and the bull fights.

The bull fights were frightening, exciting, morbidly fascinating, the crowds a huge, exuberant mass of color. The ritualistic fights, each proceeding with a rhythm long established as "the right way," were punctuated by arresting calls of trumpets. I felt I, too, should adore the fights because the Spaniards were crazy for them, and it had been the "in thing" in college to slavishly refer to Earnest Hemingway and his bull-fight writings. But for all the fights I saw–the most memorable featuring Luis Miguel Dominguin who, along with his rival, Antonio Ordoñez, was the subject of Hemingway's book, *The Dangerous Summer*–I can't honestly say that I liked them. I struggled to discover what I was missing. My employer and mentor, "Papa" Martín, finally relented to my questions one day and said, "Look, Roberto, you must understand the Spanish. We are a prideful people and we have a strong need to assert ourselves. We believe that man is the number one animal on earth. The bull is number two. That's why we fight. We have to keep demonstrating that we are number one. Sometimes the bull wins, but not often. We are meant to rule the world. It says so in the Bible, and that means we are the dispensers of death to all other things."

Sr. Martín looked at me imploringly for my understanding. I shook my head tentatively, as if I had been given some insight, but I really hadn't. It didn't seem reasonable to me that when the matador killed a bull, the bull's death signified an affirmation of life for humankind. The psychology of it all was beyond me.

If bull fighting remained a mystery, the rest of the Spanish scene didn't. I loved the slow feel of the place, the charm of dusty paths in ancient walled villages, with surprises beyond every turn of a corner. The people were friendly, and picking up enough additional Spanish to get by was no problem. The wine was good, twelve cents a liter, and there were enough tourists to give the Costa Brava a holiday atmosphere. The Martín family was very easy to live with, and I felt secure even as I lived out my dream of being swallowed up in the culture of Spain.

My letters from Europe to Barbara also showed that I was struggling with myself. Much like the Spaniards with their need to constantly prove their superiority over the rest of the animal world, I still felt a nagging need to prove myself in the world I had left at home. Europe became an increasingly empty playground for me and the superficialness of my life without work began to weigh heavily on me. Soon I was plotting my return home. My correspondence with Barbara, whom I had met in college when she dated my best friend, Glen Sparrow, was an increasingly important part of my thinking. Without realizing it, I was falling in love with the tall blonde who worked as an interior decorator in San Francisco.

Dick and I returned to San Jose for Christmas. I began dating Barbara that winter, and her mother's favorite story of our first date has been retold many times.

"Barbara and I were home one Saturday night," Ann Nagel recalls. "I knew she had a date that evening, but I really hadn't paid any attention. The doorbell rang, and I told her I'd get it, because she was still getting ready. I opened the door and was shocked to see this young man standing before me, asking for Barbara. He was dressed in the fanciest English suit that I'd ever seen!

"I forgot my manners and left him standing there while I rushed down the hall to find my daughter. 'Barbara, there's a gentleman out there to see you!' "

"A gentleman?" Barbara asked. Ann had never referred to any of her dates as "gentlemen."

"Yes, honey—he's wearing a hat!"

Ann became my most enthusiastic supporter, and Barbara and I married in November, 1962. Our wedding date was planned so that we could spend our honeymoon in the Bahamas at the Nassau Speed Week. We knew when we wanted to marry, but deciding how took some discussion.

Like so many people, I'd had an internal religious war going on for a decade. I liked Sunday School as a child, but lost interest sometime in high school. Perhaps it happened in a science class when I discovered that the creation story in the Bible couldn't be taken literally. Later, with the focused violence I experienced in the Marine Corps and what I learned in college philosophy classes, religion became pretty much irrelevant to my daily life. It was popular in school circles to poke fun at money-crazed TV evangelists who rented Sunday morning air time to vacuum up money from gullible old lady shut-ins, and I gleefully joined in the derision.

So I knew I didn't want to be married in a church. Basically, I saw them as being houses of hypocrisy. In my way of thinking, they were condemned by inconsistencies. I couldn't reconcile the wrathful, vengeful God of the Old Testament with the loving Father of the New. Nor could I tolerate the obsessive moralizing on the teachings of Jesus on Sunday mornings, and then the relegation of those same teachings to the dust bin of irrelevance for the rest of the week. And the presumed literalness of the Bible neither made common sense in my head, nor rang true in my heart.

Raised as a nominal Protestant, Barbara didn't have any religious ties at all, and laughed genuinely when I poked fun at my supposed shirt-tail cousin, the Rev. Billy Graham. He was much adored by one of my grandmothers and I suspected her of sending money to his TV show. I'd sigh to Barbara and say, "At least she's keeping it in the family," and Barb would smile at this familial foible. As it turned out, we were quite happy to be married in Ann's home by a Jewish judge, which seemed appropriately quirky to us.

After Europe and my marriage I no longer saw myself as a character in an adventure novel. The fantasy period of my life was over. Now began the time to assume the responsibilities of a householder and plant some roots.

We first lived in a cabin in the Los Gatos Mountains. I commuted to my CPA job in San Jose and Barbara to a decorating studio in Saratoga. We focused our time on fixing our place up and going to sports car races up and down California. In 1965, Barb and I took a three-week trip to Europe, and I was thrilled to show her the spots that touched me four years earlier. She loved meeting the Martíns, but she especially enjoyed the museums and cathedrals. Our far flung trips came to a halt when our three daughters arrived, beginning with Merede in 1966, followed by Lara in late 1967 and Sarah in 1970.

One of the happiest periods of our marriage was when we lived on that small cattle ranch outside Hollister. Our family was by then established, and the future looked rosy. Later my career pulled me to different locations, and five different houses in five years, but we attacked each move with relish. They were all part of a brighter future, which is the way I've always viewed life.

•••••••••

Two things happened during my time with Haskins & Sells that had a big impact on what was to come in my life. From 1972-1974, I was a member of the California Agricultural Leadership Program. Its purpose was, and is, to take promising young people (forty and under) working in agriculture and provide them with a greater depth, balance and motivation for assuming future leadership roles. At the time it was a three-year fellowship for thirty of us, and it gave us an exposure to the political, cultural, social, economic and historic characteristics of our country and others as well.

We attended seminars at a number of different college campuses, visited Washington D.C. to see the national government in action, and the poverty-ridden, cancer-struck Appalachian Mountain region to see why some of the government's actions were, in fact, needed. I came home from Washington with pictures of myself shaking hands with Vice-president Spiro Agnew and Secretary of Agriculture Earl Butz. Both were history within a year, Agnew convicted of fraud and income tax evasion, and Butz forced from office due to racist remarks that he'd made.

My time in Ag Leadership intensified my interest in agribusiness.

I especially related to the straight-ahead, self-reliant values of my classmates. Our class took two lengthy international trips, one to Latin America and the other to the Middle East and Russia.

Our trip to Guatemala in 1973 really shook me up. My cozy middle-class world, where progress and prosperity seemed open to everyone, was shaken to the core when I witnessed the conditions of poor farming families. They lived lives of extreme difficulty and quiet desperation, farming small plots of poor land, or as virtually indentured laborers on the huge plantations of the oligarchy. There were millions of them, clearly the vast majority of the population. It was no wonder that we saw their overseers wearing pistols. The local Rotarians in one of the outlying towns blamed the need on "communist guerrillas," but the problems looked deeper than that.

As I rode through Guatemala and talked with my buddies about what we were seeing, I determined that someday I would reach out and try to help people to whom little seemed possible.

The 1974 trip eastward opened my eyes to a lot of things. We were in the Kuwaiti parliament when they debated raising the price of oil to the then astounding amount of $5 a barrel, which precipitated the first US "energy shock." We went through Iran only slightly aware that something was amiss, and that the Shah of Iran would be overthrown in a few years. But we didn't have to look for subtleties in Russia. Moscow was the most oppressive city I'd been in. Interestingly, there was no litter anywhere, but the bugged hotel rooms, the restrictive regulations and the sullen and downtrodden people were a high price to pay for clean streets and roadways. Only the vodka was good.

Things were different down in the Ukraine. It was a rich countryside and the people seemed more at ease the further we went from Moscow. Many people remembered the Americans with fondness for our contributions in helping defeat Hitler.

And I had experiences in Israel that started me treating religion with more respect than I'd been giving it.

A sharply cooling wind swept across the Plain of Esderlon. Deflected by the rocky slopes of Mt. Carmel, it blew up into my thin jacket and across my bare head as I stood at canyon-edge of the ruins of Har Megiddon. The formerly massive defensive walls had been destroyed here and there, leaving an appearance of missing teeth. The fortress seemed possessed by spirits past, and now I thought I could hear voices of alarm as an approaching enemy marched steadily up the Plain. Death was again in the air, and not even my spastic shivers could shake it away.

I remembered our bearded guide's vivid portrayal of fearsome battles fought here, some of them described in the Old Testament. More importantly, he said, trying to distinguish this stop from other competing ruins, Megiddon is the origin of the word "Armageddon." This would be the site of the coming battle on the "great day of God the Almighty" described in the last book of the New Testament, Revelation. He let us know that many Christians thought it would happen in the year 2,000. Now in 1974 with the superpowers in a blind race to accumulate nuclear bombs sufficient to destroy humanity several times over, the prophecy had a certain logic to it. For an instant, I imagined I saw people exploding, smelled flesh burning and heard the bleat of dying animals. I trembled with sickened awe at the titanic foretelling of the end of time as we know it.

I shuddered again, and thought how I always seemed to shiver in deserted ruins. Why? Was I imagining time-encrusted events, or remembering them? So much of what I was seeing in Israel seemed to be nostalgically familiar to me.

My consciousness was continually shocked as our Leadership Program class made its way around Israel. We stopped at one place after another that was mentioned in the Bible. The physical existence of these sites came as a big surprise to me as I had thought that the Bible was pretty much a fabrication from beginning to end, having taken a viewpoint opposite that of fundamentalists.

Now it was Jerusalem, and I stopped at the Fifth Station of the Cross, where Simon of Cyrene helped Jesus carry the cross. Where was the Sixth? Looking forward on the crooked, narrow, cobblestone street provided no clue. The Via Dolorosa was jammed with tourists, locals, donkeys, and carts, limiting my vision. I consulted my map for the twentieth time, gave up and continued on. Slowly working my way through the river of two-leggeds and four-leggeds, I imagined I was Jesus staggering under the cross, goaded on by soldiers angry at the pause at the Fifth Station.

Each lash of a soldier's whip and the resulting roar of the blood-thirsty crowd must have carried a venting of outrage for his urging people to a higher standard of behavior, for his calling out for change. Change, the most resisted and hated word in language. How dare he! "Take that, you troublemaker!" I felt the sting, heard the guttural wrath. A thought ran through my mind: "If I die as a sacrifice, will you stop killing the lambs and the doves in the temples? It would be a fair trade."

My tour book said the stations, designated by Francis of Assisi during a 13th century Crusade, were sites of Jesus' expression of suffering on his way to the place of the skulls, Golgotha. The march to crucifixion. The whole thing had a realness for me, and I questioned my skepticism of the Bible. Perhaps...I had been wrong about some things. Maybe. Every now and then I shook again. Something had happened here, no doubt about it. I kept the picture of Jesus bearing a cross pulsing in my forehead.

Scenes from the Holy Land kept renewing themselves as we flew for Kuwait, via Cypress and Lebanon, leaving no marks in our passports to tip the Kuwaiti officials that we had been in enemy territory. Har Megiddon, Jerusalem, many other places; they were very real for me. And then there were some that weren't. The grotto "birthplace" of Jesus in the Church of the Nativity—no. The remains of the "childhood home of Jesus" in tourist-trap Nazareth—definitely not. They just didn't convey any feelings to me, no shivers. (In recent years I've learned that the authenticity of these two places is considered "very doubtful" by Biblical scholars, so it's no wonder I didn't pick up any "vibrations.")

I speculated on Barbara's reaction when I would reach home and tell her that I thought the family should start attending church. And that there were some true stories in the Bible; that they could help us. Not all of them, but some, and perhaps many. "Literally true?" she asked. What could I say? I tried, "Not exactly, not always, but true like myths—they themselves may not be strictly true, but they're based on truth. I know it's confusing. But whether they're true or not isn't the point." And what was the point, I asked myself?

I couldn't explain it. I said, "Just trust me, Barbara. Let's go to church. It can't hurt."

And that's what happened. We went. The pastor of the little Presbyterian Church in Hollister was pleased to see our five shining faces the next Sunday morning. He invited me to show my trip slides at fellowship the next week.

(I never could explain to Barbara where I was with the Bible. I only discovered it recently, finding it in a Tibetan Buddhist saying about some of the long-time-ago accounts of their religious cosmology: "You're a fool if you believe these stories—and you're a fool if you don't!")

• • • • • • • • • • •

The other thing that happened while I was at Haskins & Sells was that I met my future business partner, Dino Cortopassi, at a Harvard Agribusiness Seminar. Dino was an agribusinessman and farmer from Stockton, California. He and another Stockton farmer, John Kautz, controlled a small food processing company. They engaged my firm to perform auditing and management services. This gave me a good chance to get to know Dino, and vice-versa. Although our styles were different—Dino being an Italian with a strong Mediterranean personality, a big fellow, and myself being of Scotch/Swedish descent, small and quieter by far—we valued the same things and were both quite ambitious. We soon developed a fast friendship.

It wasn't long before Dino proposed that I join him as a partner in a situation that promised plenty of excitement and a chance to accumulate some real wealth. That hooked me. But there was a catch; I had to take a 40% salary cut! Dino requested that I take a decrease, not only because I'd been making quite a bit more than the ag community was used to paying, but also to prove how motivated I was to come on board. While I've always enjoyed the challenge of proving myself, the cut was a mild nick to my pride. So for years I kept squirreled away my last earnings statement from H&S that proved—to whom? myself?—that I had made $100,000 in my last year before joining Dino.

I also accepted the financial risk of losing my down payment on the corporate stock interest I acquired from Dino. I had been around agriculture long enough to know that there was always a chance to incur large losses, but I figured I could go back to being a CPA if things came unglued.

Barbara, ever faithful to my career moves, joined in the spirit of things. She took an immediate liking to Dino's wife, Joan, and thought that living in Stockton would be just fine. While leaving the security of H & S gave her pause, she also had misgivings about where H & S might transfer me next. It could be a long way from her family and hard on our three young daughters as well. So we decided to take the plunge with Dino, and on September 30, 1976, I resigned from H & S, five years to the day from when our old firm had joined them.

Late one evening, soon after I joined Dino, we were discussing a difficult question. Dino proposed a course of action on the issue and asked, "How do you feel about it?"

I ran down the pros and cons and ended with my conclusion. "Well, it seems to be the only option at this point."

"Yes, but how do you feel about it, Bob?" Dino asked again.

"I just told you."

"Look, what you've told me is what you think about it. I want to know how you feel about it."

I sat there stumped. How I felt about it? Did he mean, was I happy or sad or something? I didn't know how I felt. Actually, I didn't seem to feel anything at all. I tried conjuring up some feelings and took a crack at analyzing the few wisps of emotion that came my way. And what did all this have to do with a business decision, anyway, I wondered. God, this was hard work! I was embarrassed by the passage of time and blurted out, "I feel...okay. Yes, that's it. I feel okay about it."

Dino eyed me suspiciously, and I felt it. It was something I would have to get used to, this thing of feeling as well as thinking. His encouragement, actually it was a demand, that I should find out how I felt about business issues as well as thinking about them, opened me up to new dimensions of action.

• • • • • • • • • • •

"Ron, tell me more about the pickle business. You've been in it for a long time. We all know it's in decline. How do you feel about it?" I used Dino's question often, now. Actually I wasn't all that interested in Ron, and was just killing time as the two of us waited for his flight to LA. Our time together had been dry and unproductive, and now even the afternoon coffee seemed stale.

One of the businesses that Dino was involved in was a food processing firm with two divisions. Neither was doing well and I spent half my time working on their operations. When everything was sorted out, it was clear that we should sell both of them, and I took up the task. I soon discovered that selling a money-losing business with a dubious future is a tough job. Time dragged on.

When Ron P.'s resume came in response to our need for a CEO for the pickle division, I didn't see much promise. However, we had few prospects and I arranged for Ron to meet with the ownership trio of Dino, John Kautz and myself. The interview wasn't inspiring. It broke up with everyone convinced that they had seen the last of Ron.

Now Ron and I sat in the airport coffee shop. With our business agenda exhausted, the conversation drifted with little purpose. Ron talked about the history of the pickle industry, now dominated by Heinz and Vlasic, with sales of the highly salted, blood-pressure raising product going nowhere. There were understandably fewer small companies each year, and he started telling me amusing personal stories about the guys running these soon-to-be-relics. I thought to myself, "He sure knows a lot of these characters." Notwithstanding the entertainment, I told myself for the one-hundredth time that the industry was a loser for us, and thought, "I give up."

Almost as soon as I "gave up" and stopped thinking, something new popped into my mind. I had a clear picture of Ron finding us a buyer for the business! With a few minutes left before his departure, I formulated an idea.

"Ron, would you like to work for us for six months? You can do it from your home, and you won't have to move here. You can start

off by calling every pickle plant in the U.S. to see if they would like
to buy some of our inventory. In the process, nose around and if you
discover someone who is interested in buying our business, we'll pay
you a handsome commission. What do you think?"

"I think 'yes,' for the right salary and commission. Hey, I've got
to catch my plane." We nailed down the deal as we walked to the
departure gate.

Dino and John were quite surprised to hear that I had hired Ron.
They were doubtful that anything would come from it. By then my
feeling of intuition had passed, and I was privately doubtful myself.
But I stuck to my guns and implemented the plan. In fact, it worked
with precision. In four or five months Ron sold not a nickel's worth
of our inventory, but he had found a similar business in Wisconsin
where one of its owners was tired of cold winters, and willing to listen to the siren song of the warm, sweet life of California. In a few
months a deal to sell the business had been negotiated and closed.

The other division of our troubled food processing company also
was sold through intuition. It was a good thing, too, as I had no luck
using conventional tactics to get the job done.

About a year after the pickle company sale I was on vacation at
Lake Tahoe. One day I idly leafed through Fortune Magazine and
came upon an article about a management ruckus at a Fortune 500
company. I enjoyed business gossip and read it with interest. Buried
in the story was a reference to the company's former CEO, Bill B.,
who was noted to be living in Fresno, California teaching business
courses at the local state college.

Fresno was a modest valley town and the site of our pickled pepper division. I found it hard to believe that a Fortune 500 CEO
would move from Chicago to Fresno, at least willingly. He was bound
to be bored. I paused from reading and looked out over the lake, gaz-
ing unthinkingly at the Sierra Mountains circling me. I became very
excited when a picture of Bill B. buying our business came to me.

The first thing I did when I returned home was to call information for Bill's phone number. Fortunately he was listed.

"Mr. B., my name is Bob Graham. I read about you in Fortune
magazine. The company I'm with owns a specialty foods processing

plant there in Fresno. We want to expand our markets, and I wonder if you would be interested in consulting with us? You are? Good. Let's make a date when I can come in to see you with the guy who runs the plant for us."

Over the next year Bill and his partner, Fred G., became quite familiar with the business. They took a liking to Al Andrews, who was the plant's CEO. When I proposed that Bill, Fred and Al buy the business, the three were ready to talk. We soon worked out a deal that satisfied everyone's needs. The business flourished in subsequent years and everybody lived happily ever after, more or less.

As it turned out, the best intuition teacher I've ever had was Dino. When I met him, I was, by training and inclination, a rational, linear, left-brain thinker. And I'd been disconnected from strong emotions for a long time. I wasn't even very good at articulating my deep love for my wife and children. But Dino legitimized for me the experiencing and expressing of feelings, which opened me up to intuition. That, in turn, led me to many wonderful experiences of what I call nonordinary reality in the years to come. Feelings were the key.

I've never been able to figure how and when my separation from feelings actually occurred. I know we all start out as kids fully in touch with feelings, and ready to act on them at the drop of a hat. But someplace along the line I lost that. It probably happened as part of the process of becoming "a man."

4

ONE LAST LOOK

arly in January, 1979, Barbara and I attended the National Food Brokers Convention in New Orleans, along with Al and Claudia Andrews. Al ran our California Gift/Orlando Foods subsidiary and we were there to talk with key brokers and promote sales of our pickled pepper and grape leaf products. After a long day of doing business, we were ready to enjoy the food and jazz that make the city so special. Brennan's for brunch and Gallatin's for dinner; these and others like them were our landmark restaurants, and every meal was an occasion. Afterwards we hit one jazz club after another until we could go on no more. The French Quarter was delightfully different from any place I'd been in the U.S. People wandered up and down the streets, drinks in hand and spirits soaring. Sleep was the only thing that seemed in short supply.

After the convention, Barbara and I went to Natchez for a few days and reveled in the magnificent, nineteenth century homes of the rich and famous cotton barons of the time. These houses and their gardens, marvelously restored and maintained, reflected an opulence undimmed by comparison to contemporary mansions. Although I didn't particularly enjoy looking at other people's houses back home, these places had a strange hold on me. I actually enjoyed seeing several of them twice and one of them three times! I think Barb and I projected ourselves back into the prior century and somehow saw ourselves as part of the landed aristocracy. We were very happy.

Our only troublesome moment came when we called home to see how our pastor, Rev. Roger Stiers, was doing. Roger had become ill the previous spring and it took his doctors several months to discover that he had cancer. The resulting late start in treating the disease contributed to a rapid decline in his health. Now the news seemed to be worse by the day. Barbara was particularly fond of Roger and we both identified with his family which mirrored ours: husband, wife, and three pre-teenage daughters.

Back home from our mini-vacation in Louisiana, we resumed our daily life of work, school, running the house and dreaming about springtime. January in Stockton is a time of tule fog, an intense, cold, thick, grayness that forms at ground level and casts a pall over the region. The fog, which struck me in some ways as evil, wasn't limited to Stockton; it ran up and down California's long Central Valley for two or three months at a time, socking in airports and causing spectacular, chain reaction, multiple-vehicle crack-ups. Sometimes fifty, and as many as one hundred, cars and trucks would tangle on one of the freeways with devastating and fatal effect.

The most consistent result of sun deprivation, at least for us, was the onset of a mild depression which could only be lifted by a quick trip to Palm Springs, or anywhere else the sun was shining. Even the approach of my birthday on the eighteenth did little to uplift our mood. Our only solace was our quiet determination to outlast another fog season. The night before, we decided that we wouldn't do anything special on my birthday, just have an early dinner with the kids.

That morning as we finished breakfast the telephone rang. Barbara answered. It was a woman from church who told her Roger had died shortly after midnight. We looked soberly at each other.

"You never know when its going to happen," I said, sadly. We looked deeply into each other's eyes and shared a silent prayer of thanksgiving that we and the children were all healthy. We hugged, and I said to Barbara, "I love you very much," and we kissed good-bye.

"Happy birthday," Barbara's lips silently mouthed as I turned back for one last look.

The day passed slowly at work. The tule fog had everyone in a funk, and we worked at 3/4 speed. Early in the afternoon my partner, Dino, looked at me strangely and said, "Bob, what's the matter? Are you all right?"

"What?" His voice hardly registered through the sinking feeling that had suddenly engulfed me.

"I...I don't know. Maybe I was thinking about Roger." I had told Dino about Roger's death earlier in the day. "Roger was so young, my age. God, you never know!" I felt better being able to ascribe my bewildered feeling of despair to Roger's death, even though in fact I had not been thinking about him.

About four-thirty that afternoon our neighbor, Phyllis, called, very upset. Her words tumbled out. "Bob, do you know where Barbara is?"

"No, no," I stammered.

She rushed on. "The girls came home from school and they couldn't get into the house, so they came here. I called and called but no one answered. Finally I went over there. The doors are locked and there was no answer to the door bell—but the car is there. I'm worried!"

"I'm leaving now!" I hung up the phone and ran out of the office, saying nothing to the startled receptionist. The ten-minute drive home was long, even though I was speeding. Too long, for it gave me time to imagine all sorts of terrible things. Barbara had been in an auto accident and was in the hospital. She had been kidnapped. She had slipped, broken her leg and was lying in pain somewhere. God, where was she?

As I approached the last curve before our house, a brown station wagon came into view and approached. My heart was filled with relief. Barbara was okay, coming to see me about something! But the Chevy wagon met me and kept going—it wasn't our car, just a look-alike! I raced around the corner and pulled into our driveway. I ran to the door, unlocked it, flung it open and screamed, "Barbara, Barbara!" Silence. I raced through the downstairs rooms, still screaming her name. Silence. I ran up the stairs and through our open bedroom door.

She was lying on the bed with a day blanket pulled up over her waist. I took three quick steps and knelt beside her. She had no breath, no pulse. I tried mouth-to-mouth resuscitation. Nothing. In a wild panic I picked up the phone and dialed emergency. I blurted out the situation and our address. Then I was sobbing, moaning, and at the same time trying to apply every emergency technique I had ever learned and forgotten. Nothing, nothing, nothing!

After an eternity (less than ten minutes, I learned), the paramedics arrived and took over. Their efforts proving fruitless, one of them picked up the phone and called the hospital to say they were bringing her in. It was then I noticed the book she was reading, lying on the bed table by the phone. It was Elisabeth Kubler-Ross' book, *On Death and Dying*. What was that all about? My mind tried to rally out of its sheer panic and focus on the meaning of Barbara reading about dying just as she, herself, was dying, but the idea was slippery. My mind lost it, fading back into panic, back to the place where my head pounded, where I didn't have control of my body, where my heart was breaking.

The paramedics rushed her downstairs into the ambulance. Just then Dino pulled up with our partner, Gene Wallom. They had heard about my sudden exit from the office and came to see what was going on. The ambulance roared off and we jumped into Dino's Chevy Blazer for the hospital. Gene sat in the back with his arm around me, comforting me. We started praying, praying that somehow the doctors at the hospital could revive Barbara. We were both bawling.

Dino was speeding through red lights as if he, too, were driving an ambulance. He called our office on our radio system and kept up a running instruction on who was to be called and who was to do what. Phyllis was to bring the girls to his house where his wife, Joan, would look after them, and so on. As I cried, prayed, begged my Lord, I imagined that Barbara would be awake when we got to the hospital.

It seemed like we waited no time at all at the emergency room, and then too soon, far too soon, a physician came out and said, "I'm sorry. There was nothing we could do. She was gone before she got here."

He took my arm, suggesting that I sit in the meditation room to compose myself. I was trembling, on the verge of collapse, trying desperately to think of something to do or say, some one last chance! As he led me down the hall, the door to the treatment room was open.

There was Barbara, on a gurney, naked from the waist up. They had used electroshock treatments in a desperate attempt to start her heart. It was then I really knew that she was gone, and that her life was over. She wasn't going to get up from that gurney and join us, putting an end to this nightmare. She wasn't going to just have a stay at the hospital and come home in a week. She was never going to be at home again. I went numb.

• • • • • • • • • • •

The three of us sat quietly in the meditation room. The finality of it all descended on me like a large weight. I seemed temporarily out of tears, but my mind started up as if it were a washing machine. Barbara dead! Roger dead! Barbara reading a book on death and dying! ON MY BIRTHDAY! What was happening? Was any of this real or was it some horrible dream from which I would soon awaken? I didn't have time to dwell on this because a new and even more terrible thought crept into my awareness. What about the girls? Three innocents: eight, eleven, and twelve.

This was the end of a normal world for them. And I had to be the one who told them. But who would explain it to them? I couldn't explain it to myself. "Ministers," my whirling mind thought, "ministers are supposed to do this." But our minister was also dead, in the morgue, at the same hospital as Barbara!

The washing machine in my head continued its turbulent rotation, with thoughts racing around and no answers coming. I forced myself to ask, "Who can help? Who can help?"

I thought of Dr. George Davis, a psychiatrist and an elder in our church. I told Dino and Gene what I was thinking, and Dino went to the telephone to arrange for George to meet us at Dino's house. The drive there was a long journey deep into my mind's idea of what was coming. My own sense of loss was momentarily put aside as I projected the emotions I thought my daughters would experience. My gut contracted and contracted until it seemed I could hardly breath.

When we arrived, Dino and Joan's daughter, Becky, had the girls upstairs in her bedroom. Becky often baby-sat the girls and they adored her. They seemed to be having a good time when I entered the room. I asked Becky to step out.

Is there a way to do it? Do you lead up to it with a long preamble? With tears running down my face I blurted out, "Girls, something terrible has happened. Your mother is dead!"

"No, NO!" Merede, the oldest, ran sobbing from the room. I ran after her, physically restraining her as she plunged down the stairs. I forcefully pulled her back into the room where Lara and Sarah were crying with desperation and confusion, and gathered all of us into a circle where we leaned on each other, weeping the tears of pain, loss, hurt, abandonment, sorrow, and fear.

After a long while, our cries for help and our tears of anguish slowed, and were replaced by a sort of turning into each other, an acknowledgment of the love among ourselves, and my pledge that I would take care of my daughters. I would never leave them.

I stuck my head out the door and, seeing Becky, asked her to come to the girls. I slowly descended the stairs, holding the railing carefully as if I might fall and crack open like a thin-shelled egg. George Davis, the psychiatrist and church elder, was in the living room with Dino and Gene. They had told him of the events and I could only add my mumbled ideas about George talking to the girls and myself. Even as I desperately wanted George to give us the answers that would explain this nightmare, I knew he couldn't. I knew that no one could.

The girls came down and sat by me on the couch. Dr. Davis sat in an armchair by the bright, warm fire blazing in the large fireplace. After expressing his sympathies, George gathered himself to try to make some sense for us of what had happened and what was going to happen. As he did so I had an image that this is what President Roosevelt's fireside chats might have been like, the father-figure to the nation consoling and counseling his bewildered, despondent flock as they suffered the Great Depression.

But this was not the Great Depression. This was the Great Death. Roosevelt could talk about the economic factors that brought on the Depression and the measures that were being taken to restore the country to health. But Dr. Davis could not explain why a well woman had suddenly died forty years before her time, nor prescribe any medicines or methods to restore her to life. The conversation proceeded slowly.

"Girls, I've asked Dr. Davis to come help us. Do you remember him from church?" Sarah didn't look up and instead snuggled in closer under my arm, making whimpering noises. Merede kept her gaze focused on the fire. Only Lara looked up at George, but it was doubtful that she could see him through the tears which now seemed a permanent part of her eyes.

"George, can you tell us about Barbara? I mean...where she is...is she...all right?...I mean..." What on earth did George say, the poor man? I can't remember.

When we broke up, I realized that it wasn't what was or wasn't said that gave our time together meaning, it was that we had done it. Questions, doubts and fears were legitimized. Answers would only come at their own pace in their own way.

It was now eight or nine in the evening. The girls drifted off with Becky. Dino, Gene and I had a tall, stiff drink. Joan and Karen, Gene's wife, were making cooking sounds in the kitchen. They called out for us to come and eat something. I dutifully followed my friends into the dining area. As the food came around I absently put a few things on my plate. The conversation was subdued. Having nothing to say, I put some potatoes in my mouth. My first sensation was that they tasted good. Then I was shocked! What was this? Barbara had died only hours earlier and here I was enjoying food! I resorted to picking at my plate.

After a while Dino asked Gene about his day at work. Gene launched into an increasingly amusing explanation of an incident in the welding shop. Suddenly I was startled to hear myself laugh. What was going on here? I was laughing when my wife just died? Was it the wine I had hardly touched? Was I crazy? Embarrassed, I lapsed into passivity. But in my mind something began to gnaw at me. There would be a tomorrow. There would be a time after the funeral, after the burial. There might even be a time when the fog ended and the sun came out again.

The next days were a blur. I started every morning in the shower, howling my pain. After the respite of sleep, all of what happened would come again to me to be relived, accompanied by cascades of tears. Then, after those cathartic moments, the pain was temporarily replaced by decision anxiety. There is an amazing amount of things that need doing after a family member dies. Notices in news-papers, friends and relatives to be told, letters written, calls made; a funeral home must be chosen, a casket selected; the time of the ser-vice must be decided upon, as well as the time of the burial; a ceme-tery plot must be selected and purchased, along with a tombstone. What should the tombstone say? Who should perform the service, since our minister is dead? What should the service be like? Who should sing and what would be sung? Where should people go after the service?

More stuff: how will the girls be cared for? Someone needs to talk to their teachers; there is all kinds of legal paperwork to be done; what is to be done with Barbara's clothes? How can I change my work from a ten-hour-a-day job to spend time with the girls? Who will take care of the pile of work that is on my desk? Everyone is doing so much to help—how will I ever repay them? And on top of all of that, there is this burning pain in my chest. Am I dying, too? How can I survive this?

●●●●●●●●●●●●

Funerals in 1979 were, by and large, prescribed by tradition. Some music, a minister trying to make sense out of the loss of life in religious terms, some more music, and finally a procession of the mourners past the body of the deceased. The family of the dearly beloved delivered themselves beforehand into the hands of the pro-fessionals, and the results were impersonal; hearts heavy with grief found little consolation in them. It was before the time when remembrances and tributes to the dead delivered by family and friends began to be incorporated into services, and people said after-wards, "Wasn't that a nice service? He (the deceased) would have liked it."

Because the First Congregational Church was in turmoil due to Pastor Steirs' death, I agreed that the services for Barbara would be conducted at a funeral home. My family and I huddled together, gaining some support, in a side room that looked into the main hall. It was hard for me to make sense of what my friend, Allen

Christensen, was saying in the service, because I was focused on the coffin where my wife and my dreams lay inert and unmoving. When I did take my eyes from that place where Barbara lay and looked at my girls, I barely saw them through a teary blur.

Beautifully dressed by friends, their anguished looks made a sharp, gut-aching contrast. Each time I looked at them, another piece of my heart seemed to break away, rising up to stick in my throat like leaves gathering in an eddy of a pond. I stirred only when the soloist beautifully delivered "Morning Has Broken" to the packed hall. For a surrealistic moment, I thought I heard Barbara singing her favorite song right in harmony.

She looked so natural, so beautiful there in that coffin. Of course, what did I expect? It wasn't like she was in an accident or something, or that she was a ninety-year-old invalid. I wondered where they got her dress, one of her favorites. Another behind the scenes act of kindness performed by someone, I guessed. And her face was still as loving as ever, even though she had just been robbed of her life and her family. Her eyes were closed, but she had a faint smile and it seemed to be telling me something. Or did I just imagine it?

"Hi, Bob. Don't worry so. It was a nice service."

"God, Barb, what happened? Why you? Why now?"

"There's a reason, Bob. I can't explain it, but everything is for a reason. You'll understand someday."

"We'll miss you terribly, darling. Just terribly." My tears were real, and they followed two well worn paths down my cheeks.

"I won't be far. Take good care of the girls."

"I will, sweetheart. Help me with them when I need it."

"I will, Bob. Good-by...I love you."

On the fourth day after her death, a small group of us gathered at the funeral home. Scattering ourselves in four long, black limousines, we entrained to the cemetery. The fog was moderate, but it was cold and damp and we all wore coats. At the cemetery, we marched in a silent procession across the damp grass, avoiding the grave markers, to a canopy that had been placed over Barbara's grave site. Folding chairs were set up for the final prayers.

I sat in the front row with my girls. The ceremony was mercifully brief, but when the casket was lowered and we dropped flowers on top of it, I felt like jumping in the grave. In a strange way I didn't want it to end, even though I couldn't stand it. Then the first shovel of dirt was thrown on the physical remains of the most significant part of my life. I turned, gathered the girls and we cried our way to the car.

Twelve days after Barbara's death, our doctor told me that she had had a heart attack. The last time she was seen alive was at our neighborhood market around noon, when she complained of feeling very cold. She must have been losing circulation then, and went home to bed to get warm. Dr. Spracher figured that she had died in the early afternoon, about the time I had the sinking spell in Dino's office.

The doctor also told me that tests showed I had a stomach ulcer, and I needed to turn my attention to healing myself, as I was all my girls had left. The physical healing of the ulcer began right away. The emotional and psychological healing of Barbara's death would be a very, very long time coming.

●●●●●●●●●●●●

My daughters and I were devastated when Barbara died. We floundered through the next months, fortunate to be helped by many good friends. After five months or so, Joan Cortopassi decided that it would be a good idea for me to start dating. She arranged for me to meet some of her single girlfriends. It wasn't long before I fell in love with one of them, Wendy Berolzheimer. It was an exciting time for me when we started dating. She was a determined high achiever, very intelligent, and had been an art history major at Wellesley College. Brown haired and beautiful, I continue to catch men looking at her to this day.

We soon discovered we had a lot in common, especially kids! She had four children; Carin, a vivacious college freshman at seventeen; Philip, wheelchair bound with Muscular Dystrophy at fifteen and an inspiration to his high school classmates and to adults alike;

and the two little ones, Laura, five, and Michael Thomas, three. On December 1, 1979, we were married, joining two families into one with seven children. Wendy's grandmother and two other young people lived with us for the first several months, giving us a total of twelve people sometimes in the house, ages three to ninety-three!

At our wedding in the small chapel of the Congregational Church in Stockton, Wendy and I were flanked on the platform by the seven children. When the minister, Bill Chrystal, asked for the "I do's," there was a tangle of young voices chiming in. The guests roared, and Wendy and I laughed excitedly. It turned out that more than the two of us were getting married.

Our combined household was one big surge of energy and noise. It was a refreshing relief from my sober, quietly despairing home of the previous year. Our friends made favorable comparisons of us to "Cheaper By The Dozen" and "The Brady Bunch." But it wasn't all fun and games. My three daughters wanted a mother, but Wendy's children hadn't bargained for giving up half of theirs! Problems soon began to surface.

Joan had given us a wedding gift of two counseling sessions with a local therapist. I thought this was amusing at the time, but we used them quickly. In retrospect I wish that we had had enough wisdom to have supplemented them by a factor of fifty! The complexity and challenges of integrating the two families proved to be far greater than either Wendy or I had imagined. Many things didn't get enough attention, such as the full effect of their mother's death on my children or the effect of the breakup of Wendy's marriage on hers.

I was working at my office in Stockton the Saturday after Thanksgiving, 1980, when Philip's father called. Philip had been staying with him on Little St. Simon's Island, off the coast of Georgia, and had died in his sleep. He had tried to call Wendy at home but she wasn't there. Would I please locate her and let her know what had happened?

She was in Carmel with Carin, and I dialed the number there. While I waited, I thought, "Okay, here it is again. Death. It's been almost two years. Don't let it get you again. Keep cool."

Wendy answered the phone and I was calmly factual in telling her that her son had died. She said she would come home right away. When I hung up, I felt dry and emotionless. A few hours later, she arrived home. During this time, I had steadfastly refused to think of what they might be talking about on the three hour trip. When she got out of the car, I held back, mouthing only empty consolations.

I didn't want to have a damn thing to do with death!

5
KATALYSIS

After Barbara's death and my marriage to Wendy, life settled down. Wendy assumed responsibility for our home life. I was comfortable with this as Barbara and I had basically defined our roles in a similar fashion: she took care of the children and the house, and I worked away from home at my office. Back then my consciousness didn't include concepts like family dynamics or a husband-wife sharing of child care and household duties. Basically I let the family and home "chips fall where they may," trusting that everything would work out over the long haul. Things did, but, in retrospect, I can see that I could have done things a lot better in the first ten years of my new marriage.

With Carin away at school or elsewhere, and Philip gone, the five youngest children—Merede, Lara, Sarah, Laura and Michael Thomas—essentially grew up together. Today they all consider themselves "real" brothers and sisters; legally they are half-siblings as Wendy adopted my three girls. Although Carin wasn't as much a part of the process, she demonstrates the same familial feelings.

On the business side of things, I experienced a great partnership and friendship with Dino Cortopassi, which carries on to this day. We soon had a dozen corporations and partnerships involved in farming, food processing and agricultural services. Dino and I were constantly scheming new plans for tax and financial advantages; and twenty years later we are still unraveling some of the perhaps unnecessary complexities. Now it is getting harder and harder for me to remember why we did some of the things we did. (I think this is also known as the aging process.)

We expanded Dino's already-substantial farming operation to very large, and then ran into a buzz saw in the early 1980s when interest rates hit 18% and heavy unseasonable rains ruined our crops. We had no choice but to cut back, and it was bitter medicine to sell ranches and equipment that had taken years of effort to accumulate.

It rained from the late summer through the fall of 1982, or was it 1981? The year is a little fuzzy, but the picture is all too clear in my mind. I stood at my office window watching one storm after another wash down upon us, destroying our tomato crop, then our grape crop, then damaging our bean crop as it lay in windrows for drying. Each rainstorm caused me to do a new mental projection of the size of "The Hole." The Hole was our impending loss for the year, the amount of our shortfall-to-be in repaying our crop loans to the bank. The Hole had first emerged during the preceding late winter when heavy rains had virtually ruined our wheat crop. Now The Hole deepened with each new outburst from the heavens.

In between storms we headed for the fields to assess the latest damage. It was hell being out on a beautiful morning with the hot summer sun chasing off billowy clouds, and forcing myself to keep my eyes down on the muddy rows of rotting tomatoes. It took little time on the humid, steaming days after the rains for gray-black mold to climb onto the skins of red, almost-ripe fruit. An odor of garbage-needing-to-be-taken-out would waft up around us. We would eye the ever-decreasing number of still-green tomatoes, those that might, just might, have a chance of surviving until they could be picked. Then it would rain again.

Sometimes I thought the rain had a reddish tint to it. Was it from clearing pollution out of the atmosphere or was it literally raining red ink? Depression rose as the rain fell. There seemed to be no one to talk to, as no one really understood. Or worse, they did understand, and conversation just intensified the pain. Back in my office I stood by the window, running my numbers for no purpose; no one wanted to hear them. But I was not alone in the rainy vigils. Dino peered out from his office window, and the others, the guys who were normally in the fields everyday, Gene and Bob and Alvin, looked out from theirs. Watching stoically, bleeding inside.

Over the years we acquired and sold a variety of businesses that didn't work for one reason or another, including an irrigation supply business, one that processed peppers, pickles and olives, and a major investment in the citrus business. I learned the painful teaching that it is easier to get into a business than it is to get out of it, and that while good luck usually visits only those who are prepared, bad luck seems to visit everyone—prepared or not. I also learned that there are people who love being partners when things are going good, but who, when times gets rough, head for the nearest exit! Finally, I was shown time and time again that neither I, nor anyone else I knew, was perfect at the great game of business.

On the other side of the coin, we happily "hit a lick" in the tomato canning business, acquiring canneries in Modesto, Gilroy and Sacramento with investor partners over the course of five years. Although the canning business is cyclical, we experienced many more good years than bad, and our team developed a strong capacity for the business. And they are still at it. By the way, try our Muir Glen organic tomato products; they're as delicious as they are wholesome.

Our bankers at one point called us "compulsive expansionists." While my conservative CPA training occasionally held back Dino's more free-wheeling ways, we both had a driving sense of urgency, and we didn't want anything to pass us by. We looked at, and tried to buy, three times as many businesses as we actually did. Part of our acquisition frenzy was driven by the times; the 1980s were a decade of newly-invented financial instruments and schemes like "junk bonds" (debt with little security and a low credit rating), LBOs (leveraged buy-outs) and real estate tax shelters. Thirty-year-old business school graduates made six and seven figure salaries on Wall Street and the "big hitters" piled up tens and hundreds of millions of dollars.

Later, the times changed to prove the truth of the Mexican adage, "Once on the downgrade, even rocks have wheels." And when the bottom of the hill was reached in the early 1990s, many a financial genius found that the wheels had come off their money machines in a big crash!

Business school grads and Wall Street hotshots included, Dino was the best deal-maker I'd ever seen, and I learned a tremendous amount of negotiating skills, strategies and tactics from him. In our daily life, Dino generally handled operations and I took on finance and administration; but there was much cutting across those lines, and we spent a lot of time making sure that each knew what the other was doing—too much time, according to our wives. Dino was the majority ownership partner and had the final, final say, but for years our preoccupation with business and worrying at night seemed to be about equal.

I loved working with agricultural people. They are largely of good heart and quite caring. They are almost always "there" for one another. Their exposure to the constant agricultural cycles of ups and downs gives them a great sense of acceptance and carrying on, although farmers do seem to complain constantly about the weather or crop prices, in a mostly good-natured way. Being close to nature also produces a pervasive feeling of "groundedness" among ag people that is hard to find in an urban area. And "aggies" tend to stay closer to the virtues they learned at home, and move around less than other folks.

I also enjoyed this business as a wonderful playing field for personal growth, and learned a lot about myself and other people. Just as in the Marines, I saw that clear-headed persistence in the face of adversity is a powerful weapon. Frequently I experienced the immense satisfaction of dealing with a person whose "word is his bond," and always tried to be like that myself. And I was continually amazed at the spirit of team-work, loyalty and camaraderie that a well-treated group of employees would exhibit. Time and time again I saw that, if the financial rewards were adequate, it was the psychic rewards of the job that made the difference to people.

As time went on, I came more and more under the spell of my "50-50 at 50" plan. I began to find many ways to implement my vision of spending half my time and resources in assisting others when I turned fifty. That birthday happened in 1986, and my efforts were greatly aided by an Act of Congress, of all things.

Late that year Congress passed a "tax reform bill"—an oxymoron as our system is inherently incapable of passing legislation that is purely reform and free of special treatment for someone—and it created a one-time window for favorable tax treatment of corporate liquidations. Dino and I took advantage of this and dissolved our principal company. This created the opportunity for me to cash in most of "my chips." It was with more than a little regret that I reduced my role in business. But my interests and circumstances had changed so much that I knew I needed to move into the next phase of my life.

•••••••••••

"So it's 50-50 at 50, eh?"

Those words of Dino in 1983 have stuck to me like my signature. Many times I have used the term "50-50 at 50" in talks and people seemed to remember it, even as they forgot most of what I said. Once I had made my declaration to "be my own hero" and had the support of my wife and my business partner, I had to decide just what to do. I planned to contribute a significant amount of financial resources as well as time, a combination that dictated high involvement in whatever project drew me in.

Wary of nonprofits operated in an unbusinesslike manner, I wanted to be in an organizational culture that integrated accountability, cost effectiveness and recognition of the economic laws of supply and demand into its programs. And whomever I worked with—be they poor, sick or uneducated—I thought should participate in the cost of the work. In other words, they should pay something, for I saw the goal as being to increase their self-reliance. It seemed to me that just giving them something would be counter-productive toward that goal.

Beyond that I felt that the primary source of information about how to help someone would not be found in books or by asking experts, but rather by asking the person in question. I figured they would have a pretty good idea of what needed to be done, and if I hoped to aid them in building self-reliance, their knowledge, skills and resources would all have to come into play.

I began my search for a project to get involved with in the last few months of 1983, but it soon became evident that I was not going to readily fit into most existing service entities. I also had the mistaken idea that most of the local needs in our hometown of Stockton were being met by the government or established charities. So I began to look further from home.

The experience that I had in 1973 in Guatemala with The Agricultural Leadership Program emerged from my memory and pointed me to the field of international development. The plight of poor Mayan Indian farmers had never left me. Now had come the time to see the seeds of that trip sprout. The question was how to go about it. I decided to investigate what US nonprofits were doing in Central America by identifying four of them and sending each a $1,000 contribution and a request for information. With one exception, I received in return a computer generated thank-you and a newsletter. Slim pickings. The one exception came in the form of a phone call from Ed Bullard of Technoserve, in Connecticut. Ed was about my age and had left a large family business fifteen years earlier to begin his international development nonprofit. A dedicated and compassionate man, he soon became my mentor and partner.

Late in 1983 Wendy and I incorporated a nonprofit to carry out our service work. We named it Katalysis, after the Greek root word for catalyst. Being typically short of ready cash, I took out a loan from the bank for $25,000, opened a checking account on the last day of the year, and we were in business! The fall of 1984 found Wendy and me in Belize scouting out service opportunities.

"Bob and Wendy, I want you to meet my friend, Carlos. Let's have some coffee." Wizened old Bob Mahler of Belize City introduced us to Carlos Santos, a tall, black-haired, handsome Belizean about ten years younger than I.

We exchanged a warm, firm handshake. His dark, almond-shaped eyes seemed to glisten with anticipation, and I suspected mine did as well. Soon the four of us were sipping the bracing coffee of Central America on the flower-laden verandah of the Bull Frog Hotel in the capital city of Belmopan.

We spent the next two days traveling around the country with Carlos. Belize was an exciting country with huge tracts of unspoiled rainforest, magnificent mountains, and countless rivers flowing into the warm, clear waters of the Caribbean Sea. Boasting the world's second longest barrier reef which extended the length of the country, the potential for tourism seemed boundless.

Yet, in the midst of this marvelous beauty, most people were poor, at least by our standards. Belize City, population 50,000, was particularly depressing with its slums and open sewers. Housing throughout the country was often primitive; wooden shacks sat on stilts for ventilation and high water protection. Public services were in short supply, and most villages had only one telephone. There were only 150 miles of paved roads in the entire country and travel to outlying districts was an arduous challenge.

We loved the people we met. They were Creoles (African-Americans), Mestizos, (a mix of European invaders and the indigenous peoples of Latin America), Garifunas, (descendants of Africans and Carib Indians), Mayan, (the original inhabitants) and people from various Near and Far East countries. Walking down the crowded streets of Belize City, it was hard to know whether I should watch the sidewalk to avoid the garbage and sorry-looking dogs or to keep my head up to see the people colors of black, red, brown, white and yellow.

All those races appeared to be living in harmony and the country was peaceful, a sharp contrast to most other Central American countries at the time. The Mayan people especially fascinated me, retaining most of their traditional ways and living both in the worlds of "Natural Man" and the lately arrived "Technological Man."

"I lost, Bob, I lost!" Carlos called from Belize in January, 1985, with the election results.

"Oh, I'm sorry, Carlos. What happened—was the vote close? How are you feeling?"

I struggled with how to show sympathy for my new friend, when I was really feeling a surge of happiness. Carlos had heavily invested himself in his campaign, and losing was a big disappointment to him, but this meant that he would be available to become the founding Managing Director of our newly named nonprofit, "BEST" (Belize Enterprise for Sustainable Technology). We began to make plans for his new life.

BEST had an organizational meeting that February. About sixty people attended, representatives from a number of small farmer groups which would be our first client base, along with people from government, business, foreign embassies and USAID (United States Agency For International Development). Carlos used all of his political connections to draw the right speakers to set the stage for presentations by the initiating trio of himself, Technoserve's representative, Roger Anderson, and myself. We had a long and lively group dialog about what was needed in Belize and what BEST could do to help. The crowd was enthusiastic and it was an exciting time for all of us.

It turned out that Roger Anderson and I were leaving the country on the same airplane to Miami, and we were overjoyed when we saw Charlie Jenkins of USAID in the passenger line with us.

"Roger," I whispered, "Let's get seats on either side of Charlie and we'll talk his ears off about getting us a grant from AID!"

The plane wasn't very crowded and we were able to accomplish our mission. As we waited in the plane for our departure, Roger and I began our pitch to Charlie. We were so engrossed that we didn't notice how long we had been in the plane until a crew member came by and asked us if we wanted a drink, since "there has been a slight delay." Because this was the 10 a.m. flight, it seemed a little early to me to start drinking. Charlie pointed out that it was already 10:30 a.m., and in fact, it was 11:30 in Miami. Combined with the unmerciful Caribbean sun beating on me in my window seat, this was indeed persuasive. I was the first to order some rum and orange juice.

We were just taking our first sips when there was a stirring at the front of the plane, and three men headed down the aisle towards us. First came a small man in civilian clothes, and then a scowling brutal-looking guy in an orange jump suit with his hands hand-cuffed in front of him. Right behind the Orange Man came a police officer, right hand on the revolver in his open holster and left hand in the small of orange man's back. I averted my eyes from the whole lot of them and they passed by, taking up seats about four rows back of us.

The three of us, Roger on the aisle and Charlie in the middle next to me, looked at each other, grinned weakly and drained off half our drinks. It looked like it was going to be an interesting flight. We didn't know just how interesting it would be until another commotion drew our eyes out the window onto the melting tarmac. A woman ran screaming to the plane, with two customs officers behind her. They were no match for her determination and her head start, and she bounded up the loading ramp steps into the front of the cabin where the American Airlines captain restrained her.

Her Creole yells were answered by Orange Man like a bull in mating season. We looked back, saw him stand and charge into the aisle, headed forward. The policeman with the gun somehow beat him into the aisle and facing Orange Man, was back-peddling while he tried to unleash his revolver.

He freed it just at our seat, his right hand arching up with it, inches from Roger's face. Roger leaned violently to his left, away from the gun and into Charlie, who then slammed against me on his left. All this happened as if we were synchronized, a kind of timed swoon, with me sticking my head between my legs. Our rum drinks flew, showering us with their stickiness and ice.

Although the policeman had the draw on him, Orange Man didn't want to stay still and kept edging forward, shouting at the struggling woman. Not wanting to pull the trigger, the policeman kept backing up until they were all at the entrance to the cabin. By now, other officials had boarded and after a hurried conference, allowed Orange Man and the woman off the airplane. Through my window, we watched them go back into the airport. It was hard to tell who was in charge—Orange Man or the "good guys."

Roger, Charlie and I stared at each other in amazement. Thankfully the stewardess promptly reappeared and replaced our drinks. As I remember it, there were a lot of free drinks on the way to Miami. By then the three of us were "bonded" pretty good, and the USAID grant was on fast-forward.

Later I learned that Orange Man was placed on an afternoon plane to Houston, this time well guarded. The woman had been thrown in jail, just to make things easier. There was a minor ruckus in the local newspapers as Orange Man had been illegally taken to the U.S. by the Drug Enforcement Agency. Although some called it "kidnapping," on the whole most people in Belize thought they were better off without the cocaine smuggler.

That summer a Harvard Business School case writer, Mihael Kennedy, from Ireland, came to Belize for preparation of a case study which was presented at the Harvard Agribusiness Seminars in Cambridge, MA and London during the winter of 1986. The case was called "BEST—The Role of PVOs (Private Voluntary Organizations) in Developing Agribusiness," and was very well received. I was given a lot of encouragement by my peers in the agribusiness community. Some of them are still donating to Katalysis eleven years later!

It was early, but already warm, that Sunday morning in August when Carlos Santos picked me up at the Circle A hotel in Belmopan to take me to the airport. I was catching a 10 a.m. flight back to the States.

"Morning, Bob. Sleep well?" Carlos inquired.

"Thank you, I did, Carlos. Must have been all the hard work this week. Well, we sure got a lot done. I feel really good about it."

We continued chatting as we pulled out onto the Western Highway for the sixty-mile run down to the Belize International Airport. Our gay conversation was soon interrupted by a muffled explosion from under the hood.

"Damn," Carlos hissed as he pulled to the side of the road. Alarmed, I jumped out of the old Renault and reached the hood just as he did. Popping it open, we were greeted by a roll of smoke and then silence. After a moment Carlos returned to the driver's side and gingerly turned the ignition.

"Whoa, stop, Carlos! You'll tear the whole engine up!" I had never heard such weird sounds come from a car before.

As we stood forlorn by the car, a pickup came from behind us, slowed, and stopped. Carlos recognized the driver as a friend of his. "Miguel, my car has a major problem. I was taking my friend here to the airport. Can you help us out?"

"I'm going in to Belize City. I can get him that far." I didn't wait any longer and swung my small duffel bag and my heavy salesman's-style briefcase into the back of the pickup. Climbing in, I thanked Miguel profusely as there was precious little traffic on the road and this looked like my last chance of catching the only plane for the day.

As we proceeded down the road I calculated if I would make it. By the time we got to Belize City and I found a taxi to take me on the twenty minute ride out to the airport, I would be lucky to have five minutes to spare. Pointing this out to Miguel, I asked him if it wouldn't be better for me to get off at the Hattieville intersection and hitch a ride to the airport via the "back way," a shortcut we sometimes took during the dry season. "Maybe, but there's not much traffic on that road, Bob," Miguel said. "However there is a guy who lives there on the corner who will probably take you if you pay him."

It was close to 9 a.m. when we stopped at the Hattieville intersection. I pulled my luggage from the back of the truck and headed to the house on the corner with a car parked out front. Miguel waved good-bye and headed on down the road towards Belize City. He was out of sight by the time I climbed up on the front porch, and long gone by the time I discovered no one was home.

Beginning to panic, I looked around at the half dozen ramshackle houses perched on stilts around the intersection like storks at a water hole. There wasn't a car in sight! The only sign of life was at a district police station where an officer sat on the porch, watching me with interest. I rapidly made my way to him, hollering out my plight before I even made it to the porch. He looked slightly amused.

"Listen, is there anyone around here that can help me? I'll pay them well!"

The cop, in his thirties and smartly dressed in a khaki shirt and blue trousers, said, "I do know a guy with a car who might do it if he's home. He lives back up the road a little."

When I said, "Great!" the cop turned, locked the police station door and came down the stairs.

"Come on," he commanded, and strode out into the highway, looking down the road towards Belize City. Soon a pickup came towards us, screeching to a halt at the sight of the cop with arm raised high and his palm clearly showing the universal "stop" sign.

He said something into the window and we jumped into the pickup bed. The driver floored the accelerator and, after two miles or so, stopped so suddenly I fell from the spare tire I was sitting on. The cop climbed out, motioned down a dirt road and strode off. I got my bags and ran after him. Within minutes I was sweating profusely, wishing the cop would take one of my bags. Probably wouldn't be dignified, I told myself. After what seemed like a 30-minute forced hike we came to a house in the bush. The cop let out a terrific round of hollering in Creole, which I couldn't understand.

A wooden window cover was flung open and a sleepy looking woman looked out into the blinding sun.

"Wha? Wha?" The cop went on shouting in Creole and, after a minute the woman slammed the window shut. The cop looked at me and smiled as if to say, "No sweat." No sweat, I thought, with streams of it running down my face. It was now close to 9:15.

A large man in a food-stained undershirt and dirty pants came down the stairs, hollering something at the woman who was half-way out the door. He took my bags, and threw them in the trunk of a 1968 Buick Roadmaster sitting in the dusty driveway. The cop and I jumped in the back and the man struggled to start the car, succeeding on his third try. We waited until the woman, who had disappeared back in the house, finally came down and got in the front seat. She still had her nightgown on, with some sort of dust cover thrown over it. Her hair was a mess, but it made no difference as she promptly slid down the seat, out of sight.

Our driver looked back at me, smiling with several teeth missing and eyes bloodshot from the night before. "Forty dollars, man. U.S., not Belize dollars—up front!"

"Okay, okay. Let's go," I urged, handing him two twenties. What else could I say? We roared off, the Roadmaster swaying dangerously with its shock absorbers long ago exhausted. At last I was back traveling in a more-or-less direct line to the airport. As we came to the turnoff to the shortcut at the Hattieville intersection, I was surprised when we didn't stop to let the cop return to duty. I had already given him $10 for his efforts and shook his hand good-bye.

With the unmanned police station fading into the background, I asked, "Aren't you going back to work?"

"No, man, I decided that I would go to Belize City with my friends here after we drop you off."

I wondered if this happened very often in Belize. "But doesn't there need to be someone at the station?"

"Oh, nothing ever happens on Sundays this early. Another guy comes on duty at four. This way I can surprise my wife!" I nodded at this handsome guy with the compelling logic.

Leaning back into the soft cushions of the Buick, I began recalculating the time. I was beginning to panic again when a 1980 Ford, "brand new" by Belize standards, pulled up alongside us and one of the passengers threw a mango against our door, just missing our open back-seat window. The cop, sitting on that side, let out a great yell and slapped our driver on the back. He accelerated and the Ford faded back a bit on the dusty gravel road. But very soon the Ford pulled alongside us again, dangerously so on the narrow road. The swaying Buick almost collided with the other car; now the passengers in both the front and back seats were throwing mangoes.

The cop and our driver were yelling at the top of their voices and I was terrified, barely noting that our lady passenger was still no where to be seen, undoubtedly passed out on the front seat. Again the Ford faded, but before I could ask if we were in the middle of a dope fight, it came roaring back. This time the cop stuck his head out the window, brandishing his night stick and shouting in the din and the dust.

Suddenly he popped his head back in and said something to our driver. Brakes were applied hard, and we fish-tailed in the gravel. The cop got out and walked back towards the Ford. I watched anxiously, fearing that the people in the other car had guns, while the cop had only his baton. I was thrown back when the Buick roared off. Now what? Was my driver fleeing, fearful for his life?

"Hey, how about the cop? What the hell is going on?" I shouted.

I could barely understand the driver's reply, "The cop decided to go off with his other friends there. They're going to a party somewhere!"

Looking at my watch I decided I didn't have time to figure all this out. I calculated I would make it to the airport with only ten minutes before the flight! "Hey, there's another $20 for you if we make it by 9:50!" The driver nodded and the Buick surged under his heavy foot.

Soon after intersecting with the Northern Highway for the last five-mile segment of our mad dash, we heard a terrific din coming from under the car. The driver, goaded on by the prospect of an extra $20, kept on driving until the noise was unbearable. Pulling over, he and I jumped out and discovered the chrome trim along the side of the Buick had come loose and one end of it was dragging on the pavement. The Belizean grabbed it and twisted it back up at a weird angle. We quickly remounted and thundered off. Within three miles, the noise was worse than ever. This time the driver ran to the chrome strip and, cursing fiercely, ripped it from the side of the car. He tossed it into the ditch, I cheered, and we went off again at absolutely top speed.

Given everything that had happened, I was sure we would crash at the entrance of the airport. I sent prayers in the direction of every saint and god that I had heard of, especially to any of the local gods that might be watching.

People and luggage scattered as we broadsided to a stop at the terminal entrance. Almost before the car had stopped, the driver jumped out to get my things from the trunk. Just as I started to follow him, two slender brown arms appeared over the edge of the front seat. Headless, one hand pointed to the watch on the other arm, and then was held out, palm up. The woman was alive enough to claim the extra $20, and I was damn happy to give it to her!

● ● ● ● ● ● ● ● ● ● ●

"Cayetano, will women ever be allowed to have a voice and a vote in the affairs of your community?"

The question from Roy Williams, a Katalysis board member, is asked of Cayetano Ico, a Mayan Indian. We are in Cayetano's thatched roof, dirt floor home in the small settlement of Laguna in the rain forest of southern Belize. We stand or sit in hammocks with Cayetano, his wife and three of their children, midway through an hour-long visit. Smoke from the cooking fire wisps through the one-room home.

Our group of five seems to hold its breath to catch the answer to this culturally-charged question. Even the steady rain seems to pause in anticipation.

"Well," Cayetano begins slowly, glancing at his wife. I wonder if she speaks English. She has not said a word, and her face gives us no way of knowing. Gathering force, he delivers his judgment. "Soon. Within four or five years, I think."

"Why, soon, Cayetano? After all these centuries, why?" Roy asks softly.

"Because of what we're learning. We're finding out that women can be good at business, at belonging to community banks and to their cooperatives. If they can be good at business and that helps the family, why shouldn't they be good at voting, too?"

He laughs, giving everyone a big smile. It was probably the same line that he had used in community council meetings, apparently with success.

Later, as our group of Katalysis board members traveled north in the jeep on the rain-slick gravel of the Southern Highway, Roy couldn't stop talking about Cayetano. He talked about all the things the Mayan leader had told us. First was Cayetano's penetrating analysis of the local and international cocoa industry. Hershey Chocolate had entered Belize only a few years before, and although things were promising, it would be years before the right varieties were sorted out. While cocoa was being hailed as a possible gold-mine crop for Belize, the fact of the matter was that there were more cocoa trees in the world than there was need. Hershey had only come to Belize to diversify against crop failures in Africa. Cayetano said cocoa would always be in oversupply except for just such crop failures. And this kind of over-capacity always meant low prices to the grower, usually just above costs.

(As a board member of BEST, Cayetano had similarly analytical opinions of the overall state of development in Belize, about the hopes and plans of his community and the Mayan people of the region, and about his aspirations for himself and his family.)

Roy shook his head in amazement. "Here is a man living as generations of his ancestors before him, without conveniences—what we call necessities—in a remote area without communications. But he knows more than many people in the U.S.!"

From the onset of the creation of BEST, we decided that our nine-person board of directors would include representatives of our client groups. One of the first to come on the board was a fellow my age, Pablo Call, a Mayan from the remote southern area of Belize. It was readily apparent that Pablo, though a bit on the quiet side, was a tremendous leader. He was thoughtful and articulate, and a solid contributor to our governance.

We had quarterly board meetings, usually at the BEST office in the capital city of Belmopan. For Pablo and others from the Toledo District, attending a board meeting was no small matter. He had to rise at 3:30 a.m., walk four miles into San Antonio, then hitch a ride down to the Southern Highway to meet the bus going north at 6 a.m. That put him into Belmopan eleven hours later. The day after the meeting, the process was reversed. This meant that a grueling three days were devoted to a board meeting for which there was no compensation. Moreover, it meant there was much work left undone at home. I always marveled at the dedication shown by the client board members from southern Belize.

One of the benefits for me of the required two nights stay-over was that I would often room with one of the clients, thereby having an opportunity to "stand in the other guy's shoes" for hours at a time. So it was with Pablo. While I had visited the San Antonio area several times on projects, it was during the long, undistracted evenings in Belmopan that we really had a chance to talk. After dinner we would sit outside in the cool of the evening, sharing our lives.

One evening Pablo was talking about his family life. He and his wife had nine children and they lived in a typical Mayan home similar to Cayetano's: one big room, thatched roof, dirt floor, with none of our "necessities" such as indoor plumbing, electricity, phone or the like. They farmed in the typical "milpa" fashion, which means clearing a few acres of jungle, burning it off during the dry season—the average rainfall in his area exceeded 150 inches—and then planting a crop of rice to catch the beginning of the rainy season. After the rice harvest came a crop of corn, and then the land was left to go back to jungle. It was a process that, done right, requires that the land lie fallow for fifteen years after a single year of farming.

Pablo's family supplemented the rice and corn grown for their table with a few pigs and chickens. Their cash crop was honey, and they relied on this money for clothes and school costs. Pablo was determined that all his children would get at least a high school, and perhaps a junior college, education in the coastal city of Punta Gorda. However, their honey business was under attack with the invasion of the Africanized bee. BEST was helping their fifty-member cooperative cope with the invasion through special management techniques and facilitating the acquisition of specialized equipment.

"But long term, Mr. Bob (I could never get him to just call me Bob), our real problem is overpopulation. We're running out of land to farm." Having flown over hundreds of thousands of acres of jungle vacant of people, I found this hard to believe and told him so.

"You need to understand the system. First, we can farm in an area only close enough to walk to and from. For practical reasons that is about three miles, as we must carry our tools. Next, my people have traditionally lived in small villages for mutual support, and walked out to the country from there. I am one of the exceptions, living outside of San Antonio.

"We should rotate our milpas every fifteen years or so. But because we have more people farming the same amount of land, fallow periods have fallen to seven or eight years. This is not good for the land and the rainforest. And it continues to get worse. What is the answer? Disperse our people all through the bush and destroy our tradition and sense of community? I hope not! No, the answer is birth control."

"Birth control! Wouldn't that be a big change for your people?" I knew this was a highly provocative subject in the Mayan community, never spoken of openly.

"Yes...yes, it would. But it doesn't have to be done in the ways your people do it, ways that are very difficult for us to accept. No, there are ways that are in keeping with our belief system. They are natural ways. There are roots and vines in the forest that can be eaten or used in teas for this purpose." (I assumed he was referring to the Dioscorea bush, the plant that rendered the hormones for the first birth control pills.) "They have been used by our ancestors and now we must expand their use. Nature provides for all things."

Pablo then went on for another hour explaining the cosmology of the Mayan people, their spiritual practices of thousands of years, and their reverence for both God and Mother Earth. I was spellbound and, that night as I tried to sleep, I kept thinking about all that I had learned. I really felt that Pablo and his people were brothers and sisters to me. I was glad that we were trying to help them with the Africanized bee threat. Somehow, it seemed like the least we could do.

• • • • • • • • • • •

Katalysis had a fast start and it has continued to operate like a
growth business, opportunistically, enthusiastically, and with plenty
of crises. With a client base in the thousands, today the Katalysis
Partnership provides services to low income people in the way of
women's community banking, microenterprise development and
natural resource management. The four original partners, BEST
(Belize Enterprise for Sustainable Technlogy), ODEF (Organization
for the Development of Women's Enterprises) of Honduras, CDRO
(Cooperative Association for Western Rural Development) of
Guatemala and MUDE (Association of Women in Development) of
Guatemala, have formed 300 banks, each one with twenty to thirty
women members who receive business training and loans of $100-
$200 for their entrepreneurial businesses such as making and selling
food products and clothing, raising small animals and produce, or
running small stores and restaurants. They also have made thousands
of individual loans of $400-$1,000 to men and women who are
building larger businesses such as making furniture or cement blocks.
These businesses usually have three to six employees, and while they
may be microenterprise by US standards, they are big to their owners.

ODEF and Katalysis have constructed Herencia Verde, a training center outside of San Pedro Sula, Honduras, where rural residents come for training in sustainable agriculture, organic gardening
and life skills. And CDRO provides about 85% of all the available
financial and social services in over thirty villages in the
Guatemalan Highlands, taking up the slack from a non-involved
government. Undergirding these services is a practice of partnership
as a way of doing daily business in a multi-cultural, multi-racial setting. This concept, of being partners, has been heavily influenced by
my rewarding experiences in business and by the inspiration of the
book *The Chalice and the Blade*, by Riane Eisler.

For all this, Katalysis has been anything but a one-way street of
assisting other people. I've received immensely more from my
involvement than I've given. There's a lot to tell about this in the
chapters to come.

6

AWAKENING

One Saturday early in 1984 I was standing in The Pilgrim's Way book store in Carmel looking for religious books. I was struck by the face-forward display of one titled *Conscious Union With God*. Its subtitle was Oneness With the Spiritual Universe, and the author was Dr. Joel S. Goldsmith.

I picked up the book and two statements on the back cover caught my eye. "My oneness with God constitutes my oneness with all spiritual beings, and with every spiritual idea or thing." And, "When a person is able to reach the place in meditation where one becomes consciously aligned with one's inner Being, the person is automatically one with the entire spiritual universe—the universe of the past, the present, and the future."

A strange sensation moved up through my body. Inexplicably, I could feel the hair on the back of my neck; it seemed to itch. Like a blind man who could suddenly see, I stood there, stunned, as a whole new panorama of Spirit and the spiritual world unfolded before me.

I eagerly glanced at the first few paragraphs. A flood of new concepts engulfed me. "Jesus came with the divine idea of spiritual freedom...free from belief in bondage to person, place, thing, circumstance, or condition." "Spiritual healing is brought about through the realization of the Christ in individual consciousness." "When the student is ready, the teacher will appear." I immediately purchased the book, took it home, and began reading and underlining.

When I saw that if I continued to underline every other paragraph the book would be illegible, I forced myself to become discriminating. Ultimately I boiled things down to fifty-six passages which my wondering secretary, Sandy Irvine, transcribed onto 3" x 5" cards. The cards were kept in my top desk drawer at my office. When I opened the drawer for any reason, I read one of the cards, and reflected briefly. The student was ready. The teacher had appeared, and soon there would be more.

> Who ever travels without a guide,
> Needs two hundred years for a two day journey.
> Jalaluddin Rumi

I soon discovered that the spiritual journey—which might be described as a search for a profound sense of peace, ease and freedom, or perhaps as a movement from a state of potentiality to one of actuality and self-realization—is not a short journey. While seekers often experience sudden bursts of progress that feel like final destinations, within a few weeks or months one realizes the need to pack the bags and hit the road again. Why? Because not only are we not yet perfect, we're not even sure who we really are. So, considering the length of the journey—likely all of our life or lifetimes, depending on one's understanding of reincarnation—enlisting the aid of teachers and guides makes undeniable sense.

(A word of caution; while they can help take years off your journey, look before you leap. The Dali Lama recommends that a person observe a teacher for years before entering into a serious student-teacher relationship. Many other seasoned observers advise a careful check into whether the teacher "walks his/her talk." Most experienced people advise that a student not suspend critical judgment nor abandon personal responsibility in relationship to a teacher. Sri Aurobindo, a phenomenal intellect and spiritual being of the first half of this century said, "The first principle of true teaching is that nothing can be taught. The teacher is not an instructor or task-master, he is a helper and a guide. The business of the teacher is to suggest and not to impose. The teacher does not actually train the pupil's mind, he only shows the student how to perfect his instruments of knowledge and helps and encourages him in the process. He does not impart knowledge to the pupil, he shows him how to acquire knowledge for himself.")

"Meditation is the key that unlocks the door." Joel Goldsmith's statement fascinated and challenged me. I had to learn to meditate.

I tried to sit quietly and not have any thoughts. That was hardly successful, even for a few seconds. Then I tried memorizing and repeating long prayers. I was better at this, but it didn't really feel like I was meditating, feeling more like I was practicing the Gettysburg Address for a fifth grade recital. (Only later did I discover that by having repeated the Peace Prayer of St. Francis several thousand times, I unconsciously began looking for ways to console, to understand, to love, to give, and to forgive.)

Then I sat quietly and observed my thoughts, a form of "mindfulness." With this I learned that most of my thoughts were boring, repetitious and fictitious. Thoughts came and went. If I acted on them, they became the source of my behavior, but if I chose not to act, the same thoughts had no external meaning. Thus I decided there was no reason either for my randomized, unfiltered thoughts to have control over me or, for that matter, to believe that my thoughts about other people and external events had much grounding in reality, either.

In spite of these insights, my mind remained a mess. It ran this way and that. Even though I no longer gave my thoughts so much creditability as I once did, my mind continued to produce them at a rate that I could hardly keep pace with. I became anxious for better results and sometimes tried two or three meditative methods in one sitting. I was also alert for new techniques, not realizing that my mind was like a wild colt, one that needed a long period of steady and gentle training before riding.

Pay dirt was had a couple of years later when one fresh summer morning I had an experience that opened me to a new way of living my life. My journal entry describes it this way:

I've been meditating for a long, long time without much in the way of noticeable results. I began this morning on the patio just outside my study. The morning lingered in coolness before surrendering to the heat of the day, and several birds were happily telling me how special this time was. Peace seemed to surround me, so I started silently reciting the Peace Prayer. After a while I began murmuring "God, God" in rhythm with my breath.

Suddenly I was overwhelmed with a powerful sense of God in my nostrils, throat, mind and body! With it came an intense feeling of

God's blessings, of love, acceptance and forgiveness, and I experienced a tremendous sense of happiness. A bright red spot grew in the middle of the darkness of my mind. It was too powerful to stay with, for I felt I was in danger of merging into some sort of void. I shook my head like a horse trying to shake off its halter, and the spot gradually subsided.

I opened my eyes and the world never seemed more alive, brighter, fresher, or in such a process of evolution. The palpable presence of God filled me with a desire to put my personal agenda aside and to participate with God in creating whatever was to be. I wanted to get in harmony with the world instead of fighting it. When I stood, I felt an incredible lightness in my body and soul.

That short, intense experience changed me at my deepest level. No longer was God an intellectual, impersonal concept dwelling out in space somewhere. No, God was alive in me. In me! God was accessible directly by me, without the need of clergy, guru or church structure! I was in ecstasy for days afterward and today, years later, I still feel the power of that experience. It is my first and deepest anchor in spiritual bedrock, as it is grounded in knowing, in absolute certainty. The existence of a Divine Principle was no longer just a belief.

Before long, my meditations progressed to being hours and hours of boredom punctuated by brief moments of ecstasy! My wild mind was showing an occasional flash of breaking to the saddle.

For a time I focused on the early Christian contemplative meditation described in the sixth century by Gregory the Great as "resting in God." This method, as currently taught by Father Thomas Keating, is called the "Centering Prayer." In it, one sits quietly and repeats a sacred word on the out-breath, symbolizing one's intention to consent to God's presence and action within. I found it to be simple and relatively effective, and it remains one of my favorite techniques. But I was also restless and on the lookout for "a magic bullet," some form of meditation that would give me more bliss for less work.

I found a gold mine of methods in the writings of teachers from other religious traditions, especially Buddhist and Hindu. Not that the techniques seemed to work any better for me, but there were many more methods to explore as meditation is an integral part of those religions. In turn, this search for meditation techniques led me to consider the teachings and precepts of other religions. I became preoccupied with the quest for knowledge about things of the spirit. Slaking my thirst took precedence over normal work and play, and I felt eager, joyous, open. I poured time, money and enthusiasm into this newly discovered sea of consciousness.

I was excited! Each new source of spiritual teachings seemed to produce insights and new pieces of the truth. I went on a giant treasure hunt, turning over every spiritual rock I could find, and bit-by-bit building a sense of who I really was.

Soon I was devouring knowledge from every which direction: traditional and mystical Christianity commentators, Tibetan Buddhists, Hindu yogis, shamans, psychics, healers, near-death and life-after-death researchers, past-life regression analysts, transpersonal psychology writers, quantum physics scientists, Native American medicine people, Taoists and Sufi teachers, and mind-body-spirit practitioners. I retained mementos from each source, and added them to my altar of wholeness.

• • • • • • • • • • • •

My good friend, Roy Williams, gave me and several of his business buddies a book titled *Emmanuel's Book*. Looking at the back cover, I was intrigued by the assertion that a "spirit guide" called Emmanuel spoke through a woman named Pat Rodegast in the process know as "channeling." Suspending disbelief on that for a time, I moved into the book and found its material clear, refreshing and, most of all, reassuring. It lived up to its subtitle, "A manual for living comfortably in the cosmos." Its message was one of a loving God as Creator.

That was a theme that I was starting to hear more frequently— that God wasn't a wrathful, vengeful, gray-bearded old man waiting to pounce on people for their sins. I was also hearing that the concept of "original sin" was way off-base, and that we weren't born with a universal scar of damning sin seared across our souls. Rather, many contemporary theologians asserted that we were born in a state of "original innocence," and while we individually picked up some undesirable traits on our life journey—much like trail dust—we could process through our deficiencies and release them. Thus the beauty of God's creation in each of us was far superior to our dusty "dark sides" and deserved our deepest attention and affection.

While the concept of channeling still taxed my rational mind, page after page of *Emmanuel's Book* rang true to my intuition. The assertions that love is the underlying principle of existence, that our souls are eternal, that life is a school and we come here repeatedly for more classes, that there are unseen forces watching out for us and helping us, and that souls frequently associate with each other from lifetime to lifetime made more sense than most of the alternatives I'd heard when I was growing up. Quite a number of Roy's friends seemed to feel the same way, and we were glad for the opportunity when he invited Pat Rodegast to be with us for a couple of days.

There were two dozen of us in Roy and Diana's living room. We were exchanging expectations when Pat Rodegast emerged from an adjoining room. We fell into silence and stared at the light brown-haired, well-dressed woman in her forties, looking as if she was going to the office. She stepped onto a platform with cushions that Roy arranged so that she would be at the same height as those of us who sat on chairs and couches. As Roy gave her a gracious introduction, Pat looked around the room with a gentle smile. She looked a bit shy, to me. Then she said a few words about herself in a sort of soft, Carolina-tinged, East Coast voice.

Without warning, she resettled on the cushions, closed her eyes and sat still for a moment or two. When she opened her eyes, they had changed and I had the sensation that someone...something else...was looking at me through them. They seemed larger, sharper and darker. As the eyes looked at each person in turn, Pat's head nodded slightly, as if in recognition.

"I'm happy to be with each of you again." Pat's soft shy voice was replaced by one of different characteristics—it had the timbre, the strength, of a man's voice, but not the depth.

Most of us smiled and shifted in our seats, wondering if this was a joke. Was Pat, no Emmanuel, going to assert that she, no he, knew us from some far off cosmos?

"I say again, because we have touched one another during and in between other lifetimes. And here we are again, to share in the mysteries of life—but they are only mysteries when we are on your side of the curtain—on this side there are none. Here it is clear that life is lovingly supported by the Creative Urge of the Universe. And this is what I have to share with you."

The voice had an unusual inflection, as though spoken by someone from a distant land, but with a perfect knowledge of English. There was a strange cadence; it reminded me of that of a college professor who had total knowledge of the subject at hand. This was a friendly college professor, though, and there was a touch of humor sitting on top of the words, like a dollop of whipped cream on raspberry Jell-O. As the voice continued, I felt wisdom, love and playfulness, all at the same time. I had never experienced that combination before and thought it the most attractive way of being I could imagine.

Later when Emmanuel was answering questions, I screwed up my nerve and said, "Emmanuel, we're experiencing some tough times at home...with our kids and all. Is there a purpose in all this?"

"Be assured that all of the souls in your household have come together out of love and as an act of service to each other. The things that you see as insurmountable problems now will fade away as surely as the sunset. No matter what you see in the others, treat them with love as this is your promise to each other."

After a while I wanted to get at something else that was bothering me. "Emmanuel, as I've expanded my search, I keep running into different religions—new ones, to me. I've been taught that there is only one religion—ours! Which religion is right?"

Emmanuel's response sounded like that of a patiently loving parent to a small child: "To believe in God in everyone, this is the ultimate religion. It does not matter what path you take to get there. All your religions lead to God."

Does Emmanuel exist? Or does Rodegast really speak from her own Higher Self? Or does she just make it all up? An unanswerable set of questions, I suppose. I don't believe she makes it up, though, based upon "non-Emmanuel" conversations I had with her. She seemed to be just an ordinary, likable ex-secretary somewhat bemused by her life as a channeler. In any event, wherever the Emmanuel talk came from, the ring of truth came through, and it was a valuable experience for me.

•••••••••••

Stories. Don't we all love stories? Sometime in 1985 I came across a fascinating book of spiritual tall tales. Real whoppers. Couldn't put the book down.

Yogananda's book, *Autobiography of A Yogi*, had been hailed as a classic in the field of spiritual literature. I read it with disbelieving fascination and immediately began calling it "A Miracle a Minute." Here I was, a straight-arrow business man of a Midwestern background, expected to believe that miracles were being performed by dozens of people—in this century and to this day, mind you! There were accounts of fantastic healings, materialization of objects from thin air, people appearing in two places at once, people being buried alive and surviving for days, and so much communication via dreams and visions that it made the "information superhighway" look like a Johnny-come-lately invention.

I found most of the supposed incidents quite beyond belief, but there was something compelling in the book that opened me to new possibilities. Surprisingly, they made the biblical accounts of miracles more plausible for me. I started to pay attention when Pastor Fred talked about them in church, instead of dismissing them out-of-hand. And the stories, even the ones I didn't believe, prepared me to accept some miracles myself a few years later.

Yogananda, born in India and by all accounts a saint, came to the U.S. as a young man in the 1920s. He traced his spiritual teaching lineage back through a half-dozen saints, one of whom was Jesus. While his teachings contained frequent references to Jesus, they were primarily derived from the Indian science/philosophy of Yoga and from the ancient Indian scriptures collectively known as the Vedas. Yoga consists of a number of teachings and practices whose purpose is to allow the individual to grow until he or she becomes united with God. And this is what Yogananda presented to crowds in the thousands across the U.S., urging a God-centered life.

In spite of my readings, anxiety coursed through my veins as I approached the Self-Realization Fellowship Church in San Diego. I was in town visiting my daughter, Sarah, and I delighted in visiting other churches when I traveled. This was the first time, though, that I'd ventured off the conventional path, and I was nervous about what I'd find. I didn't yet have a good understanding of the church Yogananda had started before his death in the 1950s and asked myself what I'd do if it turned out to be some kind of cult. Now that would be scary!

As I approached the church patio I saw many people—all looking normal enough—standing in the sunshine, doing some sort of energy and centering exercises. I didn't want to get mixed up in that, and hurried into the sanctuary where there were already a large number of people sitting in meditation. I slipped into a chair and closed my eyes, praying that I could make it through the service without having to leave in panic.

Presently the proceedings began with singing and chanting. There was a handbook I could have used but I chose to just listen, finding it quite soothing. I was fascinated by the candle-bearing altar, above which were pictures of Yogananda and his predecessors. Yogananda's picture presented a regal-looking man with very long black hair and other-worldly smile. He projected magnetism and I understood why his personality and potent teachings had attracted millions of world-wide followers in a short period of time. The close-by image of Jesus was serenely beautiful and he stared back at me with a combination of benignness and a sort of, "Well, Bob, are you going to get with it?" questioning.

I relaxed into the service, and afterwards left marveling that there are other ways of worshipping God. And it felt good, it felt right.

A cult? No, the Self-Realization Fellowship met neither the dictionary nor the common-sense definition of the word. It doesn't embrace secretiveness, claim a totalitarian world view or practice mind control. Now when I hear someone describe something as a "cult" and realize they are talking from ignorance, I'm reminded of the saying, "Black magic is the other guy's religion!"

Yogananda, himself, was described as "the personification of love" by many who came into contact with him. It is said that the atmosphere itself became suffused with love when he entered a room. And there was something of a hub-bub after his death as his body, in care of the famous Forest Lawn Mausoleum in Hollywood, exhibited no signs of putrefaction for the weeks it was on display. The mortuary people even wrote a letter to the Los Angeles Times remarking that they had never seen nor heard of such an event.

But it was Yogananda's powerful teaching—there are integrated sets of exercises which enhance progress towards a life of daily manifestation of one's spiritual nature—that influenced me. The practices of prayer, meditation, physical exercises, breathing and study may need to vary from person to person, but their positive cumulative effect couldn't be denied. Soon I was busy remodeling various aspects of my daily life, learning what worked for me, and what didn't.

● ● ● ● ● ● ● ● ● ● ●

Now that I was digging into other religious traditions and teachers, I began to take a closer and more discerning look at the one who was first presented to my consciousness, Jesus. A mysterious figure to me as a child, somehow my adult church-going days had failed to produce a sharper definition of him.

I soon saw that the Bible attributed sayings to Jesus that make him a hard teacher and a tough guide. Some of his teachings that have bothered me the most are (lightly paraphrased in some cases):

• Don't resist violence.
• If anyone hits me, turn the other cheek.
• If anyone wants to sue me and take my shirt, give him my coat as well.
• Give to everyone who asks, and don't refuse anyone who wants to borrow from me. Give and expect nothing in return.

- Love my enemies, do good to those who hate me, bless those who curse me and pray for those who mistreat me.
  Does that make you nervous? We're just getting started. The Bible also states that Jesus taught:
- It's easier for a camel to pass through the eye of a needle than for a rich man to enter the kingdom of heaven. (Not too encouraging for me, as I'm still wealthy even if generous.)
- Pick up and leave without telling my family farewell. (There's no looking back.)
- Whoever marries a divorced woman commits adultery. (Give me a break, Jesus!)
- That he did not come to bring peace to earth, but a sword. (And I thought you were the Prince of Peace!)
- That he came to set a man against his father, and a daughter against her mother. (In this age of dysfunctional families, Jesus, you probably won't have to do that part.)

In spite of the "in-your-face" challenges Jesus presents, he remains my most influential teacher. Why? He's imbedded in my culture, and therefore in me, of course, but by choice, as well. Yes, he can be a hard man, with difficult teachings—but I learned little in school from an easy teacher.

He does say that if we come to him and learn from him, in the end we will find he's gentle, and find rest for our souls. He says his yoke—or yoga, same root word—is easy and his burden is light. I guess by that he means it's simple compared to other methods of questing for God. Besides this, he has some sort of strange hold on my psyche. He keeps popping up; he won't leave me alone.

Dum...Dum...Dum... The slow, insistent drum beat pushed me to the large animal hole at the base of a fat oak tree in the woods about a half-mile from my old Iowa home. It was a favorite place of mine during childhood. I went to my hands and knees, surprised at how easily I fit into the opening. I went down into its darkness like a gopher going home. The dirt was cool and moist, and the oak roots gave off a green woody smell. I was pleased at how well I traversed the dark tunnel, considering I was whiskerless.

A light grew before me and drew me into a chamber large enough that I could stand. Somehow I had entered the tomb of Jesus! His burial linens were laying outstretched on my left. I wasn't sure if he was still in them—but they were surely his. I wanted to stop, but my curiosity was overridden by a feeling that I was late for something and that it was urgent that I go further down into the earth. I strode on to an opening at the far side of the tomb.

This tunnel was larger than the last and I ran down it in a half-crouch, anxiety pushing me to gain time. I stepped into a large cave and looked at the dozen people gathered around a fire. It was a wild-haired bunch: early Christians. They were talking about Jesus and the persecution they were experiencing for following him. Death hung heavily in the air around them; I was surprised to find that I could really smell it. The Christians smelled it, too, but they were steadfast and affirmed their willingness to die for their beliefs.

Suddenly they looked at me with apprehension and amazement. I looked down at myself and was surprised to see that I was a Roman military officer, seemingly superior in every way to these ordinary people. My eyes went back to the group, and the moment was charged with suspense. My feet carried me forward into their circle and I drew my dagger, casting my lot with them by throwing it into the fire. Smiles of welcome crossed their dirty faces, and I couldn't tell who was more shocked—the Christians or I!

That's when I smelled death for me—my very own death odor, stronger, more stinking, than that of the others. I accepted it stoically. From afar, the drum beat reappeared in my consciousness, very rapidly now. It signaled the end to my journey, and called me to return. Reluctantly I drifted away from the gathering with a strong conviction that I had once tasted death for my commitment to Jesus.

Whoa, let's stop right there. I was in the tomb of Jesus? On a journey? Completely sober, not hallucinating? As a reader you're probably mumbling disbelief under your breath. And that's what I did the first time I participated in nonordinary reality. And I've been disbelieving many times thereafter as well. How have I handled it? By having lots of conversations with myself! For now, I'll try to reconstruct my internal conversation after the Jesus incident.

First, I need to use names for this two-way dialogue. Because I began using Robert on my sixtieth birthday—nothing Freudian, it's just my given name—Robert will be the one doing the experiencing in the events of nonordinary reality in this book. The incredulous, questioning side of me, the linear-thinking ex-accountant, the semi-hard-nosed businessman, will be the Bob I used to be. Busy Bob, I'm going to say, busy as short-hand for business and busy because that's what I was! Okay, now we're ready. Busy Bob opens with a question.

"Robert, what was that all about? What happened?

"Well, I lit a small fire in the fireplace in the living room of our Carmel cottage, put a drumming tape on the cassette player and turned off all the lights. I imagined myself entering the woods, looking for a tree with a hole at its base. That's when I knew I was looking for the tree from my childhood. You know what happened from there, Busy Bob."

"Why in the world were you doing that?"

"I had read Michael Harner's book, *The Way of the Shaman,* and wanted to experience what he called a "journey." The drumming helps get the mind off everything else, opens it up. It's something that indigenous peoples have done for thousands of years. They take journeys to obtain information, guidance, healing, that kind of thing."

"And just where did you go, Robert?"

"Another dimension of my consciousness. One not experienced by my ordinary body senses: sight, touch, smell, taste or feel. That's why it's called nonordinary reality. Dreams are a common example of nonordinary reality."

"Yeah, Robert, but when I dream I have no ability to control what I'm seeing. When you did that journey, you weren't asleep like that, you were awake, in control of your mind. I think you made it all up."

"No way, Busy Bob. Once I got through the imagining part about the tree it was like entering a movie. The cave was there on the movie screen. Only there was one difference; I was in the movie! From there on, I just watched the story unfold."

"For God's sakes, Robert, that still doesn't make it real!"

"Maybe, Busy Bob, but I have a strong feeling that taking journeys is going to have a major impact on my life."

● ● ● ● ● ● ● ● ● ● ●

Along about 1986, I became aware of Ram Dass. He was still known in the 1960s by his given name, Richard Alpert, when he achieved a certain amount of newspaper fame as a Harvard psychology professor. Harvard "invited" him to leave, because his experiments with LSD as a psychoactive agent for entering nonordinary states of consciousness had gotten out of hand, according to the powers that then were. LSD was legal then, and perhaps he could have sued the school to stay, but Dr. Alpert was probably ready to leave anyway.

Seems as how Dr. Alpert's voyages on the other side of the curtain had unalterably changed his life desires. He was madly in love with finding God. Hearing that there were yogis in India who could enter realms where they could "see God" without using any substances, he packed his bags for the East. There he met his guru who christened him Ram Dass—servant of God—and told him the place to find enlightenment was in serving and feeding people. Perceiving that as a bit ordinary, it took Ram Dass a number of years to really get it. Ultimately he co-founded the Seva Foundation, and has devoted his life to doing as his guru advised. The accounts of his journeys and experiences have filled several books which have sold in great numbers, and he has become one of the major figures in our society's disorganized mapping of consciousness.

Summertime, 1986. I had just seen my good buddies, Ray Triplett and Bill Smythe, in San Jose, and pulled onto the freeway for the drive back to Stockton in a great mood. I fished in my glove compartment for a Dave Brubeck tape and came up with one by Ram Dass instead. Well, why not? I asked myself.

There he was, sometime in the 1970s, talking at Dominican College in the S.F. Bay Area. Non-attachment to outcomes—God, but he could explain that so well! He went through several analogies, especially using water, and I drank in his every word. I paid particular attention to his analysis of how one's ego fights against non-attachment because the ego wants to be in charge of everything, always controlling every outcome.

The ego keeps up a running commentary to us—"I know exactly what should happen. I've thought it all through and it's absolutely clear. There is one outcome I want, and one outcome only. Don't even suspect for a minute that some other outcome may be acceptable. You know I know best!"

"But," Ram Dass admonished, "achievement of specific outcomes is such a dicey proposition. How many times do things turn out the way we expect, or desire? Not so often you say? Each time we allow our egos to be attached to our outcome, and it doesn't pan out, the ego takes a bruising, just like a prize-fighter up against a better boxer. Be attached to outcomes and your life will be in constant turmoil."

I nodded my head in agreement, and thought, "Yes, that's me, all right! Way too much turmoil. Now if I can just reduce my attachment..."

Ram Dass cut me off, "Therefore we must shrink the ego in order to shed our grasping of desires and outcomes. Shrink it way, way down! Shrink...your...ego!"

"Wait a minute, buddy!" I took my foot from the accelerator and spoke to the tape player. "Are you talking about my ego?" He sounded serious, and I was alarmed.

"Ram Dass, you're crazy! Shrink it way, way down?" I violently ejected the tape. "Too much dope, that guy," I yelled, glaring at the driver in the car passing me on my left. The driver caught me out of the corner of his eye, seemed to nod in agreement, or perhaps it was wonderment, and sped up to make his contact with the weirdo in the red Jaguar as brief as possible.

As I drove on to Stockton, I kept thinking I would relax, but replacing Ram Dass with Brubeck and Gerry Mulligan on the tape player didn't help at all. My ego had been challenged by the assertion that it was the source of most of my pain and confusion and the confrontation smarted because the truth had come out. My ego was frightened, squeezed, and pleaded for my understanding and sympathy. I thought maybe I would try just a little to bring my ego under better control.

But what petrified me with fear was the thought that I might go too far and lose my mind in the process. What if I shrank my ego so far I killed it? I'd worked all my life to build my ego to what it was, and the persona it projected. What if it died? Then where would the Somebody I had become, the "I" I so greatly cherished, be? Was this the price of spiritual attainment, to no longer be me? Then would I be everybody, or worse yet, nobody? The longer I thought, the more confused I became.

But before I could begin to get a handle on all this, my ego was to experience a devastating blow.

7

THE DEFENDANT
IS FOUND GUILTY

I climb up a long, sloped lawn and approach a large house. I decide to circle around the house and enter from the rear. There is no back door, so I open a cellar door and walk down the stairs. As my eyes become accustomed to the gloom, a figure stirs on my right. Startled, I see a dwarf whose fiery eyes are fixed on me. I shudder and hurry past him to stairs leading up to the first floor. I bound up the stairs, two at a time.

Our group of thirty was lying on the carpeted floor of a large room at the Pacific Theological Seminary in Berkeley, California. The sunny June morning in 1987 invited us outside, but instead we sprawled on the floor and prepared for a trip inside. We had closed our eyes, and our seminar leader told us to relax and lose ourselves in the classical music playing in the background. Presumably this experience would be helpful in the integration of our psyches for living a fuller, and more whole life.

"When the music ends, visualize yourself entering into an opening in the ground, or a structure or tree. You'll probably encounter various sub-personalities and other aspects of your subconscious. Don't be frightened and don't interfere, just follow what happens. It will be like watching a movie." I had let myself drift just as he instructed.

Reaching the landing of the first floor, I see steps to the upstairs and move up them. I want to put distance between myself and the dwarf in the basement. I continue past the second floor and climb up to the attic. It's dark again, but I hear sounds before me. I cautiously approach the noise and discover another dwarf, drinking, surrounded by wine bottles. He smells terrible, and is whimpering between drinks. I bolt from the attic back down the stairs and warily walk along the hallway of the second floor.

When I signed up for the week long seminar on "Achieving Wholeness Through Psychosynthesis," I thought it would be an interesting break away from the office and all the commotion at home. The promotional brochure said that psychosynthesis had been formulated by Dr. Roberto Assagioli as a methodology for adding the soul, the imagination and the will to the then-prevailing psychological model of libido, complexes and instincts. I had no grasp whatsoever of what any of that meant.

Reportedly, this method had been of great value in self-growth and consciousness expansion. That sounded a bit scary to me as the business seminars I was used to concentrated on facts and figures and left the "self" alone. But now a part of me wanted to risk, and I figured that I could leave early if things got too weird.

The course leader was an S.F. Bay Area minister with degrees in psychology and counseling. He started out with us in a gentle fashion and I began to trust him. I soon found myself plunged into a new world of concepts such as Higher Self, sub-personalities and a bewildering array of the conscious—sub, personal, super and the collective unconscious. The course was experiential and each concept was introduced through an exercise of one sort or another, such as techniques of self-identification, dis-identification, visualization, intuition, and auditory and imaginative evocation.

Learning about the concepts was interesting and the process was familiar—much like attending a lecture. The exercises were something else; though, unfamiliar and threatening. I had to sum up courage for each new experience, although once I had been through it, I usually liked what had happened. This was the fourth day of the seminar and lying on the floor with the music playing had been very relaxing. However, this trip into nonordinary reality was making me feel edgy.

Fearfully, I peek into a bedroom door and am pleasantly surprised to see a little boy absorbed in making a model airplane, looking every bit as I remembered myself at his age. He is dreaming of flying as he works—and his name is Courage. I continue looking in the other bedrooms and see other figures, all pleasing except for one called Anger. Going downstairs, seeing no one in the kitchen, dining or living rooms, I go out on the front porch.

Barbara is there, sitting in a swing. Her look of cold fury stops me dead in my tracks. I can't believe she is there! Her eyes lock into mine with heart-stopping intensity. I can't hold her stare, and flee down the porch steps, down the lawn, flee to the safety of the carpeted floor of the Seminary.

It had been eight years since Barbara's death, eight years of keeping a stiff upper lip. I showed the world how strong I was, and avoided talking about her death. I consciously and unconsciously kept my pain inside, deep inside. Now I was in shock. The first time I'd let my guard down, I was confronted with fear, anger and guilt that roiled in my gut like molten lava flow in the bowels of a volcano!

I was shaking and sweating, lying there on the carpet. Slowly I came out of the shock of my meeting and reflected on what had happened. I remembered three days earlier, when each person had told a little of "their story" by way of introduction. I chose to risk by going deeper than I had ever done in any group. When I came to the part of "my story" about Barbara's death and what happened after that, I was in tears, barely able to get the words out. I struggled on through, amazed that the story was as real as yesterday. In fact, my emotions around the event were literally only days old. I lay there and experienced Barbara's wrathful look again and again.

Suddenly I see myself standing before a judge in Superior Court. The judge pronounces, "Guilty of unfinished grieving. Guilty of 'leaving' Barbara too soon. Guilty of not giving your girls enough love and support." Barbara watches sternly.

Tears flowed from my eyes and I mumble, "I'm sorry, I'm sorry." I gather my voice and say, "I will give my grief full opportunity to get out. I will work with each of my girls and do something about this."

The judge slammed his gavel and said, "When you do that, I will dissolve this sentence of guilt."

● ● ● ● ● ● ● ● ● ● ●

Busy Bob had a lot to say about my experience afterwards.

"Robert, what are you trying to say here, that Barbara was actually still alive, somewhere, directing a message to you?"

"Well...I can only say it felt like someone else was directing it at me. What made it extraordinary was that I was just lying there, doing nothing, while all of this was unfolding. There was also this sense of rightness about it; that the message being given me was true, that it was right on. It was definitely nonordinary reality."

"Robert, why do you call this nonordinary reality? Look, you were emotionally overwrought. You were repressing all this stuff, and so your imagination conjured up these scenes, and they bubbled up out of your subconscious mind. You needed a stimulus to do something about it, so you imagined Barbara angry at you for holding in your grief. In fact, it was simply your subconscious mind telling you to stop repressing it. Okay, that's understandable. Why make it something mysterious? Why nonordinary?"

"I'm not deliberately trying to make it mysterious, Busy Bob. What I'm trying to say is that it didn't feel like ordinary, normal imagination. It felt real! Not that the dwarves I saw were necessarily real, but that the message being given to me about letting my grief out was. The feeling of realness about the whole thing was very strong."

"Yeah, okay, Robert. But I think you better keep this little episode to yourself!"

● ● ● ● ● ● ● ● ● ● ●

In the years following the judge's sentence, I did a lot of journal writing and visualization on death, loss, and grief. It was painful. I read books and went to seminars; somehow it seemed to help to know that grief has three stages: numbness and denial, disorganization and emotional chaos, and finally, reorganization. I tried to sort out my feelings with people who were good listeners, and I tried to express the love and support I felt for my daughters. Bringing my emotions out in the open was really tough, as I come from a family and a culture where men do not express feelings that might leave them vulnerable.

But during that Berkeley seminar, through that experience of getting in touch with a deep part of myself by exploring the nonordinary reality territory of my subconscious, I got a message. The message was that I had to do something about this dark shadow on my life.

So I did not shy away from telling "Barbara's Story," or "The Girl's Story," or "My Story." Even though each telling was an agony and left me feeling emotionally raw and vulnerable, I always learned something. Each time I felt a little stronger and a little more healed. And I didn't shy away from walking the shadow side of the street with my girls.

"Dad, you've got to come and see me. I keep having bad dreams. I'm scared. Come as soon as you can."

Now it was a Saturday, and the University of San Diego campus was sleeping in. Sarah and I walked along a rose-lined lane sheltered by stately old eucalyptus trees, with views of the Pacific calling from afar. It was typical San Diego weather, warm and sunny.

Not six inches apart physically, there was a great, dark, emotional chasm between us. I tried to name it, struggled to understand it, but no answer came.

Then, "Dad, I want to talk about Mom." And I had it. The separation between us was Barbara. Barbara, now dead for nine years, but alive between us. I looked at Sarah, saw the tears in her eyes, saw my own coloring in her skin, my own features duplicated in her face. Blood of my blood, flesh of my flesh.

Where had I been all these years?

The words...this time with more insistence. "Dad, I want to talk about Mom! I keep having dreams of her. She says I've got to get things straightened out. I'm upset about a lot of things."

The dark chasm that was Barbara wavered, relented a bit, inviting but fraught with danger.

"Okay, honey. I'm ready."

I only thought I was. My defensiveness showed otherwise. Soon I was arguing with Sarah over what had happened to her and her sisters after Barbara's death. No, I had not deserted them when I remarried. No, Wendy was not unfair to them—every normal family has disagreements over grades, work, money, lifestyles, and friends. Yes, I had tried to help the girls understand Barbara's death and no, she did not abandon the girls by dying. Yes, I was sorry that Sarah couldn't really visualize what her mother looked like. After all, she was only a third-grader at the time. Yes, I knew we should have had a lot more counseling after Barbara's death.

By afternoon I was exhausted. Sarah had to go to work and I was glad for the respite. Sleepless in my hotel bed I churned the day's conversation over and over, hoping it would turn to butter thick enough to bring my mind to full-stop. I resisted the urge to go find a bar and seek liquid relief. No, I had to be clear-headed and open-bodied enough to see and feel the healing light Sarah and I were both looking for.

Sunday morning we resumed our walking and talking along La Jolla's cliffs. I dropped my defenses and listened with my heart instead of my head. An orange sun, red bougainvillea and the blue Pacific contributed their offerings to our path. Yes, I realized, Sarah was telling the truth—her truth. I only needed to accept it as such, put it alongside my truth, and let the two truths embrace each other. I held her back, turned her to me and took her into my arms. "I love you, Sarah...I love you." An ocean-spawned breeze licked curls into her brown hair and I snuggled my face into its soft nest. Father-daughter love was once again in full flower.

●●●●●●●●●●●●

Hard Labor. I think I know the meaning of that term.

I remember the opening of the board retreat of Social Venture Network (a nonprofit business organization) where we sat in a circle, sharing our joys and frustrations. As my turn approached and I mulled over what to say, I felt my gut knot up. Only then did I know that I must tell my story again, that my sentence had not yet been dissolved.

"Today is my birthday," I heard my shaky voice. "I need to tell you what happened on my birthday eleven years ago." Responding to my distress, Burt Marks, a friend sitting next to me, rubbed my shoulders. That helped.

Choking on my still unfaded feelings, I told the story of Barbara's death, the story of my three girls, the story of what it was like for us. I didn't think about what to say, or how to say it. I let my insides do the talking. Speaking from the heart, without concern as to how things sounded or what the others might be thinking, I told it the way it was.

At the end a profound silence draped over us. I looked at each of my fellow board members, looked directly and deeply into twenty sets of eyes. Suddenly I felt a shift, a draining, and I was empty. My never-ending supply of pity for Barbara, the girls, and myself was gone. A long sigh whistled away the end of my grieving process, leaving only a soft stash of sadness for seasoning my memories in the years to come.

It had been three years since I was judged guilty and sentenced.

●●●●●●●●●●

I've had three dreams of Barbara in the last few years. One involved the girls and me meeting her, and the other dreams were of just the two of us. Each time she was warm and loving. She was especially proud of the girls and how they have turned out—as I am. I awoke joyfully, feeling I had received a positive message from her. I'm so grateful that my Berkeley journey into that house...really, just the reaches of my consciousness...has been integrated into my life. As a result of that experience of nonordinary reality, my ordinary reality has been healed, and enhanced.

There are several aspects of Barbara's death that have caused me much reflection in recent years. First was the fact that I experienced such a deep feeling of despair at my office at the time that proved to be proximate to Barbara's final moments. I believe that we are all connected in ways that we do not fully understand and can't scientifically explain. There is a myriad of reports of people sensing tragedy happening to loved ones afar, or of the idea to call someone just before the phone rings with that person on the line, or of thinking the same thoughts as another person. A recent Gallup Poll revealed that two-thirds of the respondents said that they had had experiences that would be labeled psychic, or of nonordinary reality.

This testimony to information passing via nonordinary reality composes an impressive amount of "evidence," at least as I see it. Whether we accept all this anecdotal evidence in a scientific sense or not, it seems fairly obvious that something is behind these "feelings," and we would do well to be mindful when they come knocking at our door. To do otherwise is to proceed at our own risk, and I personally have paid a high price for denying my intuition on more than one occasion.

A very mysterious event was Barbara dying only hours after Roger Steirs' death. Their mutual death day could be explained as a coincidence, although that would be at odds with the oft-repeated maxim, "There are no such things as coincidences." And, if that is true, were Barbara and Roger connected on some psychic level? At the time I had no basis for speculation on such matters. Knowing what I do now, I strongly suspect that there was in fact a deep spiritual relationship between them.

And why was Barbara reading about death and dying as she died? Was it prompted by Roger's impending death? Or did she have an unspoken premonition about her own death and was seeking information about life's greatest adventure?

And, how about Barbara's "appearance" to me? About a year ago I took a dream workshop from Dr. Brugh Joy. He is a physician who in recent years has devoted his life to working with higher states of consciousness, and he is a well known dream worker. One evening I told our workshop group about Barbara's story, my later encounter with her and the guilty sentence by the judge. Joy gave me some insight into what I had previously felt but couldn't quite explain.

He equated the judge with "the eye of God" which sees and knows everything. My coming before that eye and receiving my sentence was an archetypal "Last Judgment." Joy said that it is unusual to receive a last judgment before one actually dies. For example, some people who have had a "near death experience" report that kind of thing. But there I was, standing in the face of that tremendous force, and it delivered a negative judgment on me without preliminaries or pleasantries. The judge really "delivered the goods," Joy said. And it did feel like I was hit with an avalanche! The most important outcome was that I responded by acting to complete the lack the judge saw in my life. The results of my work generated a realization of what Joy calls "the death mystery," and a rebirth of sorts.

I see a sort of paradox here. While life is for the living, I think death is also for the living. And it's in my having an understanding and acceptance of death that I am free—free to live. That's the paradox; coming to terms with death makes us free for life. For as long as we have a great fear of death, we are not free to be fully alive.

In the years following my encounter with Barbara, I saw that there was something exceedingly important for me in the process of coming to terms with her death. I didn't know how to explain it, but I sensed that the process could be very positive, something that I should be grateful for. I could see how my entry into service and giving might have opened my heart, but I knew that it was accepting and working through Barbara's death that signaled the greatest amount of change in me. And it ushered in a large number and variety of experiences in nonordinary reality.

Now I believe that Barbara's death and her spirit confronting me gave me my spiritual initiation, that part of the initiation the Marine Corps experience lacked. Notice how the separation aspect of initiation was, in this case, my separation from Barbara. And the shattering of my life, of my ego, even, allowed me to see a new path to trod, a spiritual path. It was a tough way to be initiated, and I don't recommend that anyone go looking for the experience. But in a strange way, Barbara's death gave me a precious gift. As Martin Luther said, "You cannot know life until the taste of death is on your lips."

Recently, I met Allan Jones, Dean of Grace Cathedral in San Francisco. He has written about the three passages of spiritual life in the book *The Soul's Journey,* using Dante's *The Divine Comedy* as a guide. His reflections helped me fill in more pieces of the puzzle. I synthesized what Allan said this way. When I was separated from Barbara, I became lost and entered into the Hell described so vividly by Dante. When her spirit confronted me my initiation— incomplete in my Marine Corps experience—was now finished, and I turned away from Hell to enter the Purgatory depicted in the poem.

And when in my spiritual journey I return, I will have found home, or Heaven. Separation-initiation-return. It seems that the number two always connotes dualism—good and evil, black and white, you and me, this and that, while the number three embodies wholeness and sometimes never ending cycles: Father-son-holy spirit, you-me-both of us in relationship, creation-maintenance-destruction, and hell-purgatory-heaven.

Another learning for me in Barbara's death is that I don't want to have a traditional funeral held for myself!

I felt so constricted, choked really, being in that little side room at the funeral home. Why couldn't it have been done in a way that felt more natural, in a way that really celebrated Barbara's life and her legacy? The problem was, at that point, I only knew about one kind of funeral, the traditional kind. So it was solemn, tearful, drab, with a lot of seemingly irrelevant religious dogma and a little music thrown in. Being January, even the flowers seemed out of place. Everyone looked sober, shaking their heads in disbelief and despair, sighing. Our family was separated from the funeral-goers so that we could huddle together for strength, but we had little strength to give each other. What an ordeal!

I felt uplifted only when Barbara's favorite song was sung. The best part was afterwards when many of our friends gathered at our house for food and drink and genuine sharing. Then Barbara came back to life for a while, and the celebration of her gifts to us had a chance to happen here and there, in brief flashes and in small groups.

A few years after Barbara's funeral, I went to the memorial service of an older friend, Ira Coleman. It was held on the campus of U.C. Berkeley in a spacious, light-filled reception room looking out onto a beautiful garden. It was the first Jewish funeral service I attended, and I looked forward to discovering its mysteries. What I found was not much religious mystery, but a lot of celebration! I was amazed to be at a service where the principal activity was some of the deceased's closest friends talking about his life in an informal, sometimes joking, but always loving, way.

Ira was a very successful businessman, but his business accomplishments drew only passing reference. What did come through was a remarkably vivid picture of a warm, caring, gentle human being who had had a positive effect on the lives of many people. It was actually exciting to be there; I felt like a celebrant with a group of good friends, even though I knew few of them. When Ira's son, Don, closed the testimonies with his story of his dad, we were all rapt with attention. There was an edge of doubt as to whether Don could make it all the way through, before his grief overtook him. But, something about the light in the room, the flowers in the garden just outside the large glass doors, and the joy of the previous speakers conspired to help Don make it to the other side of the story like a small sail boat coming into dock with a trailing storm left at bay.

A final bit of traditional ceremony occurred and then, much to my surprise, lively music was heard, accompanied by wine appearing at every elbow for a fitting toast to the inspiration that Ira had given us. Now that was a Memorial Service!

This experience caused me to draw up my own memorial service instructions and to periodically update them. Currently two pages long, it includes my wishes about the last hours of life of my physical body and of the time following. The experience in its totality is of vital importance to me and I advise the person carrying out my instructions, "Please consider yourself as a midwife to my soul in its transition from this body to the next stage of my life."

It's a memorial service at Carmel Beach. There will be bonfires and people will sit on the sand, facing the ocean. There will be ceremony originating from each of the four spiritual traditions that have had the greatest meaning to me, i.e., Christian, Buddhist, Hindu and Native American. Father Charlie Moore will lead the ceremonial part of the service. Then there is to be lots of time for family and friends to speak. I hope that many of my most meaningful experiences will be relived by the speakers. Next comes music, food and drink. As the sun begins to set, someone will paddle out to the rocks and spread my ashes into the healing waters of Mother Pacific, along with dozens of rose blossoms which will wash back onto the beach to the feet of my family and friends. These roses will be my final gifts to them.

The theme of the gathering on the beach will be MISSION ACCOMPLISHED! What a wonderful send off it will be!

8

INDIA

In 1988, eight representatives of the Tibetan Government in Exile came to the U.S. to study examples of economic development that enhanced and kept a community together. Richard Weingarten, an investment banker that I had met in the Social Venture Network, was an advisor to their government and suggested they meet with Katalysis to learn about our work in Central American communities.

Our meeting in San Francisco was very cordial and informative. The Tibetans explained that there were about 140,000 of their people in India as a result of the Chinese invasion and occupation of Tibet in the early 1950s. The Tibetan government, led by His Holiness the Fourteenth Dalai Lama, fled the country and, at the invitation of the government of India, installed itself at Dharamsala in the lower ranges of the Himalayan Mountains.

The refugees were, by and large, living in settlements. With the passage of time, community cohesiveness had lessened as the younger generation was attracted to the cities of India. The Dalai Lama was keenly interested in fostering sustainable economic development in the settlements so that the younger people would be attracted to stay. In the long term he hoped for a peaceful resolution with the Chinese that would allow a return to their mother country.

I immediately developed warm feelings towards the people and their cause. When they issued an invitation to visit them in India to get firsthand exposure, Dave Brown, then vice-chairman of Katalysis, and I readily agreed. Working halfway around the world would be an immense challenge for Katalysis, but we were willing to discover if we could help.

Our trip to India early in 1989 made a lasting impression on me. Three thousand Tibetans a year were continuing to flee their country. We visited the refugee center and quickly learned that the reality experienced by these brave people was far from ours! (The U.S.

Congressional Record, August 12, 1992 describes "The sense of fear
and great suffering...the vivid, emotional and horrifying tales of tor-
ture and imprisonment....the lack of political and religious free-
doms...the environmental destruction, particularly deforestation and
toxic waste dumping by the Chinese....the apparent policy of cultural genocide practiced by the Chinese Government against the
Tibetans.")

The refugees were carrying gruesome memories and my heart
went out to them and the five million Tibetans still living under
Chinese rule. As to those who had fled their country, I was reminded of what the philosopher Euripides said sometime around 430 BC:
"There is no greater sorrow on earth than the loss of one's native
land." With nothing tangible in sight pointing to a resolution of
their oppression, one would expect the Tibetans to be a downcast lot.

Quite to the contrary, my experience of the people was they possessed a serenity and sense of peace, joy and humor that is frequently rare in my homeland. Wherever we visited—the refugee center
where new arrivals slept on thin mattresses on the cement floor, or
the Tibetan Children's Village where hundreds of orphans shrieked
with exuberance in spite of runny noses and no heat, or the nunnery
where young women who had been violated by the Chinese now
took religious instructions—we met cheerful, optimistic and humble
people.

How was it that those thin, bony refugees and those abused nuns
did not show cascading anger and hatred in their faces? They were
without material resources and comfort, and had little medical care,
but they possessed an amazing inner strength and happiness. If there
was any one characteristic that I felt in each Tibetan I met, it was
gratitude.

A social scientist could analyze the reasons for this gratitude in
great detail, perhaps reflecting that Tibetans have a highly developed
sense of family, culture and nation; that the Buddhist religion is
woven into virtually every aspect of their lives—every day is Sunday,
so to speak; and that their actions are guided by the concept of
Dharma, a twenty-five-hundred-year-old code of right living. Plus
there would be the consideration that their political leader, the Dalai
Lama, is also their religious leader, and is a singularly amazing source

of joy for all Tibetans. There would be other reasons, I'm sure, but whatever the explanations, the zest for life possessed by most Tibetans has been a source of many teachings for me!

Early on our first trip, Dave and I met with the Dalai Lama. This was a deep honor for us, and we were both nervous beforehand. His attendants gave us a quick course on the etiquette of the meeting, but I didn't really feel prepared. At the appointed moment we marched down a long porch to the door of the official chambers. The Dali Lama came smiling to meet us. A handsome man, about my age, and in ruddy good health, he had worn the robes of a monk since childhood. Dave greeted him first.

As I began to remove my gift of the traditional kata (silk scarf) to give to His Holiness, the scarf stuck in the zipper of my small traveling bag. I felt the Dalai Lama's eyes on me. As I struggled with the zipper, my camera fell out and crashed loudly on the polished wooden floor! Now I had a camera on the floor, an unyielding scarf in my hand and a beet red face!

"I'm...ah...sorry," I stammered, attempting to shake hands and free the scarf at the same time.

The Dalai Lama laughed loudly and infectiously, "Oh don't worry. This is life, isn't it?"

The thought made him squeal with laughter once more. It flashed through my mind that we had probably received a spiritual teaching on the spot, simple but profound. Amazingly, my left hand suddenly presented him the newly unfettered kata with a flourish, and he chuckled appreciatively at my unexpected recovery.

Now all I had to do was to recover the camera without the rest of the contents of my bag falling out. I slowly and deliberately squatted to the floor, focused on the task as if it were the only thing I had to do in life, retrieved the camera and put it into my bag. The zipper cooperated and I stood, trying to look more serene than I felt. This accomplished, he waved us to join him around a small coffee table. His famous warmth and unassuming personality showered upon us.

We had a relaxed half-hour conversation. The Dalai Lama spoke mostly in English, rarely consulting his English-fluent private secretary sitting off to one side. After asking our impressions of what we'd seen, he talked about the Tibetan people, their needs, the China situation, Gorborchev, the U.S. attitude toward the Tibetan situation, Tibetans living in the U.S., and his views of the monastic community.

He laughed frequently. He said that Tibetans needed to give up many of "their old habits," but to retain the gift from their Buddhist heritage of being centered and clear, of finding joy even in the most trying circumstances. This was their gift to the modern world they were now entering.

Aside from the considerable wisdom he displayed in talking about these matters, I was fascinated with the way his mind seemed to work. When we asked him a question, he would answer and then await the next question with total concentration and awareness. It seemed to me as if his mind was like a pool of very still water. A question would come, causing ripples. He would answer, and the ripples would rapidly fade away, leaving quiet water once again.

I mentally petitioned the heavens, "Oh, to have a mind like quiet water!"

There was also no evidence of strong ego identification on his part; there was no "I did this," or "I am going to do that." Nor did he use the royal "we." I couldn't get over how few times he used the word "I" as compared to the number of times Dave and I used it. I felt a strange sensation—although we were speaking largely about secular matters—it was if we were examining questions from some Olympian, or godly, perspective. It made me feel a bit light-headed and giddy. (I have heard him talk several times since then, and I have always been moved. He talks from a head and heart space that is unique from what I generally experience either from myself or others.)

As we left, he presented us with katas and Tibetan coins. Then he put his left hand on my right arm and we warmly shook our right hands, smiling all the way around. There was a gentle sweetness to the act that remains with me to this day. My journal entry of the meeting ends with, "In the presence of a high being."

• • • • • • • • • • •

Surrounded by the bracing smell of mountain pines, Dave Brown and I cautiously approached a cottage in the Himalayan foothills.

We flopped down under a shade tree in the corner of its grassy yard. It was warm, and there wasn't enough breeze to stir the Tibetan prayer flags drooping on lines running from the cottage roof to several nearby trees. I reckoned the prayers written on the flags would have to wait for later gusts for transmission to the gods. I sized up the cottage; it was large by the standards of the region, but modest by ours. A long porch spread across most of its front. A dozen or so Tibetans bowed their way off the porch and walked out to the gate, red blessing cords newly tied underneath their beaming faces.

A Tibetan boy of ten or so stood at the side of a younger boy half his size perched on a small chair on the porch. The two watched the pilgrims depart and saw us now standing uncertainly under the tree. The older boy bent to hear what the younger one was saying, then waved us over. We walked up the steps, calling out our thanks to the ten-year-old. He spoke no English and disappeared around the corner of the house.

I looked down into a warm smile splashed across the small boy's brown face. He wore a traditional monk's maroon robe over a short-sleeved golden shirt and I suspected that he would soon receive a fresh head shave. His eyes captured me. They were dark limpid pools that calmly drank me in and reminded me of who this three-and-one-half-year-old really was.

I placed my palms together and bowed to Ling Rinpoche, the intentional incarnation of a soul which keeps returning to earth to do good works, in recent centuries as the teacher of the Dalai Lamas. I softly said, "Namaste."

Ling motioned us closer and held up a handful of red strings. Yes, we nodded, we certainly wanted his blessing and a cord which symbolized good health, long life and peace, as well. We went to our knees in front of his child's chair. He placed the cords around our necks, his right hand pausing on our heads as he whispered a blessing in his native Tibetan. He did it with practiced movements—he sometimes sat for three hours doing this for hundreds of pilgrims, one at a time—but as if each of us were special.

We stood back, hands together as if in prayer, and Namaste-ed our thanks. Dave held up a camera, motioning to ask if we could take pictures. Ling nodded yes, and patiently posed with each of us in turn. As I stood taking a few extra photos, Ling's mood changed and he set aside his grown-up behavior to become a kid.

He held out his hand for my camera. I handed it over, showing him the correct button to use. He took pictures of Dave and myself, then of himself, then of the cottage, the sky...anything. Shrieking with laughter, he took pictures until the roll of film was used. Dave's was similarly shot off by Ling like a kid playing with firecrackers on the Fourth of July. It was an abandonment to excitement. Finally the cameras were emptied, and we didn't volunteer our extra rolls of film.

Ling the merry-maker took us both by the hand and led us to a door into the house. I peered into the semi-darkness and saw that it was his bedroom. But it also had something very strange in it along the back wall. We stepped inside.

He rushed to the object, a body, talking excitedly. We couldn't understand what he was saying, but his gestures told us exactly what he meant. He kept pointing, first at the figure, then at himself. Over and over. He was telling us that the body against the wall had been himself in his previous lifetime. We moved across the room for a better look.

The maroon-and-gold-garbed body of the previous Ling Rinpoche sat in full lotus position on a three-foot-high pedestal, beaming benignly at us through the glass case that surrounded him. He had died six years earlier in 1983 at the age of eighty-one, and his body had been dried with salts, preserved with herbs and coated with gold, which accounted for the smoothness of his extra-yellow skin. Although it was the first time I'd ever seen a six-year-old dead body, let alone one so well preserved as to be life-like, I accepted its presence calmly enough. I remembered what Dave had told me as we began the India trip, "You'll have to suspend judgment when you're there. Otherwise you'll miss what you're really seeing. And we're going to see a lot of wild stuff in India—at least I have every time I've been there!"

One of the wildest things we were experiencing was meeting "tulkus," or people whose spirit chose to reincarnate as the same personage, so to speak. Thus the Dali Lama, Ling Rinpoche and others we met were souls living out lives in a serial fashion—in a stream of Dali Lama's or whatever the chosen vehicle.

• • • • • • • • • • •

While I, as Robert, was more or less successfully suspending judgment on that concept, Busy Bob wasn't.

"Wait a minute, Robert. You're just getting me used to the idea of reincarnation—that our souls continuously come back to earth in a series of bodies—and now you're believing that some souls know how to target their incarnations?"

"I didn't say I believed it, it's just what the Tibetans believe. Well, maybe I do, why not? I'm getting pretty well convinced that reincarnation is the way things work, so why can't it be that souls can choose their next-life circumstances, either in their current lives or in between lives?"

"Why? Because you're a fool! You're losing your senses, just believing any old fairy tale or myth you hear. There's not a shred of proof that people can do that!" Busy Bob sounded pretty irritated with having his world-view challenged so often.

"The Tibetans think they have proof. They have a complex system to identify a child as a reincarnation of a lama, or high teacher. Many times a dying lama leaves a message about where to look for him/her next, or there are prophetic signs of that at the lama's death. Then extraordinary things happened in the family or area of rebirth, unusual phenomena at the time of rebirth itself; perhaps the baby lama recognizes people who were closely connected with the predecessor; or the baby may have the same physical marks as in his previous body. When it is thought that an intentional rebirth has been spotted, tests are administered."

"Great. I'll believe it when a scientific team from Harvard—no make that Stanford, Harvard's too liberal—supervises and verifies it."

"Aw, don't be so closed-minded, Busy Bob." Actually, I, Robert was having trouble with the concept, too. But, back to the story.

• • • • • • • • • • •

Less than two years after old Ling's death, the Dalai Lama had a vision that Ling's spirit had been reborn somewhere in Dharamsala. As a result of the vision, His Holiness sent the dead Ling's attendants on a search. Among four likely rebirth candidates, associates of the prior Ling found a little boy, Tenzin Chopak, living as an orphan at the Tibetan Children's Village. Chopak, age twenty-one months, showed that he recognized his old friends and selected various personal items that belonged to the prior Ling from groups of similar materials. Along with other actions and indications, his old associates, including the Dalai Lama, were convinced that he was the Ling's reincarnation.

Now young Ling Rinpoche (rinpoche means precious one in Tibetan) was being trained to assume his role of senior teacher to the yet unborn 15th Dalai Lama. I thought it was clever how the Dalai Lamas and the Ling Rinpoches continuously incarnated in different generations, thus creating the teacher-student relationship opportunity over and over again. Absorbed in the marvels of all this, it took the new Ling an extra tug on my hand to get my attention.

He was ready for less serious things and indicated that the three of us should sit on the floor. He brought several stuffed animals from his bed and we took turns imitating them, growling like bears and roaring like tigers, trying to scare each other out of our wits. Ling was in continuous laughter and this well-traveled fifty-some year old was surprised at how infectious Ling's innocence and joy was. He seemed to forget all about the gold-encrusted visage now towering over us as we sat.

Although I felt like I was playing with a much-loved child, the presence of old Ling looking down over my shoulder reminded me of the unusualness of where I found myself and the specialness of the boy I was with. I wondered what it would be like, living with my former body as a reminder of what I did in my prior lifetime!

It seemed like it would be bad luck for a child. I could just hear my mother saying, "Bobby, you're misbehaving, you're not living up to your old standards." Of course, if I were wise enough I could always give her a smart response, like, "If I try to be like him, who will be like me?" Maybe that would put an end to it. Still, I thought, if I were in young Ling's shoes I'd give my old body to a museum first chance I got!

• • • • • • • • • • • •

It was morning in India, one of those early mornings when you should be out on a roof-top letting the red-stained fingers of the sun strobe through your meditation-closed eyelids. One of those mornings where the lingering coolness of the night air is fighting a loosing battle with kitchen fires, but still retains power over the newly-rising heat. One of those mornings where the awakening sounds of man and beast, and your squinty sight of farmers leading their water buffalo to fields, reminds you that this is the way it has been in India for10,000 years. And in that moment you realize your life is nothing on the clock of history—yet, somehow, your soul is eternal!

I looked out the apartment window at the Himalayas and tried to discern the source of an exotic sound. It was a fog-horn moan of long pipes, blown there in the village of McCleod Ganj by Tibetan refugees just as they had been blown for hundreds of years in the beloved, and almost lost, Tibetan homeland. The pipes blew on, a half-hour, an hour, a sort of spiritual melody accompanying the words of Khamtul Rinpoche, a high spiritual teacher of the Nyingmapa Lineage. The wizened old Rinpoche sat cross-legged on his bed surrounded by Buddhas and plumes of burning incense.

Dave sat opposite me, and a handsome young Tibetan monk acting as translator sat next to Khamtul. The monk and the Rinpoche opened our time by chanting a prayer. Then Khamtul gave a long discourse on the object of the day's meditation—the Buddha of Compassion. It was touching and full of wisdom. Now came the time to meditate; in doing so I followed the instructions of the Rinpoche.

I visualized myself as the Buddha of Compassion in a celestial mandala, or palace. I pictured my four arms, my torso, my two legs, my pure white garments and my adornments. I radiated love and compassion for a long period. Then it came to me that my life should go forward totally in service—service to the poor and oppressed, service to my family and others through relationships, and service to

God and the life of Spirit.

Startled, I hear an inner voice, "My son, I am well pleased."

My heart feels as open as a sunflower on a hot noon, and tears well in my eyes. I take this to mean that God is pleased with my progress and vision for my life. The two Buddhists chant farewell and our stroll through this garden of Spirit is over.

After visiting several settlements, Dave and I concluded that assistance to the Tibetans from the local Indian NGO community (non-government organizations, or nonprofits) would be preferable to that of far-away Katalysis. The two of us helped with some basic training delivered by U.S. consultants and then introduced the Tibetans to a very competent Indian NGO. The resulting relationship has been quite successful, particularly in working with the Tibetans on a comprehensive long-term plan for the entire refugee community in India.

•••••••••••

Later in the trip, Dave and I traveled to the ashram, or spiritual community, of Sathya Sai Baba in South India. Shortly before leaving for India I had come across Sai Baba in a spiritual book which referred to him as "A Man of Miracles." According to the book, he was a very holy person, a full avatar, or incarnation of the Divine. He was said to perform miracles of many kinds, most frequently the manifestation or materialization of vibhuti, a kind of sacred ash.

The book also said he had on several occasions left his body in public view in Puttaparti, India, and simultaneously appeared in far away places in his normal body form to rescue someone in danger. The book explained in a matter-of-fact way that this process was known in metaphysics as "bi-location," inferring that it was done by other advanced souls as well, thereby generating the need for a name for the operation. Barely containing my laughter, I walked through my house looking for someone to tell about this, but no one was home.

While I didn't believe he, or anyone else, could bi-locate, when I came across a video featuring Sai Baba I settled in to see the action.

Somehow I enticed our then twelve-year-old son, Michael, to watch with me. What we saw was a strange African-looking man whose black hair stuck straight out at least fifteen inches in every direction, dressed in a red robe. The video was made on a day of celebration, and one person held a large urn upside down in the air while Sai Baba put his hand inside and preceded to generate enough ash falling to the floor to fill several large wash-tubs plus a dozen more urns the size of the first.

"How did he do it, Dad?" Michael wanted to know. "Where did all that ash come from? It's some kind of trick, isn't it? I think that would be great in the circus. Who is that guy, anyway?"

Soon Dave and I were sitting among a large crowd waiting to see the man. My excitement built as I wondered if we would see him perform a miracle. A thousand or so people were hushed, expectant.

Sai Baba drew closer to my front row seat. Dave was about ten feet away, at a bit of an angle to me as we are sitting in the apex of a curve. Sai Baba approached him and made a small circle with his outstretched right hand facing down. Suddenly gray ash began to fall from his hand, originating from the center of his palm. Sai Baba closed his hand for an instant to gather the materializing vibhuti before it fell to the ground, and distributed it into the waiting hands of Dave and others sitting nearby. I sat boggle-eyed, my mind unable to comprehend what my eyes had seen. In spite of having read about it, of having seen it happen on video, and of having heard people tell me of witnessing this phenomena, I was unprepared for seeing the materialization first hand.

"WOW!" I said under my breath. "Did he just do that? What does this mean? Who is this guy? Did the people around Jesus feel the same way when they saw him perform a miracle?"

While we were in India I bought more books to try to get a better understanding of what we were seeing. Just who was this Sai Baba? That was a tough question. I read book after book but none of them claimed to contain a complete, definitive explanation of him and his life.

However, many things were known. Sai Baba, called *Swami* by many of his followers, was born Sathyanarayana Raju to a poor Hindu family in the dusty remote village of Puttaparti, accessible only by oxen and cart. By all accounts, he was an unusual child from the beginning. Besides displaying unaccountable knowledge, he was caring, compassionate, and creative. Soon stories were being told of his magic-like powers, and his parents suspected that he was possessed by powerful spirits.

While still a lad, he announced he was really Sai Baba of Shirdi, and that he had most recently lived in another area of India. No one in his remote, illiterate village knew what he was talking about. He said it was time to stop his childhood play and begin his duties as Sathya (truth) Sai Baba. He dropped out of school and started teaching Vedic principles from pre-history at age twelve. No villager could imagine where he got that knowledge. It wasn't until outsiders came to hear the youth, that it became known that there had been a saint named Shirdi Sai Baba who, at the cusp of his death, had announced he would next incarnate as Sathya Sai Baba in 1926. That was the year that the Raju boy was born.

Since Sai Baba's announcement he has spent his life ministering to the needs of others, presenting himself to them for this purpose 365 days a year for almost sixty years. Aside from the reputed bi-locating, he travels infrequently and has only once been out of the country, many years ago when he flew to Africa. He doesn't ask for money nor does he seek to make himself known, although his fame is spreading rapidly by word-of-mouth, as one might expect of a person who performs miracles. There are reportedly more than one-hundred million followers of Sai Baba world wide. (While it is said that a prophet is never honored in his homeland, Jesus being one of the foremost examples of that principle, two million people recently traveled down the now-paved, lane-and-a half road to Puttaparti for Sai Baba's seventieth birthday, with the President of India arriving by helicopter.)

He belongs to no religion or order, or perhaps he belongs to all of them. He teaches the universality of the One God. He asserts there is no need to leave one's cultural religion as all religions lead to God. It was impressive to see Muslims, Hindus, Christians, Jews, Buddhists, Sikhs, and adherents of other religions at his ashram.

He preaches the religion of love and service, and sponsors a network of service, educational and medical organizations. He admonishes people to study and work hard for their families, neighbors and country. He stresses the need to live lives of purity, integrity, ethics and morality. In short, his is the message of Jesus before him, and Buddha before Jesus—the message of saints and avatars of all religions.

Sai Baba has been termed an *avatar* for decades. The concept, found throughout much of the non-Western world as well as in early Western cosmology, is that of an incarnation from God that appears from time to time when the affairs of the world are in especially bad shape. Avatars are born with complete spiritual knowledge, without the need for instructions, and have no teachers or gurus. To use the vernacular, they hit the ground running.

The appellation was bestowed on Sai Baba due to the highly unusual powers displayed by him—the unlearned knowledge, the extraordinary healings, the production of physical objects from thin air, knowing what's going on throughout the world as it occurs, knowing the future and so forth—in short, quite an assemblage of the miraculous.

Accounts of his miracles cause many people to check him out, and that's what happened with me. However, it's really his examples and teachings that have the staying power to sustain his position as a spiritual leader. Miracles can actually be a distraction to what he teaches. Sai Baba is really talking about spiritual food, and not entertainment.

●●●●●●●●●●●

Shortly after my return from India in 1989, I was walking around downtown Carmel and happened upon a beautiful Spanish colonial office. It had a "For Rent" sign in the window. The office was empty and I could see it had inlaid, red-brown tile floors, thick adobe whitewash walls and a courtyard with red and purple beauganvillas in full flower. The place was drop-dead gorgeous, and my dream of what an office should be.

As I looked it over, I had the damnedest feeling that I should rent it. Mind you, we lived in Stockton, almost three hours away. Yes, we had a weekend place in Carmel, and it was my fantasy that we would someday live there, but back then everything was in Stockton—my business, Katalysis, and an eighth-grader in school. But the tingles in my chest and arms kept saying, "Rent it, Bob. Rent it." I wrote down the phone number from the sign and excitedly went to find Wendy.

Looking for her gave my mind enough time to rationalize renting an office that I had no use for. I theorized that space like that was hard to find, and that if I leased it for several years I could rent it out on a short-term basis. I figured I would be able to cover my costs, even make a few bucks. That seemed to make a plausible explanation.

I negotiated a lease and put my phone number on the "for rent" sign. I was just beginning to get some serious nibbles that summer when Wendy said one night, "Bob, this year-round thing that Michael Thomas' school started just isn't working. He's got to get in a good eighth-grade year to make it into prep school. I'm going to look for something else."

Two days later she said "I've talked to York School at Monterey, and they can take him. It's a very good school, they'll prepare him well for high school. Would you be up for the three of us living in Carmel for a year?"

I said, "Well, it would mean a lot of commuting back and forth. But I could set up in the Dolores Street office and get a lot of work done there. If he needs it, let's go for it."

With that I played right into the hands of intuition and synchronicity. And my life would blossom in Carmel like it never had before.

9

NO FEARS!

Our eyes met in the mirror over the bathroom sink counter. Hers had an anxious look, and her hand applying the not-very-red lipstick was stopped in its tracks. My eyes, squinting to guide my tie-tying, questioned the strangeness I saw in hers.

She said, "You're not going to drink as much tonight as you did at the wedding yesterday, are you?"

My heart raced, but I said with a studied, casual air, "What are you talking about?" It was the first time Wendy had ever said anything to me about my drinking.

She turned to face me, and I braced myself. "You acted so...differently." There was a hesitation, a searching for the right words. She was rarely critical of me and this came hard for her. "You were...acting out of character." Her voice was concerned.

I didn't give her the chance to say more, figuring the best defense was a good offense. "I was just trying to have some fun! You know how I hate those phony social occasions where everyone stands around bragging about their kids, talking about sports, and telling dirty jokes. No one ever wants to talk about anything serious or important, so I just got in the mood to go along with the crowd." There! I thought. Did I get the blame attached to the right people? Yes. But didn't I sound just like my kids when they made excuses? I hated those whiny justifications, and mine gagged in my throat as they made their unwelcome appearance.

"Well, okay, but please be more careful. Sometimes you don't seem aware of how much you're drinking." She turned her attention back to her face which had patiently waited in the mirror for its lipstick and makeup.

"Aware!" I hissed the word under my breath, and angrily undid my almost-finished tie knot to begin again. As if I weren't aware!

Alcohol had been on my mind for much of my adult life. I had continually thought about my parents' problems, about when I was and when I wasn't going to drink, and about how my drinking habits compared with other people's. I furtively checked "yes" or "no" or "sometimes" on the "Alcohol Problems?" quizzes that appeared in the Sunday newspaper, manipulating the answers so that I never made the problem category. But sometimes fear formed unexpectedly, starting in my gut and expanding in my chest, as I thought about the odds of my becoming an alcoholic, given the rampant history of alcohol abuse that climbs up and down my family tree like strands of DNA.

The fear hadn't always been there. I grew up in the 40s and early 50s in semi-dry Iowa where there were beer-only-bars and state liquor stores for "package goods" which were consumed at home or poured into "set-ups" from brown paper bags kept under tables in private clubs. Few kids in my high school drank, probably because the opportunities were nearly non-existent.

Drinking wasn't something I thought about then. Although I noticed my parents' interest in whiskey and beer, I paid little real attention to what they were doing. Now and then my dad needed a ride home from the Elks Club, but my pleasure in driving the family car obscured any inquisitiveness I had.

My first experience with alcohol came when I was nineteen and a PFC. in the United States Marine Corps. One weekend I caught a ride with a buck-sergeant friend, Marty, from Camp Pendleton to Los Angeles. It was a warm, sunny day and we whistled up the coast highway in his top-down, cream-colored Pontiac Chieftain convertible with an imposing Indian-head splitting the wind at the bow of the hood.

About twenty minutes down the road, Marty pulled into a liquor store parking lot. Without a word he jumped out of the car, returning in a few minutes with a bag under his arm. We sped off and, on a deserted section of the road, Marty pulled two quarts of beer from the sack. He showed me how to hold a bottle between my legs, and threw me a "church key" to open the beers. I jumped to the newly-assigned duties, feeling proud to be treated as a grown-up.

The fat brown bottle was cold in my hands, a wonderful contrast with the heat seeping up through my white cotton trousers from the

Pontiac's sun-baked plastic seats. Mimicking Marty, I took a big swig of Schlitz, "the beer that made Milwaukee famous." I loved the beer from the instant it made a wet, icy path down my throat to the moment a carbonation-induced belch ran up from my stomach cavity to the freedom of the ocean air swirling around my head.

A few more big gulps and the beer had made me feel like I'd never felt before. I went right to the head of the class, from PFC. to General, to the top of the world. I had no problems, no worries, no cares; just a warm, gay, optimistic feeling that spread through me like fingers of ecstasy.

"Thanks, Sarge," I shouted. "This is the life!"

"You're right, kid. You ought to get a fake ID, so you can buy your own!"

"Right, Marty!" My mind toyed with how I could forge an ID, because as a part-time "office pinkie," I had access to the blanks in the Charley Company office. The problem was that they were prenumbered and tightly controlled. That would never work. Then I remembered that ID cards for newly discharged Marines weren't prenumbered. Jackpot!

"I've got it, Marty," I shouted, polishing off the beer with gusto. With that I yelled, "Whoopee!" and tossed the empty bottle up in the air, arching my head to follow its flight. I was terrified to see a huge truck following us. The bottle arched back to earth, then paused, seemingly waiting for the right instant to bomb through the truck's windshield into the driver's lap. But my panic dissolved when the bottle crashed harmlessly on the highway just barely in front of rushing tires.

"You're drunk!" Marty hollered. He roared with laughter and I howled with relief and triumph; together we two loud maniacs rode behind the surging Indian Chief on a modern day trail that emptied into Los Angeles—the city of cold Midwestern winter-night dreams.

After the Marine Corps came college and my beer drinking began in earnest. Friday afternoon beer busts at my Sigma Nu fraternity house were never-missed events. Brothers bonded over the rims of beer mugs bearing the fraternity insignia and initials in fancy, hard-to-read scroll. Beach parties, socials with sororities, the

Kingston Trio at the Kerosene Club—there was a drinking venue every weekend.

The socialization was very important to me, and it didn't seem to interfere with the rest of my school and work life. I came to see alcohol as a real "life-enhancer." Meanwhile my parents were stepping up their drinking, especially my father. We lived in the same town, San Jose, so I couldn't miss it. I could see that they couldn't handle alcohol, but never doubted for a minute that I could.

Of course, I conveniently overlooked the fact that in my junior year I was arrested for drunk driving. I hired my law professor to handle the case and he easily negotiated a reduced charge and a fine. Only two classmates were aware of what happened and, needless to say, I never talked about it again! I also overlooked the fact that in my senior year I ran my Morgan sports car into a ditch in the Los Gatos mountains after a party. Luckily, neither the car nor I sustained much damage.

In the next several years my dad's drinking got completely out of control. Life around him became a hell for everyone concerned, especially for my mother. Finally the family convinced him that he needed help and he agreed to go to Woodside Acres for rehabilitation.

It was a dark winter's early evening and my brother, Dick, drove. Dad sat alongside him in the front seat, and I in the rear. I looked at the back of his unmoving bald head, sickened that his once robust body was now frail. I'd actually had to help him into the car, and he was only fifty-two. Conversation with Dad had come harder and harder over the years, and the drive to the treatment facility was accomplished in a stony silence. After all, what do two young men with undeveloped capacities for feelings say to a father who admitted he was a failure?

Woodside Acres was a rambling, drab, uninviting facility. It sure didn't look like any three week vacation spot. While the man in charge worked with Dad and his admittance papers, his assistant, a fellow in his early thirties, took my brother and me for a tour. We weren't allowed in the patient quarters and the treatment area was eerily quiet, with no one about. Our guide tried to offset the grimness with a cheerful line of patter, telling us all the good things about Woodside. I wondered what qualified him to be the number two person in a facility that dealt with people committing suicide one drink at a time. Probably just a paper pusher, I thought.

But perhaps not, as he took special pride in describing their treatment methodology. This consisted of giving the alcoholics a drug that made them violently ill when they drank. The theory was that the patient would promptly lose desire for alcohol forever-after.

"There," he said, directing our attention to a large glass window looking into a almost bare room with a cement floor. "We bring them in here once a day and make them drink. We have almost every kind of booze and they can select their favorite," he sniggered, barely suppressing a smile. "They get sick, right there—on the spot. This is a one-way glass, so they can't see the staff watching. You know, we just watch to make sure they're okay."

That's when I noticed a hose coiling up to a faucet, over in a corner by what looked like a drain. Grasping the implications of the process, I imagined my father retching his guts out onto the bare concrete floor for twenty-one days while an orderly kept a camouflaged watch, waiting to perform the hosing-down duties.

I steadied myself against the wall, and turned to ask the administrator what their success rate was, and what they did if a patient refused to drink. The words choked in my mouth as I realized I didn't want to know the answers. I was afraid if we knew the truth, Dick and I would take Dad right back home with us—and then he'd never have even this lousy chance to break the iron grasp of alcohol squeezing the nape of his neck. The administrator noticed my ashen face and motioned for us to return to the office.

The burley fifty-some-year-old boss was just getting to his feet as we arrived, the paper work complete. He seemed glad to see us again, as if he were anxious for us to leave so that he could get my dad into the patients' ward and out of his hair. I noticed for the first time that he had the facial blotches of an alcoholic himself and at first was comforted, knowing that recovering addicts often made the best counselors, and then troubled at the prospect that the guy might still be drinking. Someone turned off the hall lights and the four of us and the room itself seemed to shrivel a bit.

Dad appeared unable to rise, his body slumping like a dead weight in the chair, his face in his hands on the boss' desk. The air in the room seemed dead itself, as if it contained only half the normal oxygen.

"Dad...we'd better go. It'll be late when we get home," Dick offered, his voice feeble.

Dad released his face from his hands, turned to us, and the fear jumped from his eyes into the room like an evil spirit at an exorcism. I became breathless. Dad tried to speak. "Ah...well..." but the tears welling in his eyes drowned out the plea in his throat. As one, Dick and I reached down to his pitiful figure, awkwardly hugging him, mumbling, "Good luck." Back then we could've never told him we loved him.

The silent drive back to San Jose was excruciatingly long. Dick and I didn't want to share our revulsion at what we'd seen, nor our doubts about Dad's chances; doubts that proved well founded when he began drinking heavily again within sixty days. When I reached home I surprised Barbara by telling her I didn't want any supper and went to bed. I probably shocked her by not having a drink.

As time went on, I become ambivalent about my drinking. It no longer seemed to be all fun and no harm. One year at my annual physical when the physician, going down her checklist, asked me about my drinking habits, I decided to tell the truth. I informed her that I took two drinks every night and many more at parties, when I often became tipsy and exuberant. She looked at me knowingly and said, "Oh, a social drinker," and went on to the next question.

So I proceeded along in my pattern. I drank some each night to relax—alone or not. I drank more with good friends to let my hair down and have fun. Sporting events were a great time to drink. Social occasions were mandatory drinking events, as I really didn't like most of them, and drinking made things seem more pleasant and the inane conversations somehow interesting. In short, drinking was a crutch I used to avoid uncomfortable feelings, both in a crowd and alone.

For most of my life I'd been a control freak and I managed my drinking process so that it didn't interfere with my job or my relationships in any significant way. I had always been very focused on success and it was quite clear to me that there was a fine line that could not be crossed. But I was fearful, just the same.

When I was forty-three, I developed an ulcer immediately after Barbara's death. The control freak in me was confronted with chaos in both my external and internal worlds. My doctor put me on Tagament for one-hundred days to heal the ulcer: during that time I was prohibited from drinking. Much to my surprise, I survived psychologically, and my physical health improved greatly. I discovered a clarity and freshness in each morning that hadn't been present when I took alcohol every night. After that my drinking decreased quite a bit and I no longer drank hard liquor. Basically, I became a weekend wine user.

But even as my use of alcohol decreased, my fear of it increased. With age it took ever-smaller amounts to make me feel slightly off the next day. Worse was the developing body of knowledge that showed children of alcoholics were unusually susceptible to alcoholism. Serious problems with alcohol had by then surfaced in at least four consecutive generations of my family—and there may have been more, but no one could remember our ancestors that far back.

My pride in my father, who became a local legend in Alcoholics Anonymous and sober for fifteen years before his death, and of my mother who significantly decreased the role of alcohol in her life, couldn't change my concern that I might carry a genetic predisposition as well. I harbored a fear that I, too, would someday have to go through what they did. I wondered if I could negotiate the unstructured days of retirement, or even a thirty-day boat cruise, without crossing the line from informed use to abuse?

I took to micro-managing my use of alcohol. If I had a drink, I would enter a "D" in my Runner's World training log alongside the number of miles I ran that day. For almost a decade the cumulative miles were a steady 1600-2000 per year, depending on whether or not I ran a marathon which required increased training, and for several years the number of days that I had a drink hovered around 120. I could tolerate that number of days, but what stuck in my craw was the unpredictability of the days, and the number of drinks.

All too often, "I" (my personality) drank when "I" wanted, and how much "I" wanted. The "real I" (my soul) behind the "I" thought that was inexcusable. If "I" spontaneously enjoyed some wine with friends or my wife, or if "I" had more than my self-imposed limit of two glasses, the "real I" was furious. A fierce power struggle raged, and the "real I" worried more and more that "I" would some day experience my dad's plight. At that point a psychotherapist might have contended that my fear of alcoholism was worse than alcoholism itself. (To clarify further, although connected, these two I's are very distinct; the more my personality does what my soul wants, the happier both my soul and personality are. On the other hand, if my personality does what my soul doesn't want it to, they're both unhappy.)

So there I was at the mirror, tying my tie and thinking about what Wendy had said. Fifty-three years old, and my fear of alcoholism still a constant visitor. Every day, it seemed, one way or another. A few days later, August 29, 1989, I made an entry in my journal which read:

"I've been going full blast, either packing for our move to Carmel or working at Katalysis until midnight on the USAID project. I'm overweight, tired, stressed out and full of negative thoughts. On top of all this, Wendy got on me about drinking too much. So, I paced my drinking against hers that evening at a dinner party, and felt lousy the next day.

"I must be poisoning myself with alcohol! I need help; I'll see Tim Franklin (a therapist) and do whatever it takes. I am going to ask Sai Baba for help, too. I'll write him a letter. I'm going to go for it—I know what the other side is like. I just need help to get there."

My journal of August 30th reads: "Amazing! Sheila Krystal (a Berkeley therapist friend and student of Sai Baba) called this morning and said that she is leaving for India tomorrow. She asked if I had a letter that I would like her to deliver to Sai Baba? Did I? Absolutely—I was writing one as she called! How did she know? I wrote a short note and Federal Expressed it to her immediately.

Dear Sai Baba;
    How happy I am to write this letter! No sooner than I decid-

ed yesterday morning to write you, Sheila Krystal called to ask if she could deliver a letter to you for me. So, you are thinking of me!

Well, you know my problem. I want so much to get rid of this drinking question. It is an impediment to my relationship with you, and with my spiritual and physical life. And yet I seem powerless to do so, and I ask for your help. I just have to turn it over to you.

I place myself under your care and guidance, and await your instructions.

Love, Bob

Before I received a response from Sai Baba, which came two weeks later on September 16th, I had a dream that announced help was on the way. In a dream on September 4:

I was shown a bush and told by an unidentified voice that it was symbolic of the burning bush in the Bible. I picked a leaf from the bush and looked at it closely. It burst into flames but it was not consumed, not even burned. I knew I was being shown God's power and grace. I sobbed and asked Jesus to take me into his heart. As I was struck by my great good fortune, the observer part of me started to analyze the experience and I couldn't go deeper or receive more information.

The next morning I went to the Bible and found the burning bush story in Exodus 3.2: "And the angel of the Lord appeared to him in a flame of fire out of the midst of a bush, and he looked, and lo, the bush was burning and yet it was not consumed. And Moses said, 'I will turn aside and see this great sight—why the bush is not burnt.' When the Lord saw that he turned aside to see, He called to him out of the bush, 'Moses, Moses, here I am.' "

I also read that through this sign and a subsequent dialog with Moses, God had instructed and equipped Moses to lead the people of Israel from their bondage in Egypt. I was in awe of having had a similar dream and felt greatly comforted. A day or two later I found a magazine article that said the burning bush dream, one that many people have, has an archetypal meaning—it announces the coming of the Divine. So help was on the way for me, too. Just as God came to the rescue of the Israelites, I, too, could expect to be rescued. With this information I no longer felt merely awed and comforted, I felt ecstatic. And for very good reason: a Sai Baba dream came on September 16:

I was in a pickup riding with other business people and we were just back from a deal. We pulled up in front of my house, small and rustic like our Carmel cottage. It had a wooden fence and lots of trees with pine needles on the ground. It was in India, near Sai Baba's place.

I looked, and Baba was in front of the house. I got out and ran to him, and he recognized me. We embraced heavily and he gave me a very tender smile. I kept repeating, "Baba, Baba, Baba." It seemed I would cry, but no tears came. We went into the house arm in arm. There were several people in the living room, fellow devotees of Sai Baba, except for my brother. I wondered if he thought I was strange, hanging out with a holy person from India.

Baba led me to a vacant chair. He sat and because he is so small, I sat next to him in the same chair. I asked if he had received my letter from Sheila. He smiled and nodded yes. I wondered if he was reading my mind. He asked if I had any fears. I sat and tried to conjure up the feeling of fear, but none came, not even my fear of alcohol.

Sai Baba asked me again, "Do you have any fears? You certainly don't seem to." He smiled with approval and I realized he was showing me that I had nothing to fear. Suddenly the realization hit home. No Fears! A hundred weights, some heavy, others subtle, lifted from my shoulders. It was an extraordinary feeling, yet totally natural. No Fears! I smiled back at Sai Baba and we both laughed...for a long time.

With the confirmation of No Fears! two women appeared at our side. They said a baby was in the clump of blankets that had suddenly appeared in the chair with us. They said our laughing might wake it, but Baba told them not to worry. The dream ended..

A final entry on the subject appears in my journal on October 13th: "Talked to Sheila Krystal. She looked in her diary and said she gave my letter to Sai Baba on September 15th. My dream was on September 16th! So we are well and truly in contact."

After the two dreams, my life changed for the better. I certainly expected it to, for a burning bush dream is a powerful archetype and the presence of the baby in the Sai Baba dream could be seen to signal the birth of increased intensity of Spirit in my life.

I began to feel more at peace, more relaxed in the world. If a stray fear arose in me, I'd reflect that I really had no fears in my deepest self. And since that deepest self is my true self, the twinges of fear that I experienced could only be superficial at worst, if not, in fact, false. Ultimately I came to see that the dream was about my very deep-seated fear of life, for which the fear of alcohol was a proxy.

Soon after the dreams I realized I hadn't had a drink for weeks and then months. I felt wonderful again! Still, I wondered if total abstinence wasn't just another form of fear. When I finally took a glass of wine, I half expected the roof to cave in over me. It didn't.

(I am now an occasional wine drinker. I've lost my compulsion for it, but not necessarily my taste. I feel that I don't need alcohol, but that it's all right for me to enjoy a small amount now and then For Wendy and me an occasional glass of wine before dinner can be a point of reconnection and mutual pleasure. And it's the same with family and friends, especially around the dinner table. A little wine and food blossoms and conversations flourish.)

Bottom line, my No Fears! dream told me that as long as I remain in the Spirit, I'll have no need for alcohol or any other behaviors which modify my view of what is going on around me. That's because, it seems to me, when I admitted I needed help and called out for it, a response came from the world of Spirit.

● ● ● ● ● ● ● ● ● ● ● ●

I shouldn't give the impression that I didn't have to struggle a bit with the concept that my anxieties about alcohol could disappear in a dream, just like "phoof." Busy Bob thought that entirely too easy.

"Robert, this doesn't make sense, that you can be acting differently just because you had a dream. I don't get it!"

"Well...I don't think my change of heart happened solely in the dream. I think part of it occurred when I acknowledged that I needed help...when I consciously and formally asked for it. I believe the surrendering was essential."

"Really? Surrendering...that sounds pretty wimpy to me. Just whom did you surrender to, anyway?"

"I don't know exactly...it was a higher power than me, Bob. It was a recognition that, at some point, we all need assistance from something beyond just our own body and mind. I think it's the same thing Dad talked about in the AA Twelve-Step Program, that step of 'surrendering to a higher power.' "

"Yeah, but you wrote the letter to Sai Baba. That's what gets me. Why didn't you send it to Jesus...or God? Why somebody in India?

"That's not the significant part, Bob. It doesn't really matter to whom we surrender. What matters is that we surrender."

"Hey, wait a minute...isn't the recipient important? Doesn't it make a difference if I cry out, 'Jesus save me' or 'Buddha bless me' or something else?' Or are you just going to go around calling, 'Higher powers, help me?' "

"Busy Bob, what I'm learning is that it doesn't make any difference. God...or The Creator and Sustainer...or The Universal Force...or whatever you want to call it...anyway, the Divine is like the sun. It shines all the time, and it shines on everyone.

"It doesn't think, 'Hey I like these guys in Nigeria so I'll shine on them but I don't like those gals in Pakistan so I won't shine there.' It shines on everyone—indiscriminately. That's its nature. So it's going to shine on us whether we're good or bad and whether we believe in it or not. Doesn't make the slightest bit of difference to it: It just shines. Now the same holds true whether or not we 'surrender' to it. That is, it's just going to shine on us—no matter what."

"You're losing me, Robert. First you said surrendering is essential and now you're saying it doesn't make any difference to God. You've gone off the deep end again."

"Look, Bob, what if we have an emotional shield protecting our egos, our feeling that we are strong and independent and can take care of ourselves quite nicely, thank you, without anyone else's help? If we do, and I think so, it looks to me like the ego shield is thick, really thick. So thick, it prevents much of the Divine's blessings, those sun-like rays, from shining on us. But when we realize that we can't go it alone—that we do need help—that's when, in effect, we drop that shield. Then we can receive more of the Divine's blessings which have been shining along all the time."

"But, Robert, you're describing a God that doesn't do anything but shine indiscriminately...that has no religious affiliation...that shines equally on Protestants, Jews, Muslims and heathens. No rituals needed, no intermediaries required to receive its bounty. No dogma, no such thing as blasphemy or heresy."

"Basically, that's it. Mind you ritual, guides, and even dogma can help when they assist you in dropping your ego shield. On the other hand, they're a definite hindrance when they feed your ego by insinuating, or insisting that what you're doing is the only way things can be done. But you get the main point, Bob."

"The main point, Robert, is that you're raising hell with my belief system!"

● ● ● ● ● ● ● ● ● ● ●

As one might expect, I'm wildly enthusiastic about my dreams that seem to come from Sai Baba. I've met an amazing number of people who have had significant Sai Baba dreams, and many of the more than 100 books about him relate fascinating dreams of instructions, teachings and healings. An ashram handbook advises people who have questions for Sai Baba to write him a letter; he reputedly reads scores at a time by passing his hands over the stacks, a process necessitated by the fact that he receives thousands each week. The handbook states that Swami then answers the questions, frequently through dreams, sometimes by other methods.

In spite of the availability of this avenue of communication, millions of people also "dream" of having a personal interview with him. In the early years before seriously large crowds arrived, it wasn't so hard to do, and I know many people who have. Now a seeker faces almost lottery-type odds against having a coveted face-to-face experience. I've been four times to Sai Baba's ashram and confess to never losing hope that somehow I will be chosen from the sea of humanity for a session. It's totally an ego thing, this thinking I should have an interview. I know that others seeking him have problems far more serious than my trifling concerns. Plus, I have to ask myself, why should I be selected when I've already had a dozen inner-views with him? In fact, I've had a dream that goes right to the question:

Shaking with excitement, I stand behind an Indian fellow, second in line outside Sai Baba's interview room. The door opens and our line snakes into the room, barren but for one straight-backed chair. Swami stands before it and the man in front of me asks a question. I pay no attention as I am rehearsing my four questions. Soon enough it is my turn and I step in front of Baba. He's much taller than I, and his crown of black hair almost reaches the ceiling. I crane my neck and look up into his dark African-looking face.

"Swami, I haven't had a dream of you in a year? Are you still present in my life?"

"Yes, oh yes," his high-pitched voice carries great quantities of reassurance.

"Tell me, Swami, is having a dream of you the same as having a personal interview? Do your words in a dream have the same force and effect as if you said them face-to-face?"

He looks down the line of people, "Listen. My answer is for everyone." All eyes fix on him. I feel rocky but there is nothing to steady myself on, so I stiffen.

"I want to confirm that when I speak to you in a dream, what I say is exactly what I would convey to you in person. I need to use dreams to transmit, and the dream recipient is the object of my intentions." He pauses and looks at me.

I leave my last questions unspoken. After all, I had had plenty of dreams from him. I place my hands together prayer-like, bow, and whisper, "Namaste."

My inner-views have all come from dreams—and they have been no less powerful than the in-person variety. (Recently I had the opportunity to ask a noted dream worker, Dr. Jeremy Taylor, if dreams such as those of Sai Baba, or other spiritual guides, dead people and so on, were "telepathic phone calls." He said he believes that such dreams do involve participation of the other party, but that they also contain projections of the dreamer's subconscious as well. This would seem to put a premium on interpretation to sort out the dreamer's projections and get to the sender's message, but then dreams always require thoughtful analysis.)

One of my Sai Baba dreams was a delightful illustration of the principles of karma, or cause and effect, and free will. In my dream Swami showed Wendy and me a box theater, much like a shoe box that children use for playing dolls. He asked the two of us to take turns choosing the subject of the play—he suggested we focus on elements of a virtuous life—and setting the stage. With the subject selected and the stage prepared (the karma, or cause, was in place), the dolls proceeded in their actions without our control (free will went into effect).

This was also a great illustration of why real-life outcomes are so unpredictable. Free will and free choice allow for spontaneity, not to mention chaos! In the dream we were also shown that other factors come into play—unintended consequences, synchronicity, even the karma of the other players. But, as Swami said, that's what makes our game of life interesting—each moment is heavily conditioned by past actions and unseen influences, but in and of itself the moment has an infinite number of possibilities.

There's been a number of things I don't understand about my Sai Baba dreams, but all-in-all they have helped me in many ways. I've had more than one dream response to a letter I've written him, and now and then events occur in which I have an eerie feeling that they contain his message.

Setting aside the novel mode of communications, at the end of the day my understanding of Sai Baba's teachings is that he points me back at myself—saying that Divinity is in me and around me, and that is true for everyone. One might say he keeps reminding me that I am a spiritual being having a human experience.

10

NAMASTE

"I can see clearly now, the rain has stopped. It's going to be a bright, bright, sun-shiny day!" The board room of the Monterey County Bank was filled with the upbeat tempo of Johnny Nash and his band singing a hit song from 1972.

"It's going to be a bright, bright, sun-shiny day!"

The fourteen people gathered around the long oak table looked up with surprise and curiosity. I had suggested that we experience a "transition piece" before we began the day's agenda. "Now what's he up to?" they probably thought, but didn't say. Moving to one side of the room, I had flipped on a tape player.

"I can see clearly now, the rain has stopped."

I began to dance and urged the others to join me. It took a while, almost twice through the song, but I got everyone on their feet, dancing and singing, "It's going to be a bright, bright, sun-shiny day!"

Giving money away should be fun, don't you think?

Welcome to a Namaste board meeting! Namaste is our family initiative for service and philanthropy, transacted in a way that encourages family unity and each individual's personal growth as well. Along with giving my time, sharing financial resources with others has boosted my efforts to improve myself as a person, and hopefully, has had positive outcomes for those who have participated in the sharing as well. With this in mind, Wendy and I determined to make similar experiences available to our family. Watching this unfold has been like unwrapping presents at Christmas.

All six of our children joined the Namaste Foundation Board of Directors in 1990. Their ages then were twelve to twenty-five, with half in their teens and two at home. From my perspective, the older ones had asserted independence and now stood on the outskirts of our porous family circle. The younger ones were on their quest for individuality, too. It seemed to me that it would only be a matter of time before they were as distant from their siblings and parents as their older sisters. Clearly, we needed new ways to relate to each other. But we had few clues on how to start.

Three short years later, Namaste had proven to be the vehicle for a family transformation. That was the year daughter Carin was quoted in the booklet by the Whitman Institute, *Building Family Unity Through Giving*, as saying;

"Now I think the family comes first for all of us. Before Namaste, we didn't spend that much time together. Now we're definitely closer and enjoy each other more. If the foundation was an excuse to bring us together, it worked—but I still would prefer my dream family where everyone got together just because they wanted to."

Notice that she didn't say we are a dream family—we aren't! But also note that participation in Namaste, which was one part of a comprehensive plan to teach our children about the responsible making, managing and use of money, had created something almost magical. As Carin said, it brought us together. And it was a lot more fun than eight people going through psychotherapy!

You see, in the process of the family joining a board of peers and focusing on the problems of others less fortunate, we began to treat one another differently. Everyone seemed to grow up in each other's eyes! Of course, this wasn't without confusion. After our first meeting, Lara shook her head in frustration. "The whole concept of a foundation is a mystery."

And then, from Sarah: "I feel scared and lost."

But, gradually, it got sorted out, and at our third meeting, Carin's voice cut through the generational impasse: "I get it! You want us to take responsibility for what happens."

Taking responsibility. What sweet words to a father's and mother's ears!

Roy Williams is a friend who works with families on building trust and communications, and with issues of family businesses and wealth. He worked on me for a year to get me focused on dealing with these questions within our family, and then helped us once Wendy and I decided to begin. He recently said, "You started in a hole as deep as anyone. You were a blended family with conflicts running in every direction. The kids were acting out with alcohol and anti-social behavior. They didn't trust you as parents. Your offspring said they needed an appointment to talk to you, you were so busy with business. Let's face it, you really didn't know what was going on."

Well, we climbed out of that hole. And while the giving wasn't the whole of it, it was an important part. Not only is our family now as thick as thieves, I can't describe how proud I was to read in the business plan of the Beach Chalet, a micro-brewery and restaurant that daughter Lara and her husband, Gar, are opening on the ocean-end of Golden Gate Park in San Francisco: "The partnership will contribute five cents per beer sold to a community fund. While this will adversely affect our profit margins, we believe that this fund represents an enlightened and proper way of conducting our business." And the $20-25,000 each year will certainly help people in their community who can use a hand!

• • • • • • • • • • • •

One of the advantages of intergenerational family giving is that the younger people are not yet old enough to know why things won't work. Consequently, our grant making has been more daring than if it were executed only by Wendy and myself.

In 1988, Merede put to the Namaste board a proposal for a series of photographic flights over the rain forests of Belize in Central America. There were a lot of raised eyebrows on that one! But Merede persisted. She had met with Project Lighthawk and, armed with reams of information, presented her case with entrepreneurial vigor. The board ultimately designated $8,500 for the project.

Late in 1990, an article in People Magazine about Project Lighthawk featured the results of their flights over Belize. From the Lighthawk plane, public officials had seen the scope and importance of their rain forest for the first time. As a result, they had set aside 100,000 acres as a preserve. Namaste's partial funding of this project has probably had the highest payoff of anything we've done so far!

The positive results of including the children (and spouses) in the process of sharing resources outside the family has been dramatic in many ways. We have been asked to give our story in print or in talks and seminars. After overcoming our initial hesitation, we have said yes, and the younger generation, in particular, enjoys it. We like to think that we are helping others achieve personal transformation through giving, as well as helping stimulate the flow of more resources to worthy projects.

As much as I love to promote the benefits of service and giving, both as a family and individually, I am forced to acknowledge certain complexities that seem inherent in these actions. Just how can I "see clearly now?" For example, should I, and how can I, integrate the impulses of altruism into my everyday life, and not as just special events? Am I giving because it is my duty, or my joy, or to assuage guilt of some kind or another? Who should I give to, and how?

From time to time I like to reflect on what Maimonides, the great Jewish philosopher of the 12th century, described as the eight levels of charity. His thinking seems as appropriate today as it was then. Going from what he saw as the lowest level of charity to the highest, he listed:

1. He who gives unwillingly.
2. He who gives cheerfully, but not enough.
3. She who gives enough, but not until she is asked.
4. She who gives before being asked, but gives directly to the poor person.
5. The poor person knows from whom he takes, but the giver does not know who is receiving.
6. The giver knows to whom she gives, but the receiver does not know the giver.
7. The giver does not know to whom he gives, nor does the poor person know from whom she receives.
8. And the highest form of charity is to strengthen the hand of of the poor person to help lift him out of his poverty.

• • • • • • • • •

Once I showed this list to Colin Ingram, my writing coach and good friend. That promoted a challenging conversation.

Colin said, "I've seen that list before, Robert, and it raises as many questions as it answers. For example, we often don't have the opportunity to determine the level of our giving or even whether or not we should give; we just find ourselves in situations where we react spontaneously, without a moment's thought."

"Give me a for instance, Colin, so I know what you're talking about," I urged.

"Okay, once a friend and I were walking across Union Square in San Francisco when we noticed a beggar sitting on the ground, leaning against a bench—not one of these young "spare change" hippies, but an older man, a genuine wino who looked like he had never been anything else. Dirty, unshaven, matted hair, complexion burned a deep red by weather and booze—you know the type.

"We stopped walking and began discussing what our response should be. My friend was of the mind that if we gave him money, the wino would just use it to buy another bottle; therefore, we should give nothing. I countered with the idea...actually, from Hebraic tradition...that one is required to give to anyone who asks, regardless of his or her situation and regardless of how we view his or her need. My friend suggested that we had not been formally asked, and I replied that that was merely a function of how close we passed to the wino. If we walked by the bench, he would probably ask for a handout."

"I'll bet you were right about that, Colin."

"Yeah, we walked by the bench, and, sure enough, the old man requested money. 'What for?' I asked. 'For food. I haven't had a good meal for days.' My friend started to say 'Why haven't you gone to one of the free meal—' but I interrupted him and said to the wino, 'Come on, we'll buy you some food.'

"So we helped him up and took him to the nearest mom and pop grocery store, a couple of blocks away. He chattered away the whole time about his good fortune in meeting two such admirable gents as ourselves. We came out of the store with two large bags of groceries and headed for his flop house room not far away. It was on the fourth floor, and we carried the groceries up to his room, placed them on the single table and left, ushered out with profuse thanks.

"Once downstairs, we crossed the street and stopped to look up at where we thought his window would be. Just then it opened and the two bags of food came flying out. The bags hit the sidewalk with a soft thud and burst apart. Several passersby walked around the stuff but a few of the poorer-looking ones examined the canned goods, loaves of bread, etc. and began gathering them up to take with them. In a few moments, only the torn bags were left.

"Then the old man came out of the entrance door and headed back toward Union Square, where we had first seen him."

"You guys must have felt like idiots, Colin. Obviously the guy wasn't interested in eating and was going back to try to get money for liquor."

"That's right, Robert. And it was then that my friend and I took up the discussion, once again, of the right thing to do in this circumstance. I maintained that we cannot be responsible for the results of our charitable actions. He countered by saying that perhaps that was true in general, but that we also had an obligation to carefully consider the potential effect of our gifts to the recipients.

"You see, Robert, I was trying to do what Maimonides suggested in his last (and highest) form of charity. I was trying to offer a small first step by helping lift that fellow out of his tragic position by getting him properly fed. But to this day, I don't know what the right action would have been on that day—or if there is such a thing as right action."

I tried to think of something really wise to say, something Maimonides-like. Finally I sighed and said, "Hmm. At least none of the food went to waste, Colin."

●●●●●●●●●●●

I certainly don't have all the answers, but over the years I have more or less participated in every level of giving on Maimonides' list. I have given only because I was asked, and without a feeling of commitment to the cause. I have often not given enough, or have had to be asked to give when I could have seen the need on my own. Sometimes I probably have given too much. I have gone through all the permutations of knowing and not knowing the recipients, and them me, and have wrestled with the questions of giving publicly or secretly. And, through Katalysis, I have helped people establish themselves by loans and training. My conclusion is that this list is a good set of guideposts, but you've got to trod each path a bit to really know why Maimonides said what he did.

I equate the giving of one's time with giving money. In fact I think that giving money without active service is only half a loaf. And truth is, I believe, giving time is a greater expression of one's commitment than just giving money. When you give time, it's you. When you give money, the amount may or may not be the real you.

I've thought a lot about various expressions of service and wondered whether a similar sort of Maimonides list might be constructed. Lacking his wisdom, I have come up short, but I'll make some observations. For example, I know that the time I spent beautifying the Veteran's Memorial Building as part of a Rotary project felt different from the time I spent on the hospital board of directors. And different feelings yet have come from time spent dealing directly with farmers in Belize, or taking an AIDS patient grocery shopping, or visiting a sick friend in a dreary convalescent hospital.

What this all boils down to, I think, is that the closer I come to that farmer, or that patient, or that friend, the deeper the service feels to me. Even, or especially, if there is stress and conflict, it's deeper. It all feels juicer, and where there is juice there is connection, there is involvement, and there is the chance for personal growth and transformation, not just for me, but for the other person as well.

According to a recent study, eighty-nine million Americans give four hours or more per week in service. What an endorsement! Can you think of a better thing to do with your time?

• • • • • • • • • • •

From our home town of Carmel on the Pacific Ocean, I often see ships at sea. Sometimes I speculate on what they're carrying. Perhaps autos, or oranges, or maybe oil. Whatever the cargo—manufactured, like cars, or grown, like oranges, or extracted from the earth, like oil—each object has one thing in common. At the destination, everything will be valued in the currency of the land.

We not only value goods and services in money, sad to say we also tend to value many of our actions, even a major part of our lives, in money. If love is "the tender trap," money may be thought of as the "tar baby trap." It's hard to get free of tar baby, for money has a psychological dark side. I certainly don't know many people for whom money isn't an issue!

Money carries a dynamic psychological charge in our society. It's right up there with sex! In addition to using money for the necessities and luxuries of life, and as a way to exchange our energy for someone else's, we use it for power, for mood management, for manipulation and for prestige. Even giving away money isn't as easy as it may seem at first blush. So, we need to recognize that there is a lot of emotional baggage that we need to deal with as we go about giving, not to mention in living, as well!

As I see it, there are two limiting concepts around money that come up when we give. The first is that there is not enough money in our lives, and the second is that money is often used as a proxy for the control of other people's behavior.

Most of us have spent the major part of our lives believing that we don't have enough money. And I count myself in that "we," as only in recent years did I conclude I had enough. Now, it's pretty logical that if our experience of money is that we don't have enough, we'll have a difficult time in giving. And even if we feel we have enough money now, our fear of giving too much and not having enough later is a barrier to our charitable impulses.

Interestingly, acquiring more money usually doesn't squelch those fears. Here in this country, as income levels rise, instead of the giving percentage increasing, it barely budges. Put another way, the percentage of income given by people who make less than $12,000 a year is about the same as those making $12,000 a month! One explanation given for this phenomena is that the poor are more likely to give to others that are in a bind, because they know how it feels. In any event, high income people who seemingly could afford to financially give more, apparently can't afford to do so emotionally.

I recently saw some statistics that illustrate this financial-emotional gap. The first is that only 20% of wealthy individuals make charitable bequests in their wills. In other words they don't share their lifetime's accumulation with the society that afforded them the opportunity to so accumulate. And the second concerns the 2,500 U.S. households that have a net worth of $100 million or more. (Did you know there were 2,500?) The lifetime contributions of this group are estimated at less than $500 thousand each! How much is enough, for God's sake?

I want to suggest that in this paradox lies an opportunity for significant emotional and psychological growth. A big question for all of us is, "How much should I give?" My friend Lynn Twist, an extraordinary money philosopher, says "The right amount is somewhere between a gesture and a sacrifice."

That's good, very good, but I'd like to propose a short cut to discovering what that amount is. It's called Giving Just Beyond. What we're going to do here is test the money barriers that limit us by stretching our gifts to just beyond our comfort level. For example, if we would normally give the Salvation Army $100, but believe they deserve more, let's give them $200. Now, if the gift is just beyond, it can hardly be dangerous to our financial health, and we can cautiously watch what happens next. Or if we normally give our church $10 each Sunday and would like to help support their new child care center, but are feeling pinched in the pocket book, let's go for $13, or $15. Just beyond.

Now that we've taken that extra step, and if no financial calamity has befallen us, we'll probably feel like stretching again the next time. And what happens in life when we keep stretching ourselves— mentally, physically, or emotionally? Growth! And when we taste the resulting sense of freedom from our money, we receive a wonderful boost for our sense of self worth—as opposed to our money worth!

Now are we on our way out of the tar baby's trap of accumulating money for money's sake, by sharing our money? Are we fighting fire with fire? I think so!

(And why can't we apply the Just Beyond concept to improving our relationships, our jobs, our diets or our anything? Because our lives are a series of responses to ever-changing circumstances, when we respond, let's go Just Beyond. It works like the old saying, "An inch is a cinch, but a mile takes a while.")

I mentioned a second limiting concept of money, that of using it to control the behavior of others. We often use money this way, both intentionally and unintentionally, but rarely are we clear on our motives in doing so. This is especially true in giving when our gift to charity or a family member is really conditional, but either we or the recipient fail to realize it at the time of the gift. Then, if the desired behaviors or outcomes aren't forthcoming, the seeds of conflict sprout, usually a nasty surprise to the giver and the recipient, alike.

It's a good idea to continually ask ourselves what our true motives are in making a gift. When we give to a family member, is it unconditional? What if an offspring takes our money and spends it on something that is totally legal, but which meets our disapproval—for example, perhaps they buy tons of CDs made by weird musicians? Or they invest it unsuccessfully by taking a hot tip on the stock market from a twenty-year-old friend? Similarly, do you trust a charity to use its best judgment in spending your donation? What if their newsletter is fancier than you like, or their Executive Director buys an expensive new car?

These practical questions illustrate why I believe we should strive for clarity in discerning our motives. If a person feels they might have problems in the situations I described, it says the gift is really not unconditional. The only way the recipient can keep us happy is by spending in a fashion to our liking. Now, if we discover that our motive is something less that unconditional giving, that is not "bad" in and of itself. It's legitimate to seek uses and outcomes from our money that are worthy. But we also must communicate our desires to the recipient. Then neither party will be confused about the true nature of the so called "gift," and, if the recipient chooses to accept the money under the donor's conditions, many troublesome upsets will be avoided.

For example, the next time we prepare to write a check to a charity, child, or friend, we should ask ourselves, "Do I really care what X does with this money? Is there something that they might do with it that would upset me?" If the answers are no, then proceed; we're about to make an unconditional gift (which may be as rare as unconditional love).

Now, if we really care what X does with the money, and it's an important amount to us, then before we write the check, we should ask ourselves, "Just what is it that I expect X to do with the money?" If the answer is "Spend it all on school books and none on pizza or video games," then we better tell X exactly that up front, and ask for receipts from the bookstore, as well. Or if the answer is "Spend it all on food for the poor and none for the food bank's telephone bill or newsletter or salaries," then we should say so. The people at the charity will appreciate it. After all, they want us to give more than once, and they would hate to lose that opportunity because we didn't communicate our true motives.

Service, too, presents some well disguised traps. It can be a real ego trip to serve on a prestigious board of directors or run a high-impact service project. It becomes easy to see oneself as noble savior, possessing unlimited amounts of wisdom as to what other people need and how it should be given to them. Soon we come to believe that what we and our fellow board members have to say is more important than what the people we are trying to help say. There is also the problem of sincere (and sometimes not so sincere) praise and gratitude that comes our way. By the time all this happens we are deep into what I call "ego inflation," and this enlargement is a formidable barrier to doing truly good work.

Another pitfall is that giving or serving is frequently done in a transaction that has the giver up high and the recipient down low. This can do psychological damage to both parties. I am convinced that very few people really want charity. Yes, in a disaster they can gladly receive food and medical supplies, and see it as being the neighborly thing to do. And yes, there is a positive experience if a server can help another as a friend might do, so that the one helped can say to themselves, "If the need arose and I could help someone, I would do the same thing." Otherwise charity is almost always demeaning to the recipient. Notice I said "neighborly" and "as a friend." (This personal touch is one of the reasons why governments and big institutions are rarely good at the charity business.)

As knotty as these questions are, my feeling is that the best course of action for anyone considering service and giving is to be proactive. Just go ahead and get started. Treat it as an exciting new learning experience. When you stub your toe, say by unintentionally insulting the dignity of the person you're trying to help, apologize if you can, but by all means learn from your mistake and give it another try. Or if you see your charity is creating an unhealthy dependence, bring it to an end with as much grace as you can muster and think twice the next time. (I've skinned my knees on exactly these stones in the road, and a lot more too.)

Perhaps the best way to avoid these traps is found in the advice of the Indian saint, Sathya Sai Baba, "Service is the essence of devotion, the best cure for egoism. Do not believe that you can by means of service reform or reshape the world. You may or may not; the value of service, its most visible result, is that it reforms you, reshapes you. Do service as a spiritual discipline, then you will be humble and happy."

And when you make contact, when you're invited to share a meal with the person you're helping or are introduced to their family as, "This is my friend," or exchange a long, soul-touching look of understanding, I can guarantee that you'll feel like singing,

"I can see clearly now, the rain has stopped. It's going to be a bright, bright, sun-shiny day!"

● ● ● ● ● ● ● ● ● ● ● ●

A friend once asked, "Why are you leaving so much of your estate to Namaste? Do you have a lot of guilt about money?"

That caused me to write an article for our family's newsletter to help me better understand my relationship with money. I called it:

ON HAVING MORE THAN OTHERS

The first crack in my cozy world of indifference to the relative possession of resources came when I visited Central America with the California Agricultural Leadership Program in 1973. I was shocked at how poor people lived and this experience ultimately led me to start Katalysis in 1984. During the intervening years I was dimly aware that there was a resource allocation problem in the

world, but I didn't much see it as being close to me. I wasn't confronted with the issues which we now see all too clearly: homeless
people, way too much poverty, lack of health care, violence, crime
and so on.

I don't know if I gradually became more aware of these problems,
or if they just escalated until they became "in my face." In any event
they are pretty evident to me now, and my response is an important
issue to me. It has led to my passing on to others a lot of the resources
that come to me. This passing on has been to nonprofit groups and
to my family. Over the past ten years this has been a significant part
of my wealth, and a substantial amount of what I have left will go to
charity at my death.

My experience of this has been very positive. It was once said
that a wise person can build their character with money, in contrast
to some who abuse their character to make money. I believe that in
holding my money with my hand open to others' needs, I have
expanded my personal development as the money left my hand.
Hopefully, this is a legacy I am giving my children. I would also like
to note that there seems to be some force of replenishment at work,
so that even my occasional fear of giving too much has proven quite
unfounded. A good image for this is to picture a water pipe. Until the
faucet is opened and water flows out, no fresh water can flow in.

I don't want to give the impression that I have found the perfect
balance between providing for the personal needs of myself and my
family, and sharing with the larger world community. I still haven't
overcome my confusion when I come face to face with an apparently desperate person asking me for money, whether at home or in
India. I have not given when I should have and have given when I
shouldn't. Sometimes I feel people act differently with me once they
know I have money. So money seems to be a dance of discovery and
I still feel awkward at it.

Having money also means I consume a disproportionate amount
of the world's resources. Consider this. We wring our hands at the
population explosion in India and cry that the earth doesn't have the
resources to continue supporting such irresponsible behavior. But the
average American consumes twenty times the resources as the average Indian. My wife and I have six children, so the eight of us con-

sume as much as 160 Indians! My family consumes as much of the
earth's resources as a small village in India, for God's sake! Who am
I to begrudge them an extra child, unless I do something about my
own consumption, which could be trimmed without discomfort, as
any fool can see?

To look at this consumption issue in another way, I read that if
India, as only one of the relatively poor countries in the world,
developed to the extent of the U.S., there would be no future for the
rest of the planet! I reckon this makes some sense, because if the
close to 1 billion Indians consumed the earth's resources at the rate
we do here in the U.S., it would be like having about nineteen or
twenty billion more people on the globe, or about five times what we
have now. Even Philip Morris and Coca-Cola would admit that's
unsustainable!

Shall we stop trying to develop markets in India and China and
the rest of those low income countries? Remember only 20% of the
world's population is at our standard of living, more or less, but most
people, including those other 80%, want to see that changed. And if
the wheels that are in motion now roll on as planned it won't be a
question of some people having cars and others walking, we'll all be
walking! Maybe we should just plan on rationing that 80% when the
need arises, a plan that no doubt would cause a war. Or, God forbid,
maybe we should forget abundance, which may be the flip side of
scarcity, and focus on sufficiency.

I don't know. This is a new riddle for me, one that I'm slowly
approaching like a hiker who chooses to explore all the surrounding
mountain passes before descending into the valley. Wendy and I are
doing most of the standard things like recycling and asking ourselves
twice if we really need to buy more things.

I'd like to see more written on the subject, more debate and speculation. But I doubt that there are any magic formulas or rules that
should apply to everyone. We'll each have to work through our own
stuff, so to speak. The important thing is awareness and then some
kind of positive action. The awareness is compassion and the action
is loving kindness. Not so coincidentally, those are underpinnings of
religion and the spiritual path. Awareness and action will not only
make ourselves better people and the world a better place, it may

even save it!

•••••••••••

I stand at the foot of our bed, eyeing the twenty shirts peering up at me like shrunken corpses. It's an appropriate metaphor because one-third of them, that's six and two-thirds rounded up to seven, are about to become history. For, once a year, I go through my closet, down to my sweat socks, and give the homeless one-third of everything that's there. Since I've been doing this for a few years, I keep thinking I'll get down to a minimal amount of clothes. Not so far! Even though I don't remember buying anything in the last year there is still more stuff in that closet than I need. Okay, the red shirt goes, then the blue...

After you've (hopefully) decided on how much to give, to whom to give and in what form, another interesting question is, what will happen to your charitable activities when you're no longer around to direct them?

The next item on our Namaste meeting agenda looked innocent enough: "Contingency Planning." All eyes turned to me as I took up a stack of papers and said, "Pretend that I've just died. You are meeting to decide the future of the Namaste Foundation. Here's a list of your assets. As you can see, they amount to quite a bit—a few million dollars. You'll be giving away a lot more money each year than we are now. I imagine you'll have a lot of questions. But remember, I'm gone. You'll have to figure out how you're going to get the answers on your own." With that I began handing out the documents.

After an awkward pause Lara announced that it was better to think of me as being "on a leave of absence." And with that the group proceeded to have a very productive conversation about what to do with the money from my estate.

"Does anyone know about this building in Pleasanton? All I know is that Dad said he's frustrated with all the slow-paying tenants!"

"What about this stock in the cannery? Should we keep it or try to find someone to buy it?"

"This is going to be even more complicated than it looks," attorney Geoff Way interjected. "We have to give away at least 5% of our assets each year, and I doubt that all these closely held investments either pay income or can be easily sold."

"Well, let's draw up a list of questions. It looks like Dad will have a lot of answering to do when he comes out of it." Everyone chuckled at Merede's joke.

From these questions, you can see that the "Dad's gone" or "fire drill" is a very valuable family exercise in preparing for an event that is 100% certain to happen. Since the timing is the only uncertainty, the exercise points out what the survivors know and what they don't, but should. The process is likely to result in specific actions that put the family in a better position if the need arises unexpectedly. I highly recommend doing this type of fire drill periodically.

A few years later at a Namaste board meeting, my heart was warmed again and again to hear the stories told by our younger family members of their time spent as volunteers. They were doing things like working at the Boys and Girls Club, or helping youngsters with school homework, or helping raise money for projects.

In many cases, they met with nonprofit personnel to learn the goals and objectives of their organizations and, in one instance, with a small, grass-roots group, and coached them on grant proposal writing. As we totaled up the grants that had been decided upon at the meeting, I marveled to myself at what a wonderful investment these outgoing funds were; not just an investment in the people benefiting from the projects, but an investment in the attitudes, values and emotions of our family members.

One presentation at that meeting stood out for me—that of our then seventeen-year-old son, Michael. He had served as an evaluator on a proposal from a local nonprofit, the Center for Community Advocacy (CCA), which assists farm workers in improving their housing conditions. It had been formed in response to scandals wherein farm workers were being housed in tents and caves, all within thirty miles of our affluent Monterey Peninsula!

Michael and I visited CCA's office in Salinas for a briefing by the

Executive Director, Vanessa Vallarta, and then drove to a labor camp on the outskirts of the small town of Pajaro. We followed Sabino Lopez of CCA as he walked down a dirt path to the camp. We saw lots of standing water, some from broken sewer lines. Sabino went from door to door, occasionally pointing out hanging electrical wires.

The doors Sabino knocked on differed, and I could see Michael's eyes widening. First were doors on decrepit trailers. Sometimes there was a wooden step up to the door. But where the trailers had sunk into the earth, there was no need to step up—people just shuffled from the muddy outside to burlap sacks lying inside.

Next were doors to disabled pickups with camper shells for living quarters. The shell was the family bedrooms, and the front seat of the pickup the living rooms. We saw people sitting there, resting from the day's field work.

The strangest doors had been sawed from sides of huge containers that said "American President Lines" on the sides. It must have been hard sawing as the doors didn't fit well, and had left lots of room for cold night air to flow in.

The residents gathered, and a middle-aged man wearing a San Francisco 49ers T-shirt and jeans began explaining their plight. Michael concentrated on their rapid Spanish.

"Geeze, Dad, they're paying $400 to $500 a month rent for these dumps! The owner told that guy in the red shirt that he can't afford to fix the place up. The country health inspector just issued thirty-two citations, and Sabino said they could withhold their rent payments until repairs are made without being evicted. Isn't that great?"

We felt forty sets of eyes on us. Sabino said we were "a local family who supported CCA." We heard murmurs of approval, and Sabino looked at us expectantly. "Go for it, you've had five years of Spanish," I told Michael.

He spoke slowly. "Thank you for having us here. You are facing very difficult circumstances. We are inspired by your courage. We will try to help." There was no condescension in his words nor was there timidity, just a simple reaching out from one human to another.

From the smiles around the circle, one would have thought that the help had already been delivered! And when Michael made the

CCA presentation at our meeting, his eloquence in describing the farm workers caused us to give more than had been requested!

Oh yes, the ancient Sanskrit word, namaste, is still in everyday use in India, Nepal and Tibet. When people greet one another, or say good-bye, they fold their hands together, and, with a slight bow, say "namaste." It literally means, "I salute the light within you, and when you are in that light, and I am in that light, we are one."

Namaste!

11

IF YOU'RE GOING
TO HELP ME

Ron had AIDS. I had never known anyone with AIDS. And here I was, sitting next to him in the car, breathing the same air that was going in and out of his lungs, touching things he'd touched. I know, I know, I told myself. You can't catch it that way. But still... What if he was bleeding someplace under his jacket, say from the IV tubes I knew he had to use? How did he get AIDS, anyway? Does he want to talk about it? If he does, what will I say? Will he die soon? He doesn't look too bad, but he's shaky and weak. What if he passes out when we're a long way from help?

My heart was beating faster than normal, but more than that, my mind was a polluted mess. That's why I was talking constantly...

"Bob, you ask too many questions and talk too much. Look around you!" Ron interrupted me, waving his hand toward the outside.

Sheepishly, I mumbled an apology and took note of the beauty of the day unfolding before us as we headed down Highway 1 to Big Sur and the Ventana restaurant. I took several deep breaths and tried to focus on the moments that he and I were sharing together.

Some months earlier, I had been reflecting on Biblical accounts of Jesus working with criminals, prostitutes, lepers. Although society saved its most poisonous attacks for them, Jesus seemed to prefer those outcasts to the well-behaved. It didn't seem to trouble him that his actions were scorned by so many people, especially the pious. I wondered what the reaction of pious Christians would be if Jesus returned tomorrow to spend his time with the dregs of our society, rather than "nice Christians" like the rest of us.

It seemed to me that we would have but two choices; either turn our back on Jesus as the religious faithful did 2,000 years ago (and most likely would again, given the chance), or join Jesus in his ministry to the outcasts. After a lot of thought, I decided my service life lacked the dimension of "heavy duty lifting" that Jesus practiced. So I looked for a project that would make me stretch, one that would make my heart bigger.

Our local AIDS project was promising. AIDS victims had been at the bottom of our totem pole since the disease was diagnosed. That fit with Jesus' example. The clincher was that I had been homophobic for decades. My family was well aware of this as for years I had made angry, disparaging remarks about homosexuals. Why? I think it stemmed from two incidents in my teenage years when men made sexual advances to me. One of the men was someone I trusted and admired, and I felt betrayed. Now I was asking myself if I was bigger than my fear, questioning if I was ready to let it go.

I became an MCAP (Monterey County AIDS Project) volunteer in 1990, joining the local community of HIV and AIDS people and their helpers. It would be hard to over-state the benefits I received. For brief moments, I stood in the shoes of people whose external reality was drastically different than mine. But I saw the sameness of our inner reality. The sense of connection warmed and expanded my heart. Some of my most touching moments occurred when I taxied young mothers with AIDS.

Because they are the age of my daughters, it was easy for me to get confused as we drove and chatted. Was I talking to a daughter, a daughter of a friend, or a stranger? Did it make any difference? When we parked at the doctor's office, the reality of the situation snapped me back like a whip-lash.

One day I took a young woman to the hospital to pick up her baby girl. I climbed the stairs of a small frame house in Pacific Grove and knocked on the door. It was opened by a sandy headed woman with alarmingly dark circles around her eyes. "Yes?" she said, softly.

"I'm Bob...from MCAP. I'm here to take you to the hospital." She looked at me blankly. "Oh...yes." She took a jacket from the couch by the door and followed me down the stairs. "Wait...please." I watched as she picked flowers from the yard. "For my little girl."

"That's nice." I mustered a smile and held the car door open for her. As we drove in silence, I noted that she couldn't take her eyes from the flowers; it was as if she were encoding them with a message for her daughter.

When we arrived, the mother said the baby had been in for one of her periodic blood transfusions, and left me at the curb while she went to fetch her. As I waited, I asked myself in panic—does this mean the baby is HIV positive? I certainly wouldn't ask the mother. My mind said, probably, the baby must be; why else would it be in the hospital? But my heart said, no, this can't be! God, babies with HIV—babies who will have AIDS? What kind of world do we live in?!

The mother came out with a little red-head, bundled in blankets. The baby was not interested in the flowers and flung them onto her mother and me. The baby cried all the way home. There was nothing I could do but cry silently along with her. It had started to drizzle, and the windshield wipers provided a steady counterpoint to her wails which seemed to ask, "Why? Why?"

I never saw the mother and her wispy red-head again.

Of all the MCAP clients that I worked with, I got to know Ron the best. He was short like me, in his forties, with wavy brown hair and a ready smile. Over a half-year period, I saw him as often as once a week, and we became good friends. He lived in a rather seedy motel on Fremont Street in Seaside, and I'd pick him up there for trips to the doctor, or shopping or whatever was up for the day. I found the place depressing, but he didn't complain much. He had a lot more significant problems to deal with than the ambiance of his living quarters.

After a few months, he startled me by talking about a huge sum of money that he would soon receive. He said he'd invested his nest egg in an apartment complex in Santa Barbara many years before. Now the property had been sold, and his attorney was negotiating his share with Ron's partner who had managed the investment. Ron expected to receive $1.2 million in cash within sixty days. He said he was planning to buy a house in Pebble Beach for $600,000, and described the residence in great detail. He also talked about drawing a new will as he wanted to leave half the money to charitable work.

I found this story pretty hard to believe, given his living circumstances in the dingy motel and the fact that it seemed like I always
had to pay for the pie and coffee that we had at Coco's Restaurant.

As time went on, he kept me informed on the different reasons
why his money was being delayed. I didn't press him for details, as I
figured that the story was a harmless fantasy for him. (And just what
sort of fantasies would I engage in, I wondered, if I knew my time was
running out?) Instead, I concentrated on going with the flow of our
time together.

Given his earlier admonitions, I didn't ask too many questions.
He gradually related more and more about his life, and I told him
about mine. I gradually forgot my insecurities and we became quite
comfortable together.

I know the reading I did about AIDS was part of the disappear-
ance of my anxieties. I learned enough to know that I was in no danger. But more than anything else, I came to see Ron's condition as
just being part of who he was at that moment. Except for when he
was really hurting, he was no different than a friend with a heart condition, or one who worried about his job or had a bad temper that
needed controlling. Ron became both ordinary and yet special to me,
just as any other friend. Pretty soon the only difference I could see
between us was that he knew what he was going to die from, but I
didn't know what was going to take me away.

One day after an appointment, Ron and I were driving down
Munras Street in Monterey. "Hey, Bob, I want to stop around the
corner at the Mercedes dealer. You like to look at cars, don't you?"

"Okay, Ron, I've got time." We pulled into the lot and I walked
with Ron into the showroom. A dignified looking salesman wearing
a blue blazer and club tie appeared immediately. "May I help you
gentlemen?" he asked.

Ron wasted little time. "I want to look at a coupe and a sedan.
What models do you have?"

I watched incredulously as he put the salesman through the paces
of showing him a dozen cars. Growing tired of Ron's fun, I wandered
outside for fresh air, thinking how cheeky he was. When I returned,
Ron and the salesman were filling out some paperwork.

"Okay, Bob, I'm getting the blue sedan, the one over there," he pointed to the far end on the showroom. "And I found a perfect coupe for my mother. What do you think? Do you want to see it?"

I was stunned at the idea that he was buying a Mercedes for himself, but another one for his mother? I blurted, "Oh, sure, but your mother?"

"I didn't tell you, but I just found out she's going to move here from Jersey to be with me. The silver coupe is just like her!" He turned to the salesman, "OK, I'll be back on Thursday to sign the final papers and pick up the car." The salesman beamed, giving no hint that there was anything unusual. Perhaps he was used to eccentric rich people walking in and spending $110,000 in less than an hour!

When I told Wendy about the Mercedes incident, we wondered if Ron wasn't carrying his fantasy thing a bit too far. Granted that staring at death should give him extra leeway, but misleading the car dealer seemed a bit much!

Late Thursday afternoon we were startled to hear a car honking outside our house. It was Ron driving the ice-blue Mercedes sedan! He was so proud of it and carefully pointed out all of its stellar features. I gaped, slack-jawed and dumbfounded. When he talked about his mother's Mercedes-to-be and why he had selected different options for it, I just nodded in amazed agreement.

About a week later I called Ron and said I was going to be in Central America for two weeks and wouldn't be around to help him. I suggested that we have a drink together the next day. He agreed, and I met him at his dingy motel. Not seeing the Mercedes, I asked about it. He said it was at the dealer's getting the bugs worked out.

We went to the restaurant on top of the Marriott Hotel. It was a beautiful, sunny day and we had a panoramic view of the Monterey Bay. I ordered a club soda, but Ron insisted on tap water. He raved about how good the water was, and when he ordered his third glass, the waiter looked at me strangely.

"Bob, don't you think pure, fresh water is one of the best things in life? It sure is for me. Let's talk about the best things in life. There are a lot of them, aren't there?" So we sat for two hours, talking about the best things in life. When we left, I felt full of gratitude.

When I returned from Central America, I called Ron. The motel manager said he had checked out. Surprised, I called MCAP to see where he had gone. They told me that he'd been taken to the hospital a few days after I left and died there. I softly hung up the telephone, sadly thinking, "So that's the way it happens."

I was unable to find out anything more about Ron. No one in the MCAP community knew about his mother. He had recently moved to our area from Southern California, and there was little history of him here. The "dead-end" that I experienced left me feeling very incomplete about his death. There was no memorial service for him, so I privately did my own.

I could have gone to the Mercedes dealer to find out if he'd really bought the cars and if so, what had happened to them. But I didn't want to know. It felt better to me to leave Ron's fantasy—if that is what it was—about cars, the house, and his money intact. It was one thing I had left of him.

And, what happened to my homophobia anyway? I can't put my finger on it, but it had melted away. Now I have friends who happen to be gay. I feel lighter now that my anger and resentment have dissipated and I've let go of my old attitudes and prejudices. I chalk it up as another victory for serving others as a way of self-improvement. Isn't it true that in serving others, we are really serving ourselves? Isn't it clear that giving and service are not only socially transformative, but personally transformative as well?

Several years ago we asked a physician and an MCAP AIDS specialist to come and talk with the eleven members of our family when we gathered during the Christmas season. Our daughter, Merede, wrote an account of it for the MCAP newsletter, and here are some excerpts:

"If you've been reading this newsletter you are probably already familiar with the scary facts about AIDS. But have you ever considered that a member of your family, your own child, could be the next victim? Have you thought about talking with your family about the realities of the virus and safer sex? Have you talked to your kids about sex at all?

"Most people are uncomfortable talking about sex, so the subject of AIDS is neglected. This leads to false information and, especially for young people, a false feeling of security. The truth is, it's a lot easier to talk about AIDS than to watch someone die from it.

"In order for a family AIDS talk to be successful, a feeling of nonjudgment needs to be created. This isn't about whether or not your kids have sex, but rather when they do, will they be safe from AIDS? It's not easy to ask intimate sexual questions with your father across the room, but the information we received at our family talk could make the difference between me sitting with my dad at home, or him sitting with me in a hospital.

"The good news is that AIDS is preventable. The open and honest talk we had with the help of Dr. Meg and Carie from MCAP was the most valuable and lasting Christmas gift I have ever received!"

•••••••••••

My service work at Katalysis provided me with three major tests of my ability to understand and implement the concept of nonattachment: a six-figure monetary crisis, a near-fatal auto crash and a death.

At first blush, I had a lot of trouble with the concept of nonattachment, especially as it was often presented as detachment. That word sounded irresponsible and defeatist to me. Then I came across an explanation that nonattachment meant, in a spiritual sense, to "be unattached to the outcomes or the fruits of one's actions." A further elaboration said that one should put forth their best efforts in everything they do, but not be particularly attached to the outcome. Outcomes, as we have all seen in life's school, are often unpredictable.

One of the reasons I struggled with the concept of nonattachment is that my partner Dino and I often used a phrase, "Over, under, around or through it, we're going to do it." Now that certainly sounds like high attachment to outcome, doesn't it? We were frequently successful in making the phrase come true. But not always, and maybe the reason was the "through it" part. I've read that Taoism has this to say about obstacles: "The Tao (the stream of life) desires to flow like a river. When it contacts an obstacle such as a rock or a tree, it will go over, or under, or around the obstacle, whichever comes first and easiest. It does not try to flow through it."

In the fall of 1990, I received a very good lesson in this via a dream. Katalysis, many months before, had been awarded its first matching grant from USAID (our Agency for International Development) for $600,000 over three years, beginning that October 1st. The final paperwork was in process during late August and early September. Everything had been approved and passed on to the government Office of Procurement.

Although not apparent, a disaster was in the making! The government employee assigned to our grant was brand-new at Procurement. On top of that, her communications link at Katalysis was with our part-time financial officer, Jim Renicks, who hadn't worked with AID before.

At noon on the last Friday of September, I was on my way out the door to lunch when the phone rang. My secretary had already left for her break, and I was tempted to not answer the call. But something pulled me to the phone.

"Hey, Bob, this is Jerry." It was the Katalysis CEO and he sounded nervous. "I just had a call from AID. They're pulling our grant because the procurement office hasn't been able to establish an overhead rate. He said we could apply again next year and probably get it. I'm trying to reach someone higher up!"

I jumped in my car and headed from Carmel to the Katalysis office in Stockton, stopping every thirty minutes at gas stations to call Jerry, or someone at AID in Washington, DC. What I kept hearing was that the AID Matching Grant office was sympathetic, but powerless. I cursed our helplessness! When I arrived in Stockton almost three hours later, Jerry said that the AID office had closed for the day and the last word was that our grant didn't make it!

I called our attorney, Pat Riddle, and arranged an appointment for the next morning. In a high state of anxiety, Jerry and I worked late, preparing for the meeting. That night the calamity that had befallen us was the only thing on my mind, which seethed like a boiling cauldron. I was in a state of fury and fear. Then came a dream:

In it, I met a friend, Al Drucker, and some other people in a place I didn't recognize. He said they had just returned from India, where they saw Sathya Sai Baba, a very holy person. I asked how it was for him. He said, "Beautiful, Bob—complete surrender."

I awoke the next morning with the dream fresh in my mind. It was obvious from the dream that our approach to our problem had to be "Skillful means, surrender the results." Jerry and I met with Riddle and we were able to give him a clear, unemotional picture of the high stakes game we were playing. The three of us mapped out a strategy which called for faxing a letter to AID with a copy to our Congressman in Washington. Pat contacted the Congressman's local staffer at his home and briefed him, asking him to call his counterpart in their Washington office and alert him to our fax which would arrive there first thing Monday morning.

Jerry met later with Renicks to get his side of the story, and on Sunday Jerry and I began to prepare our letter. I remember feeling very calm even as the future of Katalysis was at stake. I kept focused on our team doing its very best, bringing all its skills to bear on the process. I told myself the results would take care of themselves; I surrendered them to a dynamic that was outside my control. Jerry is an extremely thorough person and our letter was quite detailed. It recited our grant history and how AID had again and again given us assurances that we had the grant, without any "subject to this or subject to that." It pointed out that we had relied on those assurances and would be greatly damaged if the grant was not made. We copied our Congressman and faxed it out.

Monday was again a day of calm for me as I awaited the results. I was pleased with our efforts, especially those of Jerry who had once again demonstrated an amazing ability to work well under severe pressure. By midmorning, we learned that our Congressman's office had made two phone calls, one to AID and one to the Office of Procurement, expressing their concern that a misunderstanding was threatening a very fine program that had been strongly endorsed. Shortly after lunch, a happy AID official called to say that they had worked out a method with Procurement to reinstate the grant!

Use skillful means, surrender the results!

● ● ● ● ● ● ● ● ● ● ● ●

Since then I've tried to hold to the concept of nonattachment, but I've got to admit that the "Busy Bob" side of me takes great exception to it. He'll say things like:

"Robert, that's a bit of a hard nut to chew, that concept of nonattachment. Don't we need to keep that goal...that result...firmly in mind if we're to succeed? You know, like the old times."

"Sure, Bob. We only got that much-needed grant from AID by focusing intensely on our goal."

"So what, exactly, were you surrendering?"

"The result, Bob—the result!"

"I don't get it. If I'm attached to becoming an opera singer, I study and practice like crazy for ten years. If I'm not attached to becoming an opera singer, do I still study and practice like crazy for ten years? And if so, what's the difference?"

"There's no difference in your actions, Bob—only in your attitude."

"Explain, Robert, explain. And keep it simple."

"You're working hard for your goal in both cases. When you're attached to the result...that is, when you have an intense desire for that result and great anxiety over not reaching it, then you lose in two ways: first, you spend all those years worrying about making it, and second, if you don't make it, you're devastated. Now contrast that with nonattachment. You do the same amount of work. You do the very best you can, but you're not worried. If you make it, fine; if you don't make it, something else that's right for you will turn up. You see? Whatever happens, you're free of that ever-present, debilitating worry!"

"I think I understand. So nonattachment doesn't mean being passive; you're as active as ever."

"Exactly, Bob. For example, the Buddha taught detachment from the ego, and from the idea that it's 'my way or no way'; not detachment from the world."

"Well, maybe I can live with that, Robert. As long as you keep working hard...and I mean hard."

•••••••••••

It was seven o'clock on a beautiful January morning in Hawaii. I had been walking the ocean shoreline, ankle deep in warm water, for more than an hour. I'd continuously sung the same song of gratitude to God, and now the song seemed to be singing me. It was part of an altered state of consciousness which had been bought on by the unceasing singing, my unrelenting focus on the Transcendent, the healing powers of the water and the early sun. I remained in a state of bliss for more than forty-eight hours.

My daughter, Lara, then a psychology major at San Francisco State University, and I had flown to Hawaii in the winter of 1991 for a seminar presented by theosophist and lecturer, Syd Banks, and a therapist, Dr. George Pransky. I was intrigued by the psycho-spiritual content of a new psychology that was developing: one called Psychology of Mind (POM).

Opening the seminar, Pransky focused on four key concepts:
- Thoughts create our psychological experience, or our reality, and thus we each live in a separate reality.
- Thinking has a voluntary aspect, that is, we can influence what we think about.
- Emotions indicate our level of psychological functioning.
- Low moods are a sign that we are identifying with our thoughts, rather than witnessing them.

After Dr. Pransky finished, he introduced Banks, the originator of the psychology. Banks began by speaking about the importance of our feelings. He said, "Our feelings are a barometer of our thoughts and when one's mind is filled with positive thoughts, the law of cause and effect comes into play, and one sees everything in a positive way.

"On the other hand, if one's mind is filled with negative thoughts, the same cause and effect principle gives rise to seeing everything in a negative way. It has been my experience that many of us don't realize that our feelings are the most important evidence of our well-being. My advice is—try to find more positive and loving feelings. It is such a state that will guide you through life. Only positive thoughts and positive feelings will assist you in discovering the knowledge that lies within you. And the longer you stay in those positive feelings, the more knowledge you get."

Wow! There I was, wrapped up in a prolonged bliss state and Syd was describing what I was experiencing and how it had happened! By choosing what I was thinking, by focusing on the positive—singing a song of gratitude for an hour—a beautiful feeling had come to me and I had stayed with it, reinforced it. These thoughts had created a reality of expansive joy and I saw everything around me in a loving way. Could it be, I wondered, that by investing in positive thought for a half-hour each morning, I would have beautiful feelings for the remainder of the day?

As the day went on, I kept hearing what was being said in spiritual terms:

- There exists a source of the deepest wisdom residing inside each of us that is immediately accessible regardless of past events or current circumstances.
- The source of human suffering is created from our own thoughts.
- We can learn to detach from and witness our own thoughts.

Late that afternoon, I met Dr. Roger Mills, a good-natured, sincere man in his early fifties. We sat by the pool and he told me of his experience in applying POM in community based psychology. He had been working with people at the 120-unit Modello Housing Project in a poor, crime-infested suburb of Miami, a project called "one of the worst in America." The results were almost unbelievable!

In less than three years, with the program serving 142 families and 604 youth, the number of junior high students failing dropped from 64 percent to only 1 student, school delinquency dropped by 80 percent and the majority of parents returned to school, enrolled in job training or began working. Drug trafficking and substance abuse decreased by over 65 percent, severe child neglect decreased by 60 percent and teen age pregnancies fell dramatically!

"Roger, this is one of the most hopeful things I've ever heard! What are you telling these people?"

"Basically I tell them that everyone has an innate capacity to function with self-esteem, good judgment and positive motivation. This capacity is always available; it can be directly engaged without reference to their past, or their history of problems, or their current circumstances.

"I explain that each persons' thoughts create their frame of reference through which they interpret their life experiences. So if their habit is to think in an insecure, negative state of mind, that habit blocks their natural capacity for self-esteem and common sense. Why? Because, until we understand how all this works, our thoughts seem real! Once we understand we can let go of those limiting thought patterns and take charge of our lives."

"You're saying healthy thinking and healthy actions start with our next thoughts? And people change just like that?" I asked.

"Not just like that, not often. No, it takes a while—so we keep saying the same things, in different ways. You've got to have patience. Almost everybody gets it, sooner or later."

I was hooked. "Roger, please send me information on your work. If these concepts can be used to build safe and sane communities among people in desperate circumstances, I want to know about it!"

Over the next three years I participated in several projects in what Dr. Mills came to call the "Community Health Realization Model." My friend, John Goodman of Minneapolis, and I sponsored the production of a video on the Modello project to help spread the news.

One of the brightest spots of my involvement was a vivacious woman named Beverly Wilson. Beverly was from Stockton and I got to know her through a friend. When Dr. Mills offered training courses in concepts and techniques, Beverly had taken to them like a duck to water.

Beverly became one of the principal community health trainers at the Lockwood and Coliseum housing projects in Oakland. Some time back she sent me a newspaper article about her work. It described her as "a tall, vibrant woman with a diamond-studded gold front tooth who herself grew up in a public housing development in Stockton." And there was her picture splashed across one page.

According to the newspaper, the Oakland Express, in 1991, when Oakland's murder rate was the fourth highest in the nation, the rate in Coliseum and Lockwood Gardens, sister housing projects situated across the street from each other, was eleven times higher than the city at large. The projects had one murder that year for every 208 residents. Put another way, there were fifteen murders on thirty acres!

In Coliseum Gardens, gangsters drove through the complex at top speed, shooting guns out their car windows while the residents sank to the floors of their apartments and prayed. Cab drivers and pizza deliverers refused to enter, and even the fire department wouldn't come in without police escorts.

The complexes were ruled by drug dealers, or "D-Boys," young men in their teens and twenties who lived in other parts of town but used Lockwood and Coliseum as their business address. They recruited younger kids who lived in the two complexes, some of them only six and seven years old, to work as street sellers, lookouts, and even enforcers. The youngsters called themselves the Mini-Mob.

Against this grim backdrop, there has been such progress that first Henry Cisneros, Secretary of Housing and Urban Development, then U.S. Attorney General Janet Reno, visited to view the changes first hand. And as a result of Reno telling President Clinton about what she saw, Jerry Williams, the on-site police officer at the developments, was invited to Washington for the signing of the Violent Crime Control and Law Enforcement Act. Why their interest?

No murders in the last three years, and the D-Boys were gone, that's why!

According to the Express, federal grants to revitalize the complexes had been important, but the most significant changes in Lockwood and Coliseum were the ones made by the residents. Credit was given to the initiatives of Beverly Wilson and her co-workers, including Jerry Williams, the cop who had undergone a conversion of attitude and understanding in his health realization training.

One of the great things about my involvement in the Community Health Realization Model has been to know several people from the inner-city. I think all of us can learn from their experiences of generating healthy communities, and there's a lot of this that we can bring into our own lives. Here's what I mean.

We have a choice of how we treat our thoughts—by taking them personally or by witnessing them impersonally. When we take them personally we assign preemptive authority to our thoughts—we treat them as if they had some intrinsically immutable reality that demands our compliance. Or, as Alan Jones said in one of his books, "The dark mystery of human freedom is that God allows us to construct unrealities as if they are real!" And Carl Jung rendered this harsh judgment on our proclivity to get tangled up in the illusions of our thoughts, "There are very few beings capable of discriminating between a mental image and the thing itself. This primitivity is poisoning our human world and is so dense a mist that very few people have discovered its existence yet."

Such a discovery is what POM is all about. Instead of getting caught up and acting on all of our thoughts, rather we first witness them. We can then operate from a state of mind that is more selfless, compassionate and in touch with our inner-wisdom. We can sort out negative thoughts and choose not to act on them, thus denying them an opportunity to create our reality. In other words, we take responsibility for our thoughts, and this shows us how to take responsibility for our feelings as well.

Because almost all thoughts are the results of conditioned thinking (what we've thought in the past plays over and over on our inner tape players), we can change that conditioning from negative to positive by not acting on the negative and thereby reinforcing it. Its hold on us is thus dissipated through disuse. This concept of consciously using the mind to our advantage, instead of letting the mind control us, may seem novel and not up to the task of changing antisocial behavior as well. But the results of the Community Health Realization Model are a spectacular demonstration otherwise!

While social programs normally treat symptoms, but rarely the disease, POM says that negative and anti-social behaviors have, at their heart, people acting on negative thoughts. And that the way to treat the symptom of school vandalism, for example, is not through more school guards or higher fences, it's to change the thinking that causes youths to commit vandalism in the first place.

What we're talking about here is becoming free, free from the patterns of negative thought that bind us. Our minds would then no longer be our prisons!

• • • • • • • • • • •

I've got to tell you that anything as radical as controlling one's mind gets Busy Bob's dander up a bit. I hear him saying;

"Robert, do you seriously think that a change in attitude is going to change the world?"

"The evidence is there, Bob. Besides, it's all rather simple. You change the way you think, and that changes the way you act, which in turn changes the results."

"It's not that simple, Robert. Changing the way our minds work is probably one of the hardest things we can attempt. You know, old habits die hard, and old thought patterns die even harder. Besides, did you ever try to not think about elephants when someone told you 'don't think of elephants?' "

"Well, perhaps that shows we can't always keep things out of our mind, but we can certainly put things in. Say, for example, I want to feel more empowered. I can suggest to myself a number of ways to help myself feel more confident—that I can make a difference, that I can improve a situation."

"Yeah, but Robert, you're saying that we're free, that we can generate and act upon positive feelings, and thereby transcend our surroundings and our circumstances. That's fundamentally changing the way human beings operate. You're saying the will is stronger than the mind. If that were true, we'd have a utopia. But it isn't."

"It probably isn't as long as we're ignorant. But if we learned a science of mind, if we learned how we think—and to the extent possible, learn to control what we think and feel—make it as fundamental a part of our education as reading, writing and arithmetic, then we'd have a different story."

"There you go again, Robert. We start with a friendly argument and now you want to change the whole school system."

"Not a bad idea, I'd say. I can sure construct a long list of things I wish I'd learned in school!"

• • • • • • • • • • •

One of the high points of my 1991 occurred on the Saturday before Easter Sunday. There I was, sitting in the sand on the south side of the Carmel River, sponging up the weak April sun. I was hoping to capture as much warmth as possible, because I would soon submerge into the river's freezing waters. My friends and I would enter just above the place where the river gave itself back over to its progenitor, Mother Pacific.

Fr. Charlie Moore moved among the twenty or so of us waiting for baptism, making final arrangements. The really brave and the really scared wanted to go first, the latter because they wanted to finish it before they chickened out. I held back as they started to line-up at the edge of the river. Looking up over my right shoulder I saw again the large cross overlooking River Beach.

It was under its shadowless arms that the Good Friday services had been held at noon the day before. Fr. Charlie went through the Stations of the Cross, using a series of 3'x3' modern-day photographs to illustrate the agonies of Jesus as he staggered toward the place of skulls. I nodded recognition when he hoisted up the famous photo of 9-year-old Phan Thi Kim Phuc and other Vietnamese children fleeing their village as it burned from a U.S. Air Force napalm attack. In the picture she—nude because her clothing had been blown off—ran toward the camera looking if there was nothing in this world left for her, certainly a modern-day Jesus. Shocking, gut-wrenching, demanding thoughts reached up from my heart, grabbing me by the throat; it was a Good Friday service with a long, long tail.

Actually the whole of Easter week was that way. Palm Sunday with the congregation in procession carrying palm leaves through a flower strewn yard singing, "Hosanna, to the Son of David!" Seder Dinner on Thursday night with matzo-ball soup, lamb and the traditional washing of the followers' feet by Fr. Charlie. The sunrise Easter Sunday service in the park would be held the next morning, but now, the baptism.

I made move to the river side, drinking in the scene. Sand, sand everywhere, sun, water, Fr. Charlie in rabbinical garb—my dream baptism was about to come true.

Wading out chest-deep into the swift water, I reached for Fr. Charlie's hand. He cradled my upper body and I leaned back. His words of ritual blew up toward the sky and sun behind his head, and he took me backwards into the shock of ice. Three times I went down, to that place where ice is transubstantiated into fire, where my cold heart was melted into warm love for all that I knew. At long last his eyes looked into and through mine, sealing the experience forever more in my consciousness.

I fought the current back to the waiting sands of my wilderness baptism, crying with renewal and rebirth. Someone was waiting for me, their hands outstretched. At that moment, I wouldn't have been surprised to see John the Baptist there offering me locusts and honey!

I can't remember the year Wendy and I met Fr. Charlie, but I've been addicted to him ever since.

How's this for a resume? "Father Charles Moore, AB and LL.B. degrees from Stanford University, admitted to practice law in California, former District Attorney of Santa Cruz County. Ordained a Roman Catholic Priest in 1964 (after being raised in the Protestant church), with degrees in philosophy and theology from Catholic University. Studied Latin at a Benedictine monastery and Greek at a Jesuit seminary.

"Avocation: languages. He has studied Spanish, French, Italian, German, Welsh, Russian and Japanese as well as Latin and Greek, and is fluent in most of these. He is also acquainted with Sanskrit, Chinese, Rumanian, Turkish, Dutch, Hawaiian, Sioux, Black Foot and Hopi.

"He has traveled extensively in search of the ancient roots of religious practices. This quest has taken him to Britain, Europe, Hawaii, Alaska, Mexico, India, Central America and the homelands of several Native American tribes.

"He is a firm believer in Christ and celebrates the Holy Eucharist at every Sunday Gathering of the Way. However, he has found the Buddhist, Hindu, Jewish, Hawaiian, American Indian, Mayan and old Celtic religions most helpful in understanding and supporting his Christian faith."

Renaissance Man!

Not too long after my baptism, Fr. Charlie accompanied my family on a trip to India. I particularly remember our first morning there. It was really the second according to the calendar, but it was our first sit-down-to-breakfast, an aromatic Tibetan repast at that, with great cups of steaming tea. Our group of ten had the entire Kashmir cottage to itself, overlooking Dhramsala and the valley beyond, and we were bubbling with excitement. Stimulated by the travel and the exotic atmosphere we had entered, many of us had had exciting dreams. Daughter Merede told of her dream visit by a little boy who turned out to be Lama Osel, the reincarnation of Lama Yeshe, and we oohed and ahhed at that one. Fr. Charlie waited patiently, then held out his hand for our attention.

"I, too, had a visit—with a tiger! And he was real." Now he had our attention!

"Around four o'clock this morning, my jet lag would let me sleep no more. I went for a walk, guided only by starlight. I went that way," he pointed out the window across the canyon to the forest climbing up the Himalayan slope.

"After an hour's walk, the sounds of people awakening in the valley below rose up to me. I heard the reveille bugle in the soldiers' barracks and the cries from the parapets of Muslim mosques, calling the faithful to their five o'clock prayers, so I started back.

"I heard noises in the jungle behind and above me and the hair on the nape of my neck stood on end. I knew that I'd made contact with a tiger. I sped up, but I could feel that he was keeping pace, just far enough back that I couldn't see him in the dark. I don't mind telling you I was frightened, really frightened! I had all I could do to keep from running, but I was afraid if I did, he would bound out and catch me easily. After an eternity I approached the cottage area and I could feel him stop and wait. When I reached the gate and closed it behind me, I glanced back.

"It was as if the tiger spoke to me. I wrote down what he said as soon as I got in." Fr. Charlie looked at a scrap of paper and read:
Imitate the action of the Tiger,
Who, flowing in possession of his power,
Is still mindful of his fragile life.

Charlie looked up and saw nine amazed faces fixed on his, faces in awe of what had already happened in India, and of what we imagined might happen.

It would be hard to overestimate Fr. Charlie's impact on me. We've sweated together in sweat lodges, did ceremony with Mayan shamans in Guatemala, experienced the magical healing of rain forest flora in Belize, floated on the Ganges past outdoor crematoria called ghats, visited Hindu temples and Buddhist shrines, broke bread with Tibetan refugees, encamped in Sai Baba's ashram, pursued tigers from elephant-back (from a respectful distance), and planted trees in our coastal mountains! He's baptized me, washed my feet on Seder Thursday, counseled, consoled, inspired, challenged, amazed me—and made me laugh so hard I've almost fallen off my chair in church! When I think of Fr. Charlie, I think of gratitude.

● ● ● ● ● ● ● ● ● ● ● ●

I'm speaking to a group of business persons. When I'm finished a man asks: "Robert, you've given us an inspiring talk about Katalysis, but just why are you doing all of this charitable work?" Over the years someone in each audience almost always asks that question.

"Well, I've been successful in life, but only because I've been helped by many people. So I want to make a pay back for the help, and this is my way. And I've been influenced by the Bible's instructions to care for the less fortunate. Also by Gandhi, who said, 'Whatever you do may seem insignificant, but it is very important that you do it.' "

I see some smiles. But their eyes say they still don't get it. I pause, thinking I will say more. But I take too long. A man takes my hesitation as signaling I'm out of things to say and begins to clap. The crowd joins in.

As I sit down I think of the things left unsaid. I hadn't dared to say anything about the "being my own hero" motivation, lest it sound like an ego trip. And I was reluctant to reveal that my reasons also had something to do with opening my heart to other people, lest the businessmen in the audience dismiss it as unmanly fluff. Besides, I didn't really understand the heart thing. Did my heart open a little, and I started helping, or did I start helping and my heart opened in turn?

I could have, should have, said that I wanted to be part of the solution to the rampant problems we see around us, and not part of the problem. I didn't say that for fear that the people might think I was one of those zealots who thought they knew what was best for the world. I don't like those kind of people myself.

And I didn't say helping made me feel good—no, not good, great! I could have said there are so many positive feelings stemming from serving and sharing that it's more effective than psychotherapy for everyday, garden-variety blahs and blues. That might have implied that I was just doing it for selfish reasons, which is true because, in addition to making me feel better, it is in my self-interest that there is less hunger, poverty, suffering and oppression in the world. For they all threaten my security of life, my peace of mind, my home town. Enlightened self-interest, I might have called this.

Would I dare to explain what happened to me as a result of the "50-50 at 50?" That when I took those first baby steps, my interior world started to change, and with that my actions? That doing some service work led me to want to do more? That being with poor and oppressed people brought me to see that it is only external circumstances, and not internal qualities, that separate us?

And shouldn't I have also said that in my process, I discovered that the major religions of the world teach that there is a series of paths for participating in the Oneness, these being the Paths of Love, Meditation and Contemplation, Devotion, Service and Knowledge? And that without a map in hand, I had stumbled onto the Path of Service, a path leading me to marvelous, and sometimes mysterious, worlds?

To really experience all people as basically the same—and isn't this one of life's most precious lessons?—I believe we must stand in the shoes of people whose lives and circumstances are radically different from ours. We can intentionally do this by leaving our own ordinary reality behind in order to experience another person's vastly different ordinary reality. For example, through service, or just being with them in their daily lives, we can check into the reality of people in poverty, or with severe illness, or in political, racial, economic or sexual oppression. What I mean by this is "hanging out" with others in these circumstances, listening to their stories without judgment and respectfully sharing our own lives. While this may be scary and uncomfortable, it can produce incredibly beautiful and personally transformative results. In short, we benefit.

In spite of our good intentions, helping others in a way that has positive outcomes is not automatic. Often our service work is unintentionally flawed. I have received many lessons in this from the South, and sometimes they were hard learnings for me. For example, I have learned that if an act of charity or service does not feel like something a "good neighbor" would do, or does not have the possibility of reciprocity, the receiver feels inferior. The giver at worst feels superior—"I have to take care of those people because they can't do it for themselves"—and at best frustrated at the sense of resentment felt emanating from the receiver.

My friend and an early Katalysis board member, Fr. Tennant Wright, once gave a wonderful sermon on service wherein he described that kind of problem. His solution?

"If a person comes to the Rectory and asks for a meal, I ask that they mow the lawn or do some other task before eating. That way the person feels they have exchanged something of value and, in fact, they have. Charity actually isn't involved."

Similarly, when we started Katalysis we established a basic principle that all services bore a charge. Usually the charge was quite small relative to the cost, but it was what the service recipient could afford, and the transaction was transformed from giver-taker to one feeling more like a two-way street. In so doing, a barrier to a one-to-one relationship of equal human beings was overcome.

"Process" was another lesson for me. In the U.S., doing business is generally a straight-forward matter in which relationships often aren't important; but it's different in Central America. There one establishes a relationship first and then, if all goes well, does business. A few years after I started my work there, I unexpectedly discovered that I was learning this process. I was talking on the phone with a Nicaraguan, Mario Ganuza. As we finished our conversation, Mario noted that I was "a different kind of American."

"Why do you say that, Mario?" I asked. Mario replied, "Because, you asked how my family was before you started talking business!"

I gradually came to see that an effective process could greatly increase feelings of broad scale ownership of ideas and projects, something that I believed necessary for the best long-term results. For example, if the staff of BEST in a burst of over-enthusiasm did most of the design work on a rice-hulling project and presented it to the Big Falls Farmers' Cooperative in pretty much final form, the coop members might well accept their work, perhaps complimenting the staff members on it. But they wouldn't assume responsibility for implementation because they hadn't meaningfully participated in the design. They didn't "own" the idea and it wasn't theirs. Guess where the blame went when things didn't work out the way they were planned?

However, implementing a productive process is often tricky. Lots of subjective matters come up. Group and personal dynamics are a major factor. For example, if BEST worked through each stage of that rice-hulling project design in collaboration with the co-op, but one farmer always dominated the discussions, there still wouldn't be wide-spread ownership of the idea among the others. When a BEST staff member complained that they had to be "part psychologist" to get anything done, I knew we were on the right track. Still, being able to judge a process a success is more iffy than calling an outcome a success. Does everyone have to agree on a course of action to say the process was a good one? Do you know how hard it is to get thirty farmers to agree on anything?

The part of me that is outcomes driven is easily frustrated at the greater amount of time and energy often absorbed by process. Sometimes it feels as if it would be so much easier just to make the decisions and get on with the work, rather than having to listen to everyone express their conflicting ideas and opinions. When I get impatient with process, it helps me if I can remember what an anonymous person once wrote:

IF YOU ARE GOING TO HELP ME:

1. Please be patient while I decide if I can trust you.

2. Let me tell my story, the whole story, in my own way.

3. Please accept that whatever I have done, whatever I may do, is the best I have to offer and seemed right at the time.

4. I am not a person. I am this person, unique and special.

5. Don't judge me as right or wrong, or as bad or good. I am what I am and that is all I have.

6. Don't assume that your knowledge of me is more accurate than mine. You only know what I have told you. That's only part of me.

7. Don't ever think that you know what I should do—you don't. I may be confused, but I'm still the expert about me.

8. Don't place me in a position of living up to your expectations. I have trouble enough with my own.

9. Please hear my feelings—not just my words. Accept all of me. If you can't, how can I?

10. Don't save me! I can do it myself. I knew enough to ask for help, didn't I?

HELP ME TO HELP MYSELF!

12

DEATH AND REBIRTH

In the spring of 1992, Wendy, Merede and my sister Mary and I joined twenty others for a camping trip to Pine Valley in the Ventana Wilderness southeast of Carmel. The expedition was led by Tom Little Bear Nason, an Esselen Indian "medicine-man-in-training," and a resident of the land inhabited by his ancestors for 5,000 years.

One afternoon we built a sweat lodge by the headwaters of the same Carmel River where Fr. Charlie had baptized me. The lodge was built in the shape of a hut, using willows covered with tarps and blankets. There was a flap for an entrance door, and a fire pit for hot rocks in the center of the lodge. Outside, a large hole was dug for heating the rocks required for the sweat.

In some ways a sweat lodge is about water's power, for one's liberal sweat represents a great cleansing. But it's also about death, as the fourth round of a sweat is known as the "death round." That's when participants typically experience at least some small death of ego and corresponding birth of a larger space for the spirit. (Although sweats can be exceedingly hot and I've found myself literally sucking the ground for cool air, physical death in the fourth round is only a rumor, as far as I know.)

A sweat is a wonderful way to enter realms of nonordinary realities. Participants regularly report contacts with deeply buried aspects of themselves, with spirits, animals and visions. It is also a time for major league truth-telling. When a dozen people sit in a circle of darkness with the encouraging glow of super-hot rocks melting one's resistance, it's easy for heart-talk to escape its bindings and make its presence felt. That's another aspect of the cleansing.

Little Bear dedicated each round of our sweat to a ceremony or prayer. A helper pitched hot rocks into the fire pit and Bear sprinkled them with herbs. Each possessing a particular meaning, the herbs gave off wonderful smells and colors in the dark. As the heat climbed, each of us in turn gave up her or his prayer, and spoke our truth. Towards the end of half an hour or so, Little Bear threw water on the bright red rocks, creating great clouds of suffocatingly hot steam. Just when I thought I could stand it no more, Bear ordered the flap opened and we crawled out on our hands and knees, looking for water. In ten minutes, it was time for the next round.

Our death round complete, we spread out on the grass in the meadows. I watched billowy clouds drift across the sky and imagined myself being ferried away on one to unknown places. After a while Little Bear asked the few remaining people if they wanted to do a fifth round. My sister Mary and I joined two or three others, and we went back in.

Bear knew that Mary and I were grieving for our mother, who was undergoing tremendous difficulties, and he dedicated the round to her. I told mother's story in the first person, eerily feeling as if she were speaking through me. I felt as if I had been sucked into her psyche, and she was ravenous to get her story expressed. The prayers that came from our circle were the most powerful I've ever experienced.

After that final round, five of us went over to the creek for cooling water. Out of the blue I asked, "Little Bear, do you do baptisms?"

"Yes, for the sincere."

I looked at Mary, and she nodded firmly. She was probably thinking that this would really be right, given we were in Indian country and there's evidence that we have Indian blood in our family.

We found a beautiful pool bordered by mossy rocks in the creek. Little Bear, saying ritualistic words that invoked the Great Spirit (God) and Mother Earth, dunked us into the cool sun-dappled water. Feeling totally blessed, I drifted back to the meadow where my warm, relaxed body surrendered itself into the Earth. Never had I been so whole in body-mind-spirit-nature. The fullness of God's creation welcomed me home again.

It had been my fourth baptism, my fourth symbolic death and rebirth, but probably not my last!

•••••••••••

"It's about Paquita," he hissed to me under his breath. His face darkened. "She's been killed. She's dead." He looked at me stunned, the white of his eyes grown large, his ear glued to the phone.

It was a muggy Friday in June, 1992, and I was in Belize for the Annual General Meeting of BEST. Carlos Santos and I were in his office early that morning preparing for the event, during which he would hand over the mantle of Managing Director after seven years. It was a day already heavy with nostalgia when the telephone call from Honduras came. After saying "Hello," Carlos' face turned mushy, losing its features.

"God, no!" I whispered. Not Paquita, not Francisca de Escoto, the founder and Executive Director of ODEF! Not one of my best friends! I wanted to bury my face in my hands, but I couldn't stop watching Carlos frozen to the telephone. Maybe it was a mistake, she was only hurt, there was still a chance. Then Carlos mumbled a few words in Spanish, something about Saturday, and hung up.

"Paquita's dead, Bob. She was in an auto accident yesterday afternoon on her way to a meeting and now she's dead. The funeral is Sunday." His voice was weak, flat. We sat in silence for a time, lost in our thoughts. In spite of my focus on Paquita, I wondered if Carlos was thinking about his brush with death only months earlier.

March, 1992. Wendy and I flew to Belize for a BEST board meeting and a few days holiday with Carlos and his wife, Amira. It promised to be a special time as Carlos had decided he would leave BEST for another run at politics. As we exited the airport, we were met by Mervin Manute of BEST.

"Bob, we've had a spot of bad luck," Mervin said in his normal low key way. "Carlos was in a car accident and is in the hospital." He picked up our bags and headed for the car. We followed in a panicky silence.

We rushed to the Belmopan hospital to see Carlos, prying details of the accident from Mervin as we drove. When we arrived the doctor said Carlos was stable, but horribly damaged. Further, they didn't have the capacity in Belize to put his bones back together. Carlos had been asking for me repeatedly. We went into the ward where he lay with his face covered by bandages and one leg sticking out at a weird angle from the sheets.

He took my hand, repeating, "Bob, Bob." Tears flowed from both of us.

"Hey, don't worry, Carlos. We'll take care of you. The doctor said you need to go to a hospital in the U.S. We'll get you out of here right away."

Now that I knew he would live, my mind raced with thoughts of what to do next. Wendy immediately got on the telephone to her long time friend, Dr. Tom Caskey at the Baylor Medical Center in Houston, to arrange for Carlos' admittance. I worked on TACA Airlines to get us on the first flight out of Belize. Late that afternoon I looked at the remains of Carlos' car and saw first hand how close to death he must have come. It had been a two car accident, one person dead, and four in the hospital.

In the morning we flew to Houston. I had secured a block of seats in the rear that folded down, allowing Carlos to be inserted on a stretcher. Amira, Wendy and I were his attendants and we arrived at the hospital less than thirty hours after his accident. He was soon on the operating table. The operations on his face and his leg were successful and a lengthy period of recuperation ultimately put Carlos back on his feet, but scars and memories remain for the rest of his life.

Three months later, after news of Paquita's death, Carlos and I flew to Honduras and spent the rest of the day with Paquita's family and members of the staff and board of ODEF. Her husband, their three children, people from ODEF, friends—all were stunned, alternating between far-away silences and then dissolution into tears. The image of her grieving young children and the irony of her death at the same age of Barbara bit at me. That night in San Pedro Sula, I had a dream:

I stepped out of a car in front of a building. Two people came outside and told me that Paquita was inside. I was very surprised, knowing her to be dead. I went inside and she was sitting at a table with two or three others at her side. I went over and bent down to her. Our heads almost touched and we looked into each other's eyes.

"Hello, Bob, I'm glad you came," she said softly, and showed me a letter that seemed to contain instructions.

"Paquita, how I can help you?" I asked.

"Help my children, Bob, help my children."

I discretely alerted a few people about the possibility of a letter showing up at home or office, but as far as I know, it didn't. I have often wondered what the mysterious letter of instructions was all about. Perhaps instead of representing an actual letter to be found by her survivors, it was something of a check list of things she wanted to tell people as she transitioned from this level of existence. She also appeared in a dream with a request to Karie Brown of Katalysis, a good friend of hers. I wouldn't be surprised if other people received messages from Paquita in some way or another as well.

I tried to be sensitive to her request to help her children and contributed to the finances for the oldest girl's education. In addition, I shared my experiences with her husband, Samuel, who had become a widower with three young children just as I had been. We established a fine relationship, and there is a special bond between us.

Pain. That's what I mostly remember. And conflict. Especially at BEST and ODEF. There was no heir apparent at ODEF, in spite of there being a fifty-person staff. Paquita was a typical entrepreneur and had no plan in place to provide for such an emergency, although she had promised more than once to hire a second in command. And ODEF's Board of Directors didn't know much about the basics of its operations, having left them to Paquita, as that's the way she wanted it. Chaos—that's another descriptor for the ODEF transition.

And at BEST, Carlos' car wreck had thrown the Executive Director recruiting process off track. The process of "the change of the guard" went badly. Things at BEST were rough, although not as bad as at ODEF.

Losing my two partners, Paquita and Carlos, put an ache in my heart that is still unhealed five years later. ODEF was our first partner organization after BEST, and the three of us had initiated the idea of inter-country partnership. But in most respects, what we advertised as a three organization partnership was really a three-person partnership. We had strong emotional ties, and I miss them deeply, personally and professionally.

At the time, I found it damn hard to be detached from the outcomes we were experiencing. Part of me wanted to make an attempt at trying to make things be the way they used to be, perhaps by exerting my will and finding a Carlos, Jr., and a Paquita the Second. Instead, I surrendered that vanity, acknowledged the end of an era, and worked as part of a team in seeking the next iteration of all three organizations. Essentially ODEF, BEST and Katalysis underwent a sort of reinvention process, emerging with new leadership and new ways of doing things.

The transition at Katalysis was more subtle, for it was mostly a matter of my "letting go," and of letting the many players in the multiple dramas apply skillful means to the best of their ability. It was also a time for me to acknowledge that it would be best for the long range health of the organization for me to share/surrender increasing amounts of the control I wielded. I'd heard a lot of negative stories about "founder's syndrome" at nonprofits, instances where the founder had stayed in control of the organization too long, stifling fresh ideas and running promising employees off the premises. I wanted to spare "my Katalysis baby" from that malady, and began to plan the turnover of the Chairmanship position on our tenth anniversary.

I'm proud to say that many people, in the U.S. and Central America, "stepped up to the plate," and assumed responsibility and leadership. Letting go of such a deep level of involvement—birthing the organization, nursing it through infancy, taking it through childhood and delivering it into the hands of others as a late teen—hasn't been easy. As every person who has started a business and every mother who has birthed a child knows, treating the grown up offspring as an adult is a bitter-sweet proposition. Oh, the memories, and the "wish I'd done this" and the "wish I hadn't done that!"

Rarely do we adults think we've learned much from our kids, preferring to see their childhood as a one-way teaching experience. But Katalysis, its people and the experiences it presented me, will always rank as one of my greatest teachers. And I'm happy to say that Katalysis and the Partnership is bigger than I, and it will probably outlive me, although in what form or configuration I have neither idea nor desire to know.

Use skillful means, surrender the results.

• • • • • • • • • • •

On the Fourth of July, 1993, I had a dream of Fred Nason, Little Bear's older brother. He was moving towards a bright light in the upper right of my visual screen, his gray cowboy hat leading the way.

"Bob, I'm going to the Light. The ceremonies were good."

Just before he entered the Light he paused, and glanced back at me. He looked just like that familiar photo of him taken up in the mountains, a muscular, handsome man, his deeply tanned face distinguished by a handle-bar mustache. He looked serious, as if he was trying to decide which fork of the trail to take. In the picture he wore Western clothes and a gun-belt complete with a revolver. But the gun-belt and revolver were absent in the dream.

When I woke, I lay in bed thinking about Fred and the wrenching events of the prior week. Things seemed to be going so well before then. From all indications, Fred was at long last realizing his dream of having a successful trail ride business at Molera State Park down the coast, and he was very happy. His operating plan was working, and the feedback from customers was encouraging. They praised the guides' knowledge of the park's animals, flowers and natural history. For many of the guests, the ride through redwoods, meadows and along the Big Sur River to the Pacific's welcoming beach was a spiritual experience.

And that was Fred's goal—that people catch the Spirit—for the Spirit was on Fred's mind everyday. His Esselen Indian heritage seemed to give him an especially gentle manner for presenting the glories of God's nature to others. Fred had a way of looking so deeply into your eyes that you began to get the feeling that he saw something of blazing value in you. It was both disconcerting and heart-warming. So then you would look intensely into his eyes and soon see what he saw in yours, the bright light of the soul. After one of those eye-exchanges, people seemed both larger and more gentle-hearted. Dreams suddenly seemed possible. I often wondered if he wasn't some kind of shaman in disguise.

A week before the dream, I saw Fred at a business meeting at the trail rides. I'd been out of town for ten days and he looked at me as if I were a stranger. He acted uncomfortable, and wouldn't sit down as the staff talked about the influx of business that we expected for the Fourth of July holiday. He left abruptly at the first pause in the meeting, and I looked questioningly at the others. No one would look at me.

"What the hell is going on here?" I asked. Michael and another guide took off like kids running from bad news, leaving me with Ramona, Fred's wife. A small, slender woman in her mid-thirties, she reluctantly lifted her eyes to mine. The dark bags around them betrayed her worry and weariness.

"Oh, he'll be all right. It's just that he is...he was gone all last week, and this is the first I've seen of him. He...he's mixed up." She shook her black hair despondently, unable to put her words to the problem.

The Problem. Now I knew, and I swore under my breath. "Damn it all to hell, and sober for a least three years! Why now?"

"Ramona," I asked, "do you know where Fred was going? I've got to talk with him!"

"Not really. Maybe he'll call you. He trusts you." Her dejection hung heavily in the air. "I'll keep things going here."

The next day I picked up Fr. Charlie, who knew Fred well, and we drove through Carmel Valley and up to the Nason home place. There were no traces of Fred, and we figured he was in the mountains somewhere. All we could do was hope he was holed up praying to the ancestors and not being a threat to himself.

Surprisingly, Fred called me Wednesday. He was at a pay-phone by Albertson's Supermarket. I asked him not to leave, made a quick call to Fr. Charlie and made a dash for the shopping center.

Fred was sitting in the cab of our business truck, engine running. He got out when he saw me, and we shook hands. He was in his familiar Western garb, and he looked tired, a bit haunted. It was worse when he talked; he rambled disjointedly about life being a mess. Not just his life, but life in general. He seemed sober enough, but I was terrified that he would jump in the truck and take off.

Thankfully, Fr. Charlie and Rudy Proctor, another friend, arrived. Now there were four of us around the back of the truck and I breathed a little easier. It seemed everyone had a lot to say. I surreptitiously reached in the Ford and turned off the ignition. That's when Fred said he'd kept it running because the starter was broken.

"Now I won't have wheels," he complained.

"Sorry. Just saving gas." I wasn't sorry at all. "Fred, you said you need help. How about some time at the recovery unit? They've got a good program, people who can really help you. I checked into it yesterday and have all the details. What do you say? Let's all go down there together." I looked at Fr. Charlie and Rudy, and they nodded agreement.

"No way, Bob. Those places don't do me any good. I've been there before. No, I just need some pills for my nerves, and some time away from everything, far away." Fred didn't sound very convincing to me, and I remembered some of my dad's binges. Time away—presumably drinking—and pills were not what a fallen-off-the-wagon alcoholic needed, especially one that required daily insulin shots to hold diabetes at bay.

"Look, Fred, as your friend I'll do anything you want to help you." Fr. Charlie and Rudy asserted that they would do the same. Then I played my trump card. "But we've got a real problem with the trail rides business. You've left without warning and no one knows what's going on. You're supposed to be in charge! We can't have that kind of example. I hate to say this, but as Chairman of the company, I have to suspend you from your job unless you go for professional help. The company will pay for it."

"Suspended? I'm suspended?" Fred shook his head, squinted at me and chuckled with amusement. The threat of suspension carried absolutely no weight with a man walking on the precipice of life itself. He looked at me appraisingly.

"You've got to do what you've got to do, Bob, but it doesn't make any difference to me. I'm going to the mountains. Why don't you go with me, and we'll camp out for a few days?"

I eyed the grocery bags in the bed of the truck. Well, I thought, maybe I could talk some sense into him. And keep him from drinking. If he wouldn't go to rehab...

"Sure, Fred. Good idea. Let's go home and get my gear."

"Wait a minute. I want to give each of you some of my medicine." He rummaged in his bag and gave Fr. Charlie and Rudy talismans. There was a mortar bowl and an oblong grinding stone lying in the truck bed and he gave them to me. As I held the bowl in my hands, it was easy to image an Esselen using it to grind acorns into flour, hundreds or thousands of years ago.

"Gosh, thanks, Fred. But are you sure you want to give this away? I know how important it is to you." He gave a faint smile, and nodded. The other three of us looked uneasily at each other. It seemed an ominous sign, a man giving away his medicine.

"I just want to be with people who will speak the truth. Why is everyone so scared? Why is everyone looking out just for themselves and not thinking of others? I'm so tired of living this way!" Fred kept up a steady wail of laments as we rolled down the coast in my Jeep. There had been a change of plans. He wanted to go to the mountains alone, insisted on it. Now I was taking him home to the trail rides so he could get some personal items and his pickup. Maybe Ramona and the kids could get him to stay the night, I thought. Maybe he'd agree to go for help when he's back in the warmth of his family.

Looking out the window, Fred turned passionate. "Look at the mountains, the trees, the rocks and the ocean! People don't pay any attention to them. People don't take care of them. Can't they see that they are part of us? The sea water is the blood in my veins, the rocks are my bones, the tree bark is my flesh. I and all these things are made of the same thing—we're all connected."

"Yeah, Fred." Pretty good analogy, I thought to myself. His long, contented sigh took my attention back to him.

"Bob, I think I'm joining Mother Earth and the spirit world. It's good."

An alarm buzzed in my head. Spiritual emergency! He's losing his separate sense of self—his ego boundaries are dissolving! Do something, I told myself.

"Fred, you're talking heavy stuff. We've got to find someone who talks that kind of lingo." Now his analogy twisted in my mind to blood becoming water, bones becoming rocks, flesh becoming bark.

Dust to dust, ashes to ashes. The problem is more than drinking, I thought. Perhaps it wasn't a drinking problem after all.

"Sure, Bob, maybe when I come back." I glanced into his eyes and saw the Mona Lisa look of someone who knew something that I didn't.

I tried a different tack. "Fred, since you've been giving away your medicine, let me give you some." I held out a little box containing vibuthi produced by Sathya Sai Baba, and explained, "This is sacred ash from Sai Baba. You can put some on your tongue if you're feeling spiritual pain. I've heard a lot of stories about people using it and they say it helps."

Fred said, "Oh, yes, I know about Sai Baba. I had a dream where he told me about you. He said you were a good person to be involved with. Later I heard 'a voice' telling me that you would take care of things. So, thanks for the vibuthi." He put it in his jacket pocket.

When we reached the trail rides, Fred talked a long time with Ramona, and gave presents to their little girls, Riana, eight, and Jana, six. Then he said good-bye to the three of them, our friend Michael Ignacio, and me. It was all very tender—as if he were going off on a trip for a year, and there was no use arguing with him. He gave Michael the last part of his medicine, and told Ramona that I'd given him my vibuthi. He said he was going to find new medicine for his life. He left in his pickup, explaining that he was heading to Miller Canyon. We left-behinds looked long and hard at each other in the fading Wednesday light, hugged, and went on our ways.

About ten-thirty Thursday night I was dragged up from sleep by the ringing phone. Fred's brother, Little Bear, was calling, sounding as if someone were strangling him. "Bob...Fred's gone...he's...dead! The Highway Patrol said his pickup...ran off a curve in Indians Valley!"

I was unprepared for the sight of Ramona, Riana and Jana in the faint light at the trail rides. They stood in the yard just about where I had left them the night before—but their life wasn't the same anymore. As I walked to their fixed figures, I tried to think of something both wise and comforting to say. Their forlorness ripped at my heart; and they were lost and drowning in grief. I imagined that Merede,

Lara, Sarah and I must have looked the same way to our friends fourteen years before when Barbara died. I was crying, and blindly stumbled on a tree root.

There were no words in my mouth. Tears and hugs were all that
came—and they seemed enough. As we stood pressed together in the
pale moonlight, I felt myself grieving not only for Fred and his family, but for me and my family, and for Wendy and Philip as well. In
that moment, I realized that this is what I should have done for
Wendy when Philip died, that my loss for words then was the clue to
forget words, to just reach out, hug and cry.

There were three or four other friends of Ramona's in the yard
and soon one of them took the girls off to bed. The rest of us huddled there in the chill of the night for hours, as if holding vigil. The
moon surrendered to clouds and now only the red embers of ciga-
rettes marked our place. Ramona smoked one after another, thirsty
for a drug of numbness.

Friday was a blur of dealing with legal requirements. The coroner's demand for an autopsy was a big problem. Ramona insisted that
Fred would not have wanted such a thing as it was contrary to Native
American beliefs. The coroner was indifferent to her appeal. After
consulting with attorneys, we realized that we couldn't win the battle, and gave up. Ramona moved on to preparing for a ceremony the
next day in a Salinas funeral home.

It was done in the traditional Native American style. Fred was
known and loved by many—it was amazing the number who said
"He was my best friend"—and people crowded into a big circle with
his body on a table in the middle of the large room. The funeral people had done their job well, and he was in his favorite cowboy
clothes.

There was singing and drumming to start, then Grandmother
Bernice, an Indian shaman, told the story of the migration of the
soul after death. Standing beside her was Fred's brother, Little Bear.

"It takes eight days for the soul to complete its journey," she
explained in the voice of a woman wizened by age and experience.
"The soul travels through a dark tunnel, and then is met by welcoming spirits of departed loved ones. Ultimately the soul will be

drawn to a brilliant, loving light and when it chooses to leave all attachment to physical things behind and join that light, the journey will be complete. Meanwhile the soul needs special nourishment and support for its travels. Little Bear and I will be doing ceremony and food offerings up in the mountains each day from now until the eighth day which is next Friday."

Little Bear, ironically a large, powerfully built man, added, "Next Friday there will be a feast in the roundhouse at Pachepus, the sacred land at the Ventana Wilderness Ranch. You are all invited."

Grandmother Bernice finished the explanation of the rituals around the eight-day journey. "On that day we will offer Fred's soul the final meal of food for the spirit: deer meat, strawberries, bread and water. After the feast day ceremony, Little Bear and I will take that meal high into the mountains and leave it for the soul, and burn flowers around it, completing our service."

Then, with Little Bear standing at the head of Fred's body and Grandmother Bernice at the foot, Bear held up a feathered talking stick. "We'll pass this around the circle and those who wish to talk can do so as the stick comes to them."

People spoke from their hearts. When the talking stick made it all the way around, people came to the body to leave a flower or special gift or remembrance. I felt like melting into the floor as I watched Fred's little girls came forward to touch their father and stroke his hair for the last time. I had to struggle to gather myself and approached Fred, whispering "I love you. You were a beautiful guy. I'm sure we'll meet again."

Three days after Fred's death was when I had the dream, the one in which Fred told me he was "going to the Light." The next day, David Hesse, a good friend of Fred's, and I went to King City to the wrecking yard where the pickup had been towed. David was an auto body specialist and it only took a minute for him to pronounce the blue truck, "totaled." The front right-half of the vehicle was bashed in about three feet where it had hit a tree. The driver's side had been compressed by half that amount, and it was the steering wheel that got our friend.

We took what personal belongings we could find to give to his family. A worker in the yard told us where the crash occurred, at Indians Valley on the Ft. Hunter Ligget Army Reservation. David and I looked at each other. No, we didn't want to see it. Yes, we were going to go there.

The further west we went from King City and the Salinas River, the drier the landscape became. It was a hot day and waves of heat rose from the highway, distorting our view ahead. David and I, previously in non-stop conversation, became silent as we approached the crash spot.

Was it a jack rabbit bursting from the shoulder of the road or the wounded oak tree right behind it that I saw first? David braked and we pulled over. Papers were strewn around the base of the tree, nothing important: Fritos sacks, grocery wrappers, California lottery tickets. We retraced the route of the truck as it missed the curve, the faint tire tracks giving no indication that Fred had tried to avoid the tree. It'd been pretty much a straight line to death.

"I'm sorry, Mr. Graham, but your doctor's appointment was canceled. Isn't that what you wanted?" It was the afternoon of our visit to the wrecking yard. "You say you didn't call in? Gosh, did someone here goof up? I'm sorry. How about next Monday?"

I sat in my car, feeling very frustrated. Why had my appointment been canceled? I hated to wait at a doctor's office, but wasting time like this was even worse. Relax, I told myself. Was this a sign that I was supposed to be doing something else? Suddenly, I had a strong feeling that I should go back to Fred's wrecked pickup. For what? I wondered.

I repeated the long drive through the hot, dry landscape. Again I went through the ugly wreckage, finding nothing special. The over-sized attendant who had waved me through the gate on my return, came over after a while and asked what I was looking for. Not knowing what to say, I mumbled something about a notebook. He seemed bored and volunteered to help. I explained where I had looked so far.

"Maybe it's in the glove compartment," he suggested. With that, he partially squeezed through the passenger window, his striped overalls covering his ample behind. "Go around up in back there," he instructed, as he pried opened the jammed compartment door just a bit. I reached though the busted window and wedged my left hand into the glove box, holding myself carefully so as not to get cut on the broken glass. My fingers groped, carrying out their part of the charade I felt I was playing.

Suddenly I felt something familiar—it was my little wooden box of vibuthi. I could feel the small heart inlaid in the cover that slid back and forth. I carefully withdrew my hand, pleased at recovering that special box that Wendy had given me, and its contents.

I told Mr. Moonface, "Well, this isn't the notebook, but it's important." He grunted his satisfaction and I left soon.

I tried to figure out some of this as I drove home. I marveled that there was so much unexplained! Why had my appointment been canceled? So I would come back and recover the vibuthi? I vowed not to lose that box again. And Fred, an Indian, crashing in the Indians Valley. Ironic, wasn't that? I shivered and recalled that Ramona told me that Fred had once said on an outing there, that "the Indians would be a good place to die." Did he know something, all those years before? And Ramona also told me that in the months preceding his death, Fred had two or three times pointed to his left shoulder and said, "My ancestors are there watching." In retrospect, she was sure this was prophetic of his approaching death.

And what was it—suicide? Drove straight off the road into that tree, almost as if fulfilling a prophecy? I don't believe that. Most likely he had a diabetic seizure bought on by his erratic eating, drinking and sleeping habits of the prior ten days. It had happened before when he'd forgotten his insulin.

No, I shook my head, not suicide. But on a deep level he knew he was going to die, I was sure. The loss of ego boundaries and the merger with all things is an experience often reported just prior to death.

Of course, those experiences are usually preceded by terminal illness or fatal accident. It's highly unusual for this kind of change in consciousness to occur in someone who is in a more or less normal physical condition. However, Fred, for all his human shortcomings, was a very spiritually advanced soul and perhaps that explained his experience of transition twenty-four hours before it happened.

I sighed, and told myself that it all added up to one more chapter in the mystery book called death.

There was a postscript to Fred's death. Ten months after he died, I had a dream in which I met him at the Molera Trail Rides.

We walked the area and he reviewed the staff, the horses and the condition of the corrals and trails. "Bob," Fred said, "I'm pleased overall, but Ramona has too much to do and needs help."

I agreed, "You're right, Fred. She needs a second in command to support her in the business."

Two days later I told Ramona that I'd had a dream visit from Fred. She exclaimed that Fred indeed was in the area as that very same night she had felt his presence so strongly that she had cried for two hours! Further, the next morning Michael Ignacio reported that he had seen Fred's outline in the dim light of the night.

When we discussed Fred's message in my dream, Ramona realized that while she didn't feel she had too much to do, in fact she had no one to be in charge of the business in case she needed to be gone. She agreed to plan for such a contingency.

Extraordinary that Fred had "appeared" to the three of us, wasn't it? Or was it?

● ● ● ● ● ● ● ● ● ● ●

> The Body
> Of
> Benjamin Franklin
> Printer
> (Like the Cover of an Old Book,
> Its Contents Torn Out
> And Stript of its Lettering and Gilding)
> Lies Here, Food for Worms.
> But the Work Shall not Be lost
> For it Will (As He Believed) Appear once more
> In a new and More Elegant Edition
> Revised and Corrected

By
The Author

(From the gravestone of Benjamin Franklin.)

Just like Busy Bob, you might be wondering why I've come to believe in reincarnation. Let's see what I can do on that score.

To begin with, you might be surprised at how many people believe in reincarnation. It's the majority of the world's population, the way I calculate. Actually, it's only our Western culture that excludes reincarnation from its cosmology, and if you go back to the time of Jesus, even our ancestors believed in it then. Moreover, your own neighbors might believe in it; a 1994 Gallup poll found that 27% of adults in the U.S. believe in reincarnation, and the figure continues to rise.

You might be thinking, "All right, Robert, but most of the world might also believe in 'knocking on wood.' Do you have anything more rational than that?"

I've learned that there are many, many case studies of reincarnations, where the individual had knowledge of events and places from the past that he or she could not have learned otherwise. And there are large numbers of people who are able to recall past lives while in a hypnotic state. Many of the world's great spiritual leaders—Buddha, Socrates, Plato, the sages of India and China—spoke of past lives. And reincarnation was part of the Christian tradition until Emperor Justinian's guilt-ridden wife, Theodora, made him get rid of it at the Council of Constantinople II in 553 AD. Even so, remnants of the concept can be found in the Biblical words of Jesus.

I just heard Busy Bob say, "That isn't exactly hard scientific evidence, Robert."

Well, I think one of the great shortcomings of modern science is the discounting of personal impressions. Here we are, equipped with marvelously sensitive minds that can pick up the most subtle nuances of feelings...and science ignores this; it rejects the perceptions of the mind as evidence. For example, at various times in my life I've had a feeling...or a vision...of a past life. I describe some of them in this book. And the feeling that accompanies them is a very powerful sense that it is true, that it really happened.

If I pick up this piece of paper and hold it in my hand, and then I stop and reflect on whether or not I am really holding a piece of paper in my hand, I know that I am. I know that it is true, real. It's that same sense of knowing that a vision of a past life is also true.

If you're at all like Busy Bob, right about now you're probably saying something like, "I'll believe it when it happens to me!" And I'll accept that as long as you promise to let me know when it does. I plan to live at least another forty years, so there will be an opportunity for some of you.

●●●●●●●●●●●●

I must confess there is another reason why I'm so interested in this reincarnation thing. It has to do with a vow I took, not once, but twice. It's a vow that has Busy Bob fit to be tied.

A few years ago Wendy, Sarah and I went to Arizona for four days of teachings by the Dalai Lama. There, the large meeting room was jammed with people. His Holiness sat on a chair on a well-decorated stage with a Buddha looking out over the audience. He wore his familiar tinted glasses, the ever-present maroon and gold robes of a monk, and a smile.

The last morning, he was especially eloquent as he finished our period of "bodhisattva training." A *bodhisattva* is a person who renounces nirvana (a state of tranquillity beyond Self and the physical senses) in order to help all other beings attain nirvana. Over the course of training, the Dali Lama stressed the practice of the six perfections: giving, ethics, patience, effort, concentration and wisdom. If an aspiring bodhisattva toils in the vineyard of these attributes through enough lifetimes, he/she will accumulate sufficient merit and wisdom to become a Buddha, and be of immeasurable service to others.

At long last, His Holiness was ready for those in the audience who wished to take the bodhisattva vow. It's obviously a very profound vow because as it applies not only to how one's present life is lived, but is a commitment to all future lives as well. Two years earlier I had received bodhisattva training from Chagdud Tulku Rinpoche, and, at the conclusion, thought long and hard about making that pledge. It was certainly like no other I'd taken or would likely take in this lifetime. The stakes seemed as high as they could be, but for the life of me I couldn't think of any reason not to do it. It was how I wanted to live my lives, present and future. It felt like exactly the right thing to do. So, just like baptism by immersion, I took the plunge. "I vow to continue to return to this plane of existence until all beings are liberated." My voice seemed unnaturally clear to me, and my journal reads, "My hair felt like it stood on end, a hair at a time."

Now the Dalai Lama was asking if there were any last minute questions.

"Your Holiness," a man in the clerical garb of a priest called out. "Your Holiness, is it all right for a Christian minister to take this vow?"

"Do you wish to live this life as a bodhisattva would, living in accordance with the precepts we have studied this week?" the Dalai Lama asked kindly.

"Yes, they are excellent precepts and certainly in keeping with those of my order. I pray that I have the strength to live my life in such a fine way."

"Do you wish to work for the liberation of all sentient beings, now and in the future, wherever you may be?"

"Yes...well...wherever I may be." I suspected the priest was struggling with the concept of reincarnation, but he ended on a firm note.

"Then WHY NOT?" The Dalai Lama slapped his knee with a peel of laughter. "Okay, let's begin."

I rose from my seat to renew my vow. Sometimes I thought I'd follow that man anywhere.

So that's what got Busy Bob in an uproar. "Robert, what in the hell did you do that for?"

"I already told you, it seemed like the right thing to do."

"What you just did was to vow that, after each lifetime on earth, you would continue to return here to help others until the last 'sentient being' is liberated...that is, is united with God. Mind you, not that I believe in this coming back stuff, but, just in case, that means you promised that we would just keep showing up to wallow in the miseries of the earth. I mean time after time after time..."

"Yes, Bob, it means that the bodhisattva vow is essentially forever."

"That's a long time, Robert."

"I know."

●●●●●●●●●●●●

Let's play with this a little further. Let's imagine that you say, "If reincarnation exists, what are the ramifications for our lives...and for society?"

I would say that, "It seems the purpose of reincarnation is to allow our souls to continually progress and evolve through a process of comparing the results of the life we've led with what we've set out to do, and then making adjustments for the next life. For example, maybe this time around I set for myself the task of learning how to deal with money and the power it possesses without it possessing me or my using its power to exploit other people. When I die I will be able to evaluate how well I did and decide what I need to learn in the next lifetime."

And because you've been doing a little reading on the subject now, you say "How does karma fit into all this, Robert?"

"To me, karma is the concept that each of us is responsible for all of our actions, and that our actions come back to us in the form of new circumstances that either reward or punish us for past deeds. It's 'as ye sow, so shall ye reap.' Now, karma is also inter-lifetime as well as intra-lifetime. We're creating tomorrow's karma today, not just the karma for the next lifetime."

Because you probably accept that what you do today has a strong bearing on what happens to you tomorrow, you're beginning to think about your next lifetime, assuming there is one. You remember what you heard in church about what happens after death: judgment. "Wait a minute," you say, "how is the judgment handed down that sets the karma for the next lifetime?"

Since we're on more speculative ground than when we were

talking about the probability of reincarnation itself, I'd have to say something like, "Well, I think that each of us decides what our situation will be in the next lifetime."

Now you'll probably jump up and say, "Then...by an extension of that logic, there is no heaven or hell. There is no Great Judge in the Sky, we are our own judge."

So I better make a distinction here. I'm not saying there isn't a God; and I'm not saying that there aren't other entities or spirits who help us look at our actions—because I believe there are—but what I'm saying is that ultimately no one judges us but ourselves. The love of the Divine is unconditional, it's beyond judgment.

But let's go back to your original question, when you asked what the ramifications of reincarnation are for society.

It seems to me that society will slowly evolve for the better on the backs of souls who are gradually progressing lifetime after lifetime. And there is evidence that crime rates are less in societies where the people believe in reincarnation and karma. It's harder to do wrong when you understand you're going reap exactly what you sow, as Jesus said. But I think the overall progress of society is limited as there are continually new, relatively unevolved, souls entering the picture—remember the population explosion! That's probably why society still seems a mess after so many millennia, although social scientists might say there has been some progress. Slavery has been pretty well extinguished, for example, and there is a case to be made for the evolution of consciousness.

Even if this is a not-so-very-pretty picture, I believe we don't have any choice about it. We're going to keep coming back until we've learned everything we need to learn. So we might as well take on the tough assignments now, while we're in a good space to deal with them. Our circumstances may not be so favorable the next time around.

If you think for a while about unfavorable circumstances, you might say something like, "Robert, presumably then, souls know what's going to happen to them when they reincarnate. They can see, in some way, their future prospects. If...if all of this is true...why are some babies stillborn? Or born horribly deformed? Or brutally murdered at an early age, before they have a chance to learn any lessons of life? Are these mistakes? Does the Creation make mistakes? Is the system fallible? Why would souls choose to reincarnate, knowing that a premature death or a maimed body lies in store for them?"

To which I reply, "I've read that human souls sometimes voluntarily incarnate into these kinds of situations in order to help others learn a lesson. For example, a wise and kind soul might intentionally take on a deformed body in order to help its parents learn compassion. Look, I don't have all the answers. At this juncture these beliefs are speculative. But for me, my view of myself is that I am a spirit, a spark of the divine, who is merely using my present body, my mind and my personality like one would use a bathing suit."

If you've had enough of this reincarnation stuff, Busy Bob would like a few words. "Good work, Robert! Now you've helped explain how a lowly, naive, uncultivated, conservative Midwesterner came to embrace every radical, far-out, guru-led, mystical teaching that California has to offer—which probably number in the thousands! God, but you embarrass me sometimes. What are you trying to do, encourage people to try everything spiritual that is available? Is that what you're advocating? Why isn't just believing what our old churches said good enough?"

"Bob, we've had this conversation before. Because too many religious institutions practice religion rather than spirituality."

"Ahh...and what's the difference between religion and spirituality?"

"John White says 'Spirituality is, in simplest terms, the effort to bring every aspect of your life into alignment with your own highest understanding of the nature of God.' Rachel Naomi Remen goes at the definition in another way. She writes that it's easier to say what spiritual is not than what it is. For example, spiritual is neither the moral nor the ethical (which can change with different cultures); it is not the religious; and it is also not the paranormal. She goes on to say that a religion is a dogma, a set of beliefs and a set of practices which arise out of those beliefs. After setting forth what spiritual is not, Remen says that spirituality is not an option, as is religion; that there is no place to go and be separated from the spiritual, that we all participate in it at all times. As Fr. Charlie says, 'Religion is for groups and is for the benefit of society. Spirituality is for the benefit of individuals.' "

"Yeah, but..."

"Look, it's not my intent to put down religion—just to differentiate it from spirituality. Religion at its best can be a wonderful bridge to the spiritual. The danger in religion is that in seeking the spiritual we may fall in love with the bridge and forget what its purpose is."

"Robert, you've gotten so tangled up in this stuff that I can't understand what you're saying." Busy Bob sounded very frustrated.

"Then, try this one on for size. God and the Devil were walking down the street together. Ahead on the sidewalk they saw an object emitting an extraordinarily brilliant white light. On reaching it, God picked it up and examined it in wonder. The Devil asked impatiently what it was. God spoke in a hushed tone, 'This...this is the truth!' And the Devil blurted out, 'Oh good! Give it to me and I'll organize it for you!'

"And so it is with organized religions; they always begin with the highest of ideals and intentions, but the Devil is in the details!"

13

NORTH MEETS SOUTH

It's springtime in 1994, and I am in a small restaurant in the village of San Esteban, high in the scruffy hills above San Pedro Sula, Honduras. The tables are rough hewn, like unfinished picnic tables; the walls are white-painted boards climbing up rows of two-by-fours. From one of them a properly dressed, attractive young woman smiles at us from a Coca-Cola calendar written in Spanish. The floor is cement, and clean, but its surface is covered with unintentional ridge lines running in wildly different directions. Candles are on each table to defend against the frequent power failures in the village. The restaurant has a frontier feeling.

Doña Ofelia joins us. She is a thin woman probably in her early forties, but looks fifteen years older due to difficult living conditions. She is the owner. Someone in our small group asks how business is.

"With the loans from Nuestro Triunfo (Our Triumph) Community Bank, and the training from ODEF, I've built this business. I've had four loans so far: $37, $65, $102 and $190. Each time I got one paid back, I borrowed more and kept improving this place." She looked around, smiling with pride and satisfaction. "Now I'm going to expand again as I have many customers, especially from the sewer construction project. I need another employee, though."

Doña Ofelia sighed in the universal language of employers that indicates "good help is always hard to find."

"How about me?" I ask. There are smiles all around our two tables. "What would my hours be?"

"The same as mine," Ofelia replies. "Four in the morning until nine at night."

"Days off?"

"No, everyday."

"Hmm . . . Pay?"

"Fifteen Lempiras a day ($2.17) and something to eat."

"Well...I'll have to ask my wife, Wendy!" Everyone laughs, especially Doña Ofelia. It seems a novel idea to her–a man asking a woman's permission.

Even though our conversation was light-hearted, it illustrates some sobering facts. In the Majority World, the non-industrialized countries where 80% of the world's population lives, a typical woman works sixteen hours a day. And she doesn't make much either. Women perform two-thirds of the world's work but earn only one-tenth its income! And the lot of women is getting more difficult due to worldwide cuts in spending on health, family planning and education, and the proliferation of cash crops and increasing population pressures on the environment. The latter means that women must walk miles further to find safe water, firewood and land suitable for farming. Theirs is a tough life, indeed.

It's no different in Honduras. Women work longer hours than men—an easily discerned fact when you notice that men have time to sit around gossiping with their buddies, but the women rarely do. The woman is responsible for the house, the cooking, the children and whatever job she has in addition to her homemaker duties. The man is responsible only for working when he can, which in the seasonal agricultural business is never full time. All in all, men work only two-thirds as much as women.

But, notice the hopefulness at the restaurant. Doña Ofelia owns her business, and she is expanding. She has taken loans from her community bank and paid them back. As part of that program, she has a savings account. She is making money–money which she is both reinvesting in her business and using to benefit her family. Do you sense her entrepreneurism?

Later, a friend and I stopped at Gloria Paz's house near Yojoa, Honduras. A large opening had been cut in the side of the house facing the dusty road. Here is where one could buy the fresh, hot tortillas that are Gloria's specialty. As we munched our way through two apiece, we talked about her business.

"Mmmm...are these ever delicious. What's the history of your business, Gloria?" I asked.

"I've made tortillas for many years. My mother and grandmother were well known for theirs. But I only made a few for sale. I couldn't afford to buy the things I needed to make more. Oh, I could have borrowed money from a coyote (money lender), but they charge 15% interest per month, and there would have been no profit, and little to show for my labor."

"So what changed?"

Gloria, dark-haired, dark-skinned and in her thirties, broke into a smile. "You know about our bank, 'Union y Esfuerzo?' " Union and Effort, what a great name, I thought, and nodded yes.

"With a loan from the bank I have been able to buy my corn meal, delivered to my door. It used to be that I could only afford the little bit I carried home on the bus. And what a savings! It's the same with the firewood necessary for the cooking. Now that I make the tortillas so much cheaper, I can make a good profit on every one I sell."

"You mean you know how much each tortilla costs you to make?" I asked incredulously.

"Certainly. Here, let me show you." She reached below the counter and hauled out a bound, blue ledger emblazoned with "Gloria Paz Tortillas" proudly written in white ink. Flipping the pages, she said, "See, this is what I spent last month. And over here is the number of tortillas I sold. When I divide my expenses by the number of tortillas, I determine how much each one cost. Then I compare that to the selling price and get my profit percentage. I want at least 30% profit."

"Beautiful work, Gloria, beautiful." I appreciated what she was doing as only an accountant would. I wondered if she had more than a third-grade education. Doubtful, I thought. I'd ask later. Right then I wanted to pursue the matter of profits.

"And did you make a profit for the month, Gloria?"

"Si—here it is." She pointed at a number at the bottom of the page.

"That's an impressive amount! Is it good pay for all your hours of work?"

"No, you don't understand, Roberto. That's my profit. My wages for the hours I worked are over here, in my list of expenses. I took the minimum wage here in our country for my pay."

I whistled softly. This was as sophisticated business thinking as I'd seen in the U.S.!

"But Gloria, where did you learn all this?"

"It's in our training by ODEF. As we learn the principles of community banking, and are making the rules for our organization, each member is developing a business plan with an ODEF trainer. Before any of us can get a loan, all of us must have an approved plan. In that plan, we are taught that we must show our labor as a cost, not as a profit. Is this not right? In your country, do people think wages and profits are the same thing?"

"Oh, no, no, Gloria." I didn't want to cause even the slightest doubt in her thinking, but as I said it, I wondered just how inaccurate this might be. How many people in business at home did think of them as the same?

"What do you do with the profits? Put them all back into the business?"

"Some of them I put over our heads!" She laughed gaily, and pointed up. We craned our necks and admired the well-fit tile roof, a sharp contrast with the ugly, hot, leaky tin roofs of most of her neighbors.

"Now I can afford medicines for my children when they are sick. We will be able to keep our kids in school longer, instead of them having to go to work. And I have a secret fund," she grinned mischievously and put a finger to her lips to seal the secret. "If you come back in two years, we will have a new house!"

On this high note we said good-bye. "Muchas gracias, Gloria. I'll be back."

"Si, si, but only come when I'm open for selling the tortillas, Roberto." She pointed at a sign with the selling hours on it. "The rest of the time I'm making them. It's more efficient that way, don't you think?"

Sometimes one person can change the world. In doing so, they provide an inspiration for the rest of us who think we can do little or nothing about the world's problems. In this case, the person changing the world is Muhammad Yunus, a one-time college professor in Bangladesh, one of the poorest countries in the world. He had an idea—an idea that is now sweeping large parts of Asia, Latin America and Africa. (It's even threatening to catch on here in the U.S.!) Called the "Grameen," or "Peoples" Bank, in less than twenty years Yunus' bank has grown from its first borrower to two million impoverished clients.

One afternoon in 1976, Yunus was taking a walk in a village about a mile from Chittagong University, where he was head of the Department of Economics. He happened upon a widow, Sufiya Khatun, who was trying to support herself by constructing and selling bamboo stools. She earned two cents a day. When Yunus asked why her profit was so low, she explained that the only person who would lend her money to buy bamboo was the trader who bought her final product; and the price he paid barely covered her costs.

If you believe the saying, "necessity is the mother of invention," Sufiya had the need—capital—and Yunus made an invention, a bank with many differences. First, the loans were to be repaid, and on time; surprisingly, in many countries of the world, the bank gets repaid only if the borrower does very well and is so inclined. Second, only the poorest villagers, the landless, were to be eligible. Third, loans were to be made primarily to women who were socially, as well as economically, impoverished. And last of all, the loans were to be made to groups of women who would be collectively responsible for their payback.

The rest is, as they say, history. Today there are two million borrowers like Sufiya Khatun in Bangladesh, well over two million in Indonesia and another four million in the rest of the world. A graph of the growth of this movement looks like a ski hill, rising slowly at first, then shooting up at an impossibly steep angle toward the sky. Even the World Bank, traditionally mired in financing large-scale infrastructure development projects of dubious value, recently announced the launch of a drive to raise more than $200 million for Grameen-style lending. And the idea has been imported by other visionaries world wide.

One of those visionaries was an American by the name of John Hatch, who started the first Latin American community bank in Bolivia in the mid 1980's. John had plenty of problems in adapting the Grameen model to Latin America, but he persevered, started his own non-profit named FINCA, and preached the gospel of empowering masses of would-be entrepreneurs through small loans.

I met the charismatic Hatch a couple of years after he launched FINCA, and in 1988 he helped Katalysis start two community banks in Honduras. Now the banks served by our partner organizations, CDRO and MUDE in Guatemala, ODEF in Honduras and BEST in Belize, number in the hundreds. Community banking has always been my favorite program. We operate on certain principles:

1. We focus on assisting business development among women in the lowest income levels who operate in the cash economy and who lack access to credit.
2. Each borrower is co-responsible for the group's entire borrowing, thus ensuring peer pressure to repay.
3. The loans bear market rates of interest, without subsidies. We strive for sustainability for all participants.
4. All borrowers are required to become savers.
5. The banks have democratically elected management committees.
6. Each bank has an educational component for community development and social transformation. This builds group solidarity and empowers the women, who learn new skills such as leadership, household finances, gardening, nutrition and better environmental practices.

Lets walk through the steps of operating a bank.

First a group of twenty to thirty women in a village come together at the invitation of community leaders and a local non-profit such as ODEF, and the concept is explained. They can choose to start their own bank, elect their own officers, make their own rules and borrow a lump sum from the nonprofit, usually $2-3,000 to start.

In turn, their bank makes a loan to each member, usually about $100. But this happens only after the members undergo ten weeks of training in how to run a bank, and in developing a business plan for the use of the loan proceeds. After the loans are made, the bank members meet each week to make payments on their loans, to work with the trainers on their business questions and to talk about their community problems. Along with the loan payments, each member makes a pre-determined deposit into her own savings account. These meetings continue until the members loans are repaid to the bank, and the bank in turn repays the nonprofit.

Assuming all of this proceeds satisfactorily, and the world-wide repayment rates average around 98% (a figure achieved by few commercial banks), a new cycle is started with increased loan amounts to accommodate growth in the women's businesses. Over time, each woman establishes an increasingly profitable business plus a significant savings account.

After three years or so, a bank is usually ready to "graduate," or re-examine its relationship with the nonprofit. Sometimes they choose to continue the relationship, sometimes they continue on their own and sometimes they disband, the credit needs of their members having been met through their own savings or by their new ability to borrow individually from commercial banks.

Now that the Katalysis Partnership banks have thousands of members (and these numbers are growing rapidly), we have noted many wonderful results beyond just the economics. Many social issues are identified and initiatives created to solve them; things like drinking water projects, the need for better information on infant care, and literacy classes. In the long run, the economic and community improvements may well be overshadowed by the transformation of the participants, the elevation of their abilities, self-esteem and confidence, and the feeling that they have the power to personally improve their lives and the lives of their families.

Here's an example. Danelia Lopez is the mother of six children and lives in the town of Choloma, Honduras. Her business is the preparation and sale of pastries and other foods. Danelia writes:

"My greatest accomplishments have been to open a large market for my product, and to achieve my supreme goal of educating my children. Part of my success I owe to ODEF, not only because of the credit and training, but also because they have helped me value myself as a woman."

Community banking! Destined to be one of the most powerful, world-wide concepts of the 21st century!

• • • • • • • • • • • •

Dum...Dum...Dum...Dum...Dum...Dum....Dum....Dum
Dum, Dum, Dum...Dum, Dum, Dum...Dum, Dum, Dum

The drum beat turns from a steady rhythm to staccato bursts. It is the signal to return from our journey of psycho-navigation, to break off our adventure into a different stage of consciousness, and to come back to ordinary reality. Our group of twenty has been lying on the carpet of a room in the Hotel Andes in Quetzaltenango, Guatemala, for a twenty-five minute exploration of the wonders of inner-space, drawn down into ourselves by the insistent drum beat. We gradually stir, sit up, and peer into the candles burning in the center of the darkened room.

A door opens a bit and a line of light cuts across our circle. Two people slip into the room and take their place with us. One is Bridget Cullerton, the Executive Director of BEST of Belize. Our session leader, John Perkins, pauses and takes particular note of her presence. Bridget has been having an enormous struggle with cancer, and has just completed six months of intensive chemotherapy following a mastectomy.

John, a member of the Katalysis board of directors, quietly explains to Roberto Poz that Bridget has been in a meeting with the executive directors of all the Katalysis Partnership organizations and could not come when we started some two hours prior. Roberto is a Quiche Mayan shaman who works closely with Katalysis' partner organization, CDRO (a shaman is one who enters different stages of consciousness to obtain information, especially for healing). He looks piercingly at Bridget and motions for her to sit by him in the circle.

Bridget slides over and faces Roberto. He studies her face deeply and then asserts, "You're cured, you don't have cancer anymore. However, there is a difference between being cured and healed. While you're cured of the disease, the healing of the underlying causes is still underway." Bridget's gaze upon Roberto never waivers; she is mesmerized by him.

"What is your birth date?" She tells him and he looks the date up in the Mayan calendar for her astrological reading. After a long pause, he interprets what he has seen.

"You are yourself a shaman and have a tremendous power to heal relationships. But at some point you have rejected your calling due to fear of what people would say about you. This has thrown your body out of balance. You need to accept this part of yourself, to have faith and to move with the process. That will help your healing," Roberto concludes with a smile. Waves of strong emotion sweep through the group as we all want to believe that Bridget is, in fact, cured of cancer. We reluctantly move on to other aspects of the shamanic work.

In planning our 1994 Katalysis board meeting in Guatemala, we sought to experience as much of the country's culture, history and daily life as we could. It was to be our first board meeting there, and we decided to include a group of Katalysis donors. This meant there would be more than twenty of us coming from the U.S. and another half-dozen from our partner organizations in Belize and Honduras.

Our two Guatemalan partners, CDRO and MUDE, were eager to show us their programs—community banking, food processing, community health and reforestation—and for us to meet the project participants. Would it be possible, we asked, to have an introduction to their spiritual and religious life as well?

Our group strained to hear the man from Guatemala City talk about his country. He spoke softly, his face at an angle to the group, as if he were afraid of being heard. I could certainly understand that, given what he was saying.

"Guatemala is opening back up after forty years of a bloody civil war that produced 150,000 dead, 47,000 disappeared, 250,000 refugees fleeing to other countries and 1,000,000 people internally displaced. Most of these, including the dead, were innocent civilians; men, women and children—lots of women and children.

"The civil war was fought between the military and maybe five thousand guerrillas at their peak. It was really a metaphor for the struggle between the ruling oligarchy and the poor, and between military dictatorships and the people. It was primarily fought in the rural areas of the country, although life was dangerous here in Guatemala City as well.

"The Mayan people, who comprise more than 60% of the population of our country, suffered the majority of the casualties in the war. Something like 100,000 of them were killed by the military and the civil patrol, more commonly known as death squads. Four hundred Mayan villages were wiped out in an effort to destroy potential hiding places for guerrillas. The military massacred the villagers and buried them in mass graves, which are only now being uncovered, much to everyone's discomfort. You see, the common citizen knew little of this.

"This reign of terror has understandably made the Maya, and really all of us, very suspicious of outsiders. Complicating things for you is the fact that it was your CIA's coup in 1954 which installed a military government that touched off the bloody business in the first place. The common explanation for CIA involvement was that our then-President's land reform measures impinged upon various U.S. business interests, especially those of the United Fruit Company. Of course the threat of communism was thrown up as a smoke screen as well.

"The world is now aware that the CIA's secret liaison with the forces of oppression continues to this day. So perhaps you can see how brave it is for the Maya to open their hearts to you, you people from the U.S." Our unofficial briefing officer turned his head and looked into our eyes for the first time. I wondered if he was looking for disgust at or complicity in our country's actions, but perhaps it was sympathy and understanding he hoped to find.

I prayed that he saw abhorrence, shock, and betrayal in my eyes, for that is what I felt. How could our country, founded and supposedly run on principles of democracy, participate in forty years of fighting democracy in the homeland of a neighbor? A nauseous vapor of anger rose from my gut and settled in my throat. But our speaker was right; the New York Times and the local newspapers were full of revelations that certain notoriously brutal generals and colonels were still on the CIA payroll, betraying their comrades-in-arms and their country!

(Almost two years later the U.S. public learned that even those disclosures didn't keep the CIA from secretly flowing more millions of dollars to Guatemala's military commanders, until they finally stopped in 1995. It would be interesting to know why they were discontinued after forty years of lying and cover-ups. Surely the CIA hasn't been brought under democratic control or discovered religion!)

In spite of this history, John Perkins gradually built trust with the Maya on the issue of their spiritual life over the months preceding the trip. John is a businessman, but also a shaman himself, albeit one who happens to be from the U.S. We were deeply honored when we received an introduction to the Mayan spiritual system. While in many respects I am sure it was just "getting our toes wet," what we did learn touched us deeply.

When we arrived at CDRO's headquarters in Totonicapan, we were greeted by the CDRO leadership and given beautifully hand-embroidered note pad holders to use during our stay. After some introductory remarks about the activities planned for the next three days, spiritual leader Roberto Poz was asked to give a prayer and discourse.

A broad shouldered, handsome man, Roberto donned the shaman's head-dress before he spoke. What was planned for thirty minutes became two hours, as Roberto held us in rapt attention. He was often eloquent, as we found many of the leaders to be; they had paid the price of struggle to obtain an education. From the talk, it quickly became evident that the Mayan religion is fundamental to their social system, values, morals and to their everyday life, including the development work being carried on by CDRO.

"The relationship of humans and nature is sacred," Roberto explained, "as neither can exist without the other. We are not superior to nature, but part of it, and we both are products of the Creator. The Mayan ancestors established nature as Mother, and they realized that destroying nature would destroy themselves as well, due to the total interconnectedness.

"We honor the sacredness of the Creator in our daily life. When we cut a tree or begin our harvest, we first ask the Creator's permission and give our thanks. Our religion is based on an agricultural life and it tells us how to successfully carry out that life in partnership with the Creator. We have devised calendars for religious, agricultural and social purposes. Our sacred calendar contains thirteen periods of twenty days. There are twenty types of personalities fitting therein, with thirteen scales of behavior, each beginning at the moment of conception. Every day is special to us, containing importance of one kind or another. Therefore we harmonize our activities around the specialness of the day.

"The Mayan view is that all religions believe in, and are inspired by, the one God. The use of fire in a ceremony melts any differences among us and acts as a purifier; that is why we always use fire in our rituals. Our religion is holistic and non-exclusionary." (I made a note to myself, "This non-exclusionary outlook is probably why many Maya have incorporated Catholicism into many of their religious practices.")

Then Roberto delivered a brief critique, "There are, however, some basic conflicts with European views on the issues of time and nature. It seems to us that Europeans believe in the domination of time and nature by mankind. On the contrary, the Mayans believe in working within the framework established by time; day and night, sun and moon, and the seasons...and nature. We believe that we must care for nature, and we do not see it as something to be subjugated and exploited."

Roberto concluded by offering up a magnificent prayer:
"May the heart of the earth
Flow to the heart of heaven through my heart
And my heart be the heart of mankind."

Afterwards I had a marvelous exchange with Roberto. I assured him that my work in the major Western and Eastern religions had convinced me that they all shared the same God at their roots, a conclusion the Mayan shamans had reached without the necessity of studying all the other religions!

On our last night in Guatemala, Bridget Cullerton told an amazing story.

"I had a dream the night of our experience with Roberto. In the dream, a black rock was given to me, symbolizing my shedding of this awful cancer disease. The rock was so tangible in my dream that once in the night I thought I awoke and found the rock was there in my hands as I lay in bed. So when I actually did wake in the morning, I looked around, expecting to find the rock close by. I didn't, and I thought it was just a dream, but a very nice dream.

"That morning I was having breakfast with some members of our group when one person, Lowell Brook, excused herself and asked me to wait until she returned from her room. Soon she was back with a gift for me—a beautiful black rock!

Bridget held out her hands and displayed the rock. "Lowell told me that she had been hiking in the Sierra Mountains a few weeks before and found herself drawn to a small area strewn with black rocks. Something told her that she must select a rock and give it to me. As Lowell said this, I could only stare at her. I was struck dumb! There it was, the rock of my dream, cradled in Lowell's hands! And then it was her turn to be shocked when I told her about my dream just a few hours earlier."

I think we all were in shock as we thought about this remarkable chain of events. Talk about synchronistic and nonordinary reality! A month later, Bridget returned to the Baylor Medical Center in Houston for follow-up tests. Although the doctors had been highly suspicious of cancer in her remaining breast during the months of chemotherapy, all of her tests were negative. Given the extreme virulence of the disease and the possibility of reoccurrence, they decided to remove her other breast as a precaution. In November she had a successful, and final operation. Cancer gone.

Healing next. What Roberto said sounded to me like Bridget should become a shamanic healer herself. The last time I talked to her about this, the thought was gnawing around the edges of her mind.

• • • • • • • • • • •

While I was willing to accept these curious events more or less on their face, my sometimes alter-ego, Busy Bob, wasn't.

"Robert, I think I can explain all of this without the mumble-jumble of shamans, Mayan calendars and so on. Let's see, the story goes that Lowell is hiking in the Sierras and something tells her to pick up a rock and give it to someone in Central America that she has heard of but has never met before. Bridget then meets Roberto and he tells her she is cured of cancer. That night Bridget dreams she is given a rock to symbolize her cure. The next morning Lowell gives Bridget the rock that was in her dream.

"Now, Robert, there is no need to suppose that any divine or otherworldly intervention has occurred. In fact, if we merely stretch the limits of traditional science a bit, there's a simple solution.

"Have you ever noticed that…say…you and Wendy think of something at the same time? For example, Wendy thinks, "Mmm, it's a nice day for a walk on the beach," and before she has a chance to mention her thought to you, you think the same thing."

"Of course, Busy Bob. Many times. I think everyone has experienced that."

"Well, let's assume for a moment that it's more than coincidence."

"That's a big stretch for you, Bob, isn't it?"

"Now let me finish, Robert, let me finish. If it is more than coincidence, what is it? The answer seems simple. It's telepathy."

"But Bob, if it was telepathy, wouldn't we be aware of it?"

"No, not according to what I've read about it. In fact, some investigators claim that 95% of all the thoughts we think, all the ideas and pictures that come into our heads are from someone else. But when this happens, we aren't aware of it because we can't tell the difference."

"You mean we can't tell the difference between our own and someone else's thoughts?"

"Exactly. When someone else's thoughts come into our awareness, they don't feel any different than our own; they don't feel as though they're from someone else—they just come into our awareness and we think those thoughts."

"But Bob, that would mean there are basically no secrets; that everyone knows what everyone else is thinking…all the time."

"Whose secrets, Robert? I might pick up your imaginary thought that Mary is attracted to Howard, but that doesn't necessarily mean it's true. If we understand that we're just receiving all kinds of thoughts but we can't always verify their accuracy, and we often don't know who originated them, that still leaves room for secrets."

"Busy Bob, how can the mind tell which of the thoughts we pick up are important?"

"That's easy, Robert. By the strength of the emotional content."

"That's great, Bob. That would explain why predictive messages about an imminent accident or something like that are the ones that get through. Because the transmitter, the person transmitting, has a strong emotional attachment to the person receiving and is worried about something happening to that person. That explains why telepathy is more common between a husband and wife, and between a parent and child."

"Yes, Robert. It also gives a possible explanation of why so many of the parapsychology experiments have had mixed results. It's why when two unrelated persons, in separate rooms, are trying to transmit and receive numbers, names, playing cards, visual scenes, etc., they don't have as good results as do people who have a relationship. It's the emotional content that is the carrier wave, so to speak, the energy that creates the link between minds. So, because your group was emotionally connected, everyone was communicating with each others' subconscious minds."

"Why, Busy Bob...that's brilliant. Are you starting to come over to the side of mystery?"

"Robert, it's no longer a mystery when people with Ph.D.s are doing the experiments. It's getting more like...scientific."

● ● ● ● ● ● ● ● ● ● ●

Picture a Bald Eagle, the symbol of our country, soaring grandly in the sky. The white plumage on its head and neck and its white tail feathers give the bird an appearance of royalty, and its unusual third eyelid permits it to look directly into the sun as if looking squarely at the blinding splendor of the Creator. Now imagine seeing an Andean Condor with a seventeen-foot wingspread, flying alongside the eagle. The condor's wings would stretch across most living rooms! What a sight it would be to see these magnificent birds soaring together.

Did you know that indigenous peoples of the Americas have long held a prophesy that when the Eagle of the North and the Condor of the South fly together, the birth of a new age of harmony and prosperity for the hemisphere will occur? What they see in this prophetic flight is that a blending of the best attributes of the two birds will manifest in the blending of the best attributes of our two civilizations.

And what are the attributes to be blended? I have heard shamans in Central and South America say that our culture is like the eagle, with maturity and sophistication in its intellectual, industrial, and mechanical development. They see their cultures signified in the condor—well developed in awareness of spirit and emotion.

When I first learned of this legend in 1994, I thought of how much the metaphor of a joint flight of the eagle and the condor fit with the dream of the Katalysis North/South Development Partnership. In Katalysis we have people from the North and the South joining together for their common good, acting on their hopes and plans in a way of partnership that is much more inclusive and bonding than is normally the case. We have so much to give each other!

Virgilio Alvarado Ajanel, the Administrative Director of CDRO, prepared a paper for our group on the philosophy and methodology of CDRO in its work with more than 400 Mayan community-based groups. In it, he contrasted several aspects of the world views of the Maya Kiche and Western Capitalism. A few examples are instructional.

"The Maya are oriented to cooperation through social groups and communities. The West is oriented to action through individual competence. The Maya have a holistic view, taking into account the needs of humans, both material and spiritual, of animals and nature; the West tends to take into account only the material needs of humans. The Maya are mostly generalists while the Western worker tends to specialize. The Maya model themselves on the cyclical structure of nature, while the West is patterned on linear thinking with a great deal of hierarchy and top down activity.

"While the Maya do not seek rapid progress as an overarching goal, the West generally prizes speed of action in whatever task is at hand."

And in a most revealing commentary, Virgilio said "The Maya see that humans exist merely as a part of—one might say in the middle of—nature. On the other hand the West understands humans to be superior to, or above nature."

Our group quickly saw that just those few thoughts could produce hours of discussion, and Virgilio had several more as well. So we chose not to analyze what he had said, but rather to focus on ways that North and South could help each other that weren't currently part of our process. Referring to the legend of the North and South coming together, someone jokingly said, "What would the Eagle and the Condor say to each other on their maiden flight together?"

The Eagles from the U.S. spoke first—wouldn't you know it? What we lacked, and what we thought the Condors could help us with, was:
- a sense of community
- compassion
- earth and nature connection
- spiritual connection

Then it was the Condors' turn, and they said they hoped the Eagles could help them with:
- bilingual education
- rediscovering their heritage through historical analysis
- codification of their spiritual system
- researching more ways to use what resources are at hand
- the Eagles' opinions. They wanted to hear them and reflect upon them

(As a comment on the Condors' wants, one needs to understand the terrible repression that the Mayan people have experienced in the 500 years following the invasion of the Spaniards. During this time, the best treatment they have been able to receive from the Guatemalan government has been hands-off neglect.)

● ● ● ● ● ● ● ● ● ● ● ●

"This palm is called 'Give and Take.' " Dr. Rosita Arvigo motions to a tree about twelve feet tall, with many spines on its trunk.

"Don't touch the trunk," she raises her voice to our group of twenty as we come closer to inspect. "Its thorns can give you a very bad stinging cut! But if you accidentally cut yourself, the remedy is taken from the inner portion of the leaves. This remedy is highly effective when applied to fresh wounds from any source to staunch bleeding, prevent infection and alleviate pain. Do you see why the common name is 'Give and Take?' "

Dr. Arvigo, a slender dynamo originally from Chicago, lead us to a taller tree in the jungle along the McCal River in Belize, close by the Guatemalan border. It was April of 1995, and our group from the U.S. was experiencing a powerful example of people from the North receiving from the South, reminiscent of the legend of the Eagle and the Condor flying together.

Rosita continued, "This is the Negrito tree. Its bark and roots produce a powerful astringent used for dysentery, diarrhea, hemorrhage, and internal bleeding. The wood is used for house frames and broomsticks." We crane our heads up to see its long, and sometimes crooked, branches.

We are on the Panti Medicine Trail, named for Don Elijio Panti, a legendary shaman known throughout Central America. Panti is now 101 years old and Rosita had apprenticed for ten years with him, learning the traditional ways of healing with herbs. She also experienced his great prowess in spiritual healing. We all wanted to meet Panti, but he stays in his village, a two-hour hike away, and is thought to be coming to the end of his time.

"This is a Fiddlewood tree," Rosita continues. The tree has dainty blue flowers. I move deeper into its shade, thankful that we are on the Medicine Trail in the morning. The rain forest will be hotter than blazes before noon.

"Powdered bark from the Fiddlewood is used to treat fungus, ringworm and infected sores. The bark is also useful for washing wounds. You can boil the leaves and use the water as a bath for asthma, malaria and chills. The wood is used for lumber and making musical instruments such as drums, flutes, and sometimes marimbas. That is why it is called Fiddlewood, but as you can see it does so much more.

"Now when you're in the forest, and out of water, just look around and you will soon see this—a Water tree. See these vines? Swing your machete at the height of your head and it easily slices through the vine. Now pull the severed vine towards you and you can drink pure, cool water as if it were coming from a hose." The water tasted as good as any spring water I'd had.

"Cut the vine at ground level, tie it around you with the ends up and you will have enough water for a day's travel." Rosita marched on.

"Wow, the rain forest suddenly seems much friendlier," someone murmurs.

Another person chimes in, "It's all here...it's all here. Why are we cutting it down?"

Indeed it all seems to be there. In a stunning display of biodiversity, we see over fifty types of plants and trees with medicinal and other valuable properties in a small area. Only two of them have been planted by humans—the rest are just there in accordance with nature's plan!

Five of these plants alone: Allspice, Baby's Tears, Buttonwood, Calabash and Contribo, are used for digestive upsets, gas, infant colic, rheumatic aches, pains, exhaustion, low energy, kidney stones, internal infections, skin sores, swellings, sleeplessness, toothaches, headaches, constipation, sedation, menstrual cramps, snakebites, coughs, lung congestion, bronchitis, flu, hangovers, colds, high blood pressure and loss of appetite. If that's not enough, teas are made from them, their spicy flavoring is used in stews and other foods, and their woods are used for making bowls and containers.

The rain forest is indeed nature's pharmacy! We also learn that plants with harmful properties frequently have warning signs—their branching patterns appear as crosses, while heart-shaped leaves are good for the heart, and so on. This is a pattern that ethnobotanists call the "doctrine of signatures." So while nature can be dangerous to the uninitiated, it is also compassionate and generous to those who take the time to understand it.

Our favorite example of nature working in harmony is that of the Poisonwood and the Gumbolimbo trees. Often growing together symbiotically, their roots intertwine and provide specific sustenance to each other. Above the ground, contact with the Poisonwood sap causes blistering, swelling and severe discomfort, while the bark of the Gumbolimbo provides the antidote to the Poisonwood sap.

We walk for two hours along the Medicine Trail, and we come away with a more profound vision of why rain forests need to be protected and preserved. We are excited to learn that Rosita's Ix Chel Tropical Research Foundation is supplying plants to the National Cancer Institute in Washington, D.C. for testing purposes, and the initial results are promising. But many of the rain forest's secrets have already disappeared with the loss of species. Indeed, we keep asking ourselves, just why are we so rapidly destroying the rain forests of the world? I say we, because we are the ones who eat the beef of the cattle raised on cleared lands that were once rain forest. And we use the wood products from the clear-cutting operations that denude the forest. We are thus creating the demand that results in the destruction of one of the life arteries of our world—a world whose disappearing secrets might have been used to save our own lives.

We gathered in an open-sided, thatched roof pavilion at the Chaa Creek Lodge next to Rosita's trail. We were from the South and the North, all connected to Katalysis in some way. Most of the people were donors; the managers of the five organizations belonging to the partnership and some staff members rounded off the group.

"When we started Katalysis," I opened the workshop, "the concept of partnership was chosen as our operational mode. That was because my business life had been spent in partnerships, and I believed that it was the most effective way to get things done, as well as being the most emotionally rewarding. Let's quietly consider for a few moments what partnership has meant to each of us and then share our reflections."

When the group was ready I volunteered to go first. There was no clue in my voice that the workshop was about to take an unexpected turn for me. I had looked around at the circle, thinking about what I was going to say. I started to speak, but all that came were a few strangled words.

"Oh...no...this is very...emotional for me! Something happened out there on the trail!" Then the only sounds were those of Wendy soothing me as I choked back tears.

"My God, what is this all about?" My voice quavered as I went on. "This morning on the trail we heard so much fascinating material from Rosita. But it was mind talk, wasn't it? Why was it that every now and again in the forest, I would feel near tears and have to stop to compose myself. Something was going on in my emotions, my heart and my body. But what was it?

"I think the forest was speaking to us through our cells, and our cells were listening and remembering ancient information. Sacred information, really, information about the way things are supposed to be. Everywhere on that trail we were seeing partnership in action. Wasn't it beautiful? Partnership must be the Law of Nature!

"It's why we have male and female. It's why we have the intertwining of the Poisonwood and the Gumbolimbo. It is the key to living in harmony. It's why our work at Katalysis is so special and important. Partnership is not anything new, but I feel like I just rediscovered it today!" My voice choked off. What I had planned to say about partnership was long forgotten—my heart had done the talking. I felt like a great truth had broken through the rugged membrane holding my separate-self reality together, and the truth's beauty was so stunning I had to cry.

After Ella Alford related her beautiful experiences of partnership of humans and nature in her remote Missouri countryside, Joan Cortopassi wanted to speak. She managed to get her words out, but in short phrases.

"I don't know why I keep crying. I knew all this once before. It's so sad we lost our connections with nature. It was all forgotten. Now it came back to me on the trail! When I was young I would become excited with the concepts of rhythms and cycles and systems. I tried to explain this once at college, but the class made crude sexual remarks. I forgot it. I just forgot it."

"Love...is...love is the ecstasy of bonding," Fr. Charlie Moore spoke powerfully. "The ecstasy we experience for loved ones is the same as for everything that participates in nature...the bonding of heaven and earth. That's what we experienced on the trail—the trees, the river, the flowers, the insects, the animals, the rain, the hot sun...they're all in love...they're all connected in some great forest ecstasy. Everything here is love!" We sat silently for a moment, listening to the sounds of the rain forest, singing loudly as if in confirmation of what Fr. Charlie had said.

Don Gregorio Tzoc, the Executive Director of CDRO in Guatemala, said earnestly, "It is our obligation to take care of nature, just as nature takes care of us; and through acts, not just in theory. We must eliminate the boundaries between us and nature as the Almighty created all without boundaries!" I could tell that he was excited that so many of us from the North had felt a deep connection to nature, that we were in harmony with his Mayan heritage.

Pim Chavasant spoke next, "On the trail this morning, sadness came up in me several times. It was the kind of sadness that you have when you've been away from home for a long time, so long that you forgot just what it looked like. You're sad, but glad. After Rosita told us about that 300-year-old tree and everyone passed it by, I touched it with my face. I felt it say, 'It's been a long time. It's been so long since anyone remembered. Come back. Come back again.' "

Later, when the workshop ended, I was reluctant to leave. After hugging one and all, I sat back down, sprawling comfortably in a chair. I closed my eyes, listening to the chirps, cackles, whistles and buzzes of the rain forest. Passionately said words from our session flashed through my consciousness..."I knew all this once before...It's been so long... Partnership is the Law of Nature...Come back again...Everything here is in love..." I was one of the lovers, ecstatically bonded. My body trembled. Every nerve ending felt like it was simultaneously sending and receiving. I'd never felt more alive in my life, more a part of everything around me! Tears of gratitude welled in my eyes.

The feeling stayed with me until I left the rain forest.

14

PARTNERING AMONG HEAD-SHRINKERS

Miners going into the mines often used to carry small birds, such as canaries, which were highly sensitive to the buildup of toxic gases. If the birds died, the miners quickly fled. Today, the world's 500 million indigenous peoples, living in some 15,000 distinct groups, are the miner's canary; and the Earth—particularly the tropical rain forest—is the mine. That the canary is dying is a warning that the dominant cultures of the world have become toxic to the Earth. In this case, however, we cannot flee the mine.
— Jason W. Clay

• • • • • • • • • • • •

Shell, Ecuador, June, 1995. The fourteen of us waited at a military airstrip for the plane which would fly us east into Achuar Indian lands lying close by Peru. The border war between Ecuador and Peru had just finished three months prior, and the military was keeping a tight rein on who went into the disputed territories.

John Perkins, Wendy and I relaxed under a tin roof and watched fellow travelers Lynne and Bill Twist having their picture taken by a camera-laden Jim Gollin. The Twists posed alongside an old single-engine Cessna. Its nose was so far caved in that the propeller was pushed against the cabin window. It was the same window where the pilot sat as he headed the plane into a tree, rather than going over a cliff into the rushing river far below the airstrip. Failed brakes, he had reported to the passengers, all of whom had survived.

"We're going to use this for our annual Christmas card," Bill yelled playfully. "We survived the jungle, that sort of thing."

"John, did you do any flying when you were here in the Peace

Corps twenty-five years ago?" I asked the leader of our group.

A big smile spilled onto John's face and his curly brown hair nodded assent. I could never get over how youthful the Florida businessman turned shaman looked. On this trip he had brought along his
thirteen-year-old daughter, Jessica, and they almost could pass for
brother and sister.

"Oh yes, this brings back fond memories. Fond, because I survived those flights! When I got time off from my work at El Milagro,
I would come to Sucua to catch a plane for Cuenca, the city in the
Andes where Peace Corps had its regional headquarters. It was a real
treat to come into Sucua as it had a couple of restaurants and a
Saturday night movie powered by a generator at the mission. These
were absolute luxuries!

"Anyway, you never knew when the DC-3 was coming. There
was no radio tower or anything like that. So I would go early in the
morning to the dirt airstrip, mud if it had rained a lot the night
before. The Shuar Indians would always be the first to hear the
plane. They'd set up great cries and someone would fire a shotgun.
Then people would flock to the strip, and what happened next
was...well, unbelievable.

"There would be a lot of cattle grazing at the edges of the strip,
animals that had been herded there from miles around. Someone
would start shooting the cattle, and others would fall upon the dying
and the dead with huge knives, cutting off their heads and hooves,
scattering their guts everywhere. The din of the dying cattle and the
yelling people was deafening. And the stench of hot blood flowing
and the sight of the carrion gathering...it was something out of
Dante's inferno."

"Wait, I don't get it." I stopped John's headlong plunge into his
memory bank. "Was this for a big celebration?"

"No, no. See, the plane would land and a couple of men would
count the passengers going to Cuenca. There might be one or two,
maybe five or six. They would bolt in enough seats for us, and then
the fun really began! The Indians would drag the bleeding carcasses
to the plane and pile them in as fast as they could. The pilot was
always hurrying to leave, because rains could set in at any time. And
the Indians were anxious for him to leave, too, because if the plane

was grounded by weather the carcasses would rot, and that might be their only cash income for the year.

"When the plane was stuffed, we passengers would climb in and take our seats surrounded by the sight and smell of blood and flesh fast aging in the hot, humid jungle air, not to mention the flies. If the ride was bumpy, and it usually was climbing the 8,000 feet to the Andes, well..."

"God, John, that sounds like a nightmare. I can't believe you're not a vegetarian after that!" I thought of how my experiences in visiting cattle and chicken slaughter houses had contributed to my forsaking meat.

"Hey, Bob, I was young! I could take it. Besides, when you're in the jungle, you've got to do what you've got to do—or else you don't survive."

Survival: the premier topic in the Amazon Basin. We were on our way to meet the leaders of the 4,500-person Achuar Indian Nation because they are very, very worried about survival. They didn't think they could survive the onslaught of Western culture, not unless some very different ways could be found.

It wasn't the survival of their physical bodies they were worried about. For example, take their linguistic cousins, the Shuar. Because they lived further to the west, closer to the colonized areas of Ecuador, the Shuar came into contact with the forces of the future a few decades before the Achuar. At the time of John's Peace Corps experience, the late 1960s, there were less than 20,000 Shuar, just as there had been for centuries before, according to anthropologists. Today those 20,000 people have exploded into 50,000!

Why? They have the missionaries to thank for that, for they brought with them a new way of life, one in which the territorial warring and the revengeful head-hunting were cast aside. And one in which modern medicine played an important role. Infant mortality went down and life expectancy went up. Natural forms of birth control were discouraged by the church. Results: a burst of population increase.

But it is not altogether a happy model. The rain forest territories of the Shuar were perfect for 20,000 of them to hunt and gather, but

not 50,000. Along with the missionaries came economic development, and as a result, the rain forest is steadily shrinking, denuded by
cattle farming, logging and oil production. Now the Shuar must have
cash to live, and they are largely reduced to being beggars. The hand-
outs come from the government, NGOs (non-governmental organizations), the oil and timber companies, and the missionaries. The
developed world takes the resources of the indigenous peoples and
puts them on the dole. The question for the Shuar, and other tribes,
is: will the dole continue after the resources are gone?

The Achuar contemplate what has happened to their Shuar
cousins. What they see is the destruction of the Shuars' economic
independence, of their rain forest and their culture, for not only did
the missionaries make them wear clothes and stop fighting, they
refused the teaching of native traditions and history in school, sub-
stituting instead the learning of European geography and the
Western creation myth. The missionaries condemned their spiritual
system, their shamans and magic and healing, and introduced them
to the foreign concept of sin.

The Achuar can see that there are a lot more Shuar than there
used to be and that they live longer. Death has been postponed for
many. That may sound good to a Northerner, but not necessarily so
to the Achuar. For them, and other indigenous peoples of the
Amazon, death can be welcomed as a good thing. It's a chance to
move on to another life as a spirit, plant, or animal. And it's a natural part of life. It's far worse to become dependent on others, a beggar or a prostitute.

So the Achuar worry about the survival of their way of life, of
their culture and spiritual beliefs, and of the rain forest. But, as we
were to learn, they know they cannot resist all change. They have
only to look westward to see, hear and smell the advance of
"progress" and "civilization"; it seems inexorable.

•••••••••••

While I was sympathetic to the Achuar cause before I even met
them, my resident skeptic, Busy Bob, was trying to reign me in.

"There you are, going off half-cocked again, Robert. You're making those Indians sound like 'noble savages,' living in their unsullied utopias. Admit it! Progress has brought some good things to the Shuar and Achuar, hasn't it?"

"Yes, there are lots of practical things they appreciate. Like rubber boots and flashlights. And for the first time, villages are in contact with each other by radio."

"And commerce. You described a plane coming and hauling away fresh beef carcasses to market."

"Yeah, but that's needed because they are now dependent on cash supplements; they are no longer self-sufficient."

"Medical care, Robert?"

"They still prefer to use herbal medicines where they can, but the availability of emergency medical care has certainly saved a lot of lives."

"And schools? The missionaries have brought a lot of claptrap with them, but they have also built schools."

"Bob, there's no arguing the fact that modern culture has brought some benefits, but—"

"Robert, Robert! Look around at the world. The same thing is happening everywhere. It's called progress, and you can't stop it. Forests are cut down to make more agricultural land; agricultural land is developed and turned into industrial, commercial and residential areas. Then more forested land is converted to agriculture."

"But, Bob, aside from the fact that earth's resources are finite— we can't just go on using everything up—what about the quality of life? Look how these people are changing. They have more comforts now, and they live longer, but they're less happy. And you talk about looking around the world; well, look around the world! What do you see? Overcrowding, increasing crime. Most of us have already lost touch with nature. Where are we heading? In a few years, the world will be one giant, never-ending shopping mall!"

"That's right, Robert! We may become one giant shopping mall...because you can't keep people from doing what they want to. People don't buy fast-food burgers because they're forced to—they buy them because they taste good; and they're cheap; and they're convenient. I mean, it plays very well on TV to see a native woman pounding meal with a stone. But give her a chance to buy it already ground at a nearby store and she'll take it in a heartbeat."

"Are those the criteria for progress, for the advance of civilization? Cheap and convenient? What about preserving traditions? What about individual dignity? What about the pursuit of excellence? What about courage and creativity and compassion? What about all the virtues we value?"

"Not lost, Robert. Not lost. Just concentrated. Each year there will be a small minority creating new movies, designing bridges, developing new medicines—and controlling the flow of capital. The rest of the people? They'll all be eating hamburgers in shopping malls—the Shuar and Achuar included."

●●●●●●●●●●●●

The two-engine plane disgorged us and our luggage onto a dirt strip at the village of Taisha. We were in Shuar territory and still had many miles to go to reach the Achuar. It was our first look at a typical Amazon village. Typical, but not traditional. For the Shuar and most rain forest residents have traditionally lived in extended family groups of twelve to twenty people, miles from the next family. Every three years or so the group would move to a new territory to plant their food crops, gather, and hunt. This is because the rain forest, for all its stunning abundance, is a fragile and infertile place. The incessant rain washes needed nutrients into streams, and in turn into rivers and, ultimately, into the sea. The relocation by the inhabitants allows the clearings to regrow and the soil to regenerate. The law of the jungle is that you have to keep on the move.

But the missionaries have changed that traditional way, attracting people to come into permanent settlements for the benefits of school and an airstrip, and, a few would say, the benefits of a church. And now, in Taisha, we watched the plane leave and turned to see thirty or so people watching us with great curiosity. John Perkins, looking a bit like Indiana Jones, motioned us to a small, thatched roof lean-to out of the blazing sun. We would wait there for a smaller plane as the airstrip at our destination wasn't big enough to accommodate the twin we came in on. We left our luggage at the side of the strip and followed him, surrounded by Shuar adults and children.

It was a bit uncomfortable as John had warned the men in our group not to look into the eyes of any female. It was a capital offense, he said, slithering his index finger across his throat. Given that head hunting still occurred from time to time, I over compensated and tried not to look at any women at all. That left a few men and a number of children to look at. But I tried not to stare at the young man with cat whiskers painted across his cheeks, or any of his friends, fearing my looks would be interpreted as a challenge.

That left me with the kids to look at. They were like kids anywhere—cute and giggling—but they were very wary of us. Their brown bodies were in various stages of dress, just like you'd see in any place where the style and cost of clothing was not thought to be a proxy for the worth of a child. The reluctance of our group to invade the eye-space of the Shuar didn't prevent them from doing just the opposite. All their eyes fixated on us, probably wondering what distant lands we were from.

As for us, we thought we knew where we were from, but we definitely didn't know where we were! So we huddled in small groups, compared notes, and slyly looked over each other's shoulders to glimpse these people from the middle of the earth—the people we had come 8,000 miles to learn something from and, hopefully, to help in return.

Another airplane ride and a short trek later, we were in Achuar territory, enjoying some welcoming hospitality. Now three Achuar women were making their rounds again, their bowls of chicha extended before them. It was definitely not polite to refuse and I braced myself for more of the fermented brew. It wasn't that I minded drinking beer in the steaming jungle, it was just *this beer*. As I kept my head down, avoiding the first woman's eyes, the sight of the lumpy white liquid reminded me of how it was made. I could imagine a mother teaching her daughter how to do it.

"Okay, you take these roots from the manioc plant and wash them in the river. Boil them for awhile. Then you chew the stewed mash and spit it into this container. Chew it good, you hear? The men don't like their beer all lumpy. Now, you let the container sit.

Two days for ordinary day-time beer, three or four for night-time beer and five or six for party-time beer. The longer it sits, the stronger it is! Now when the mash is fermented, add water from the river and mix it in with your hand, like this. And don't think you can get away with doing a poor job, or serving weak beer at a party. Each woman's chicha tastes different. I guess it's because our saliva is different. So take pride in what you do, as you will be known for it."

I tried to analyze why I was so reluctant. The women's mouths, their saliva? Probably okay, even though they brushed their teeth with a stick. I'd heard that a dog's mouth is as clean as a human's, and I'd yet to see a dog brushing its teeth. No, I speculated, it's the river water. John told us under no circumstances were we to drink the water, and here he was drinking chicha just like he knocks back a Sam Adams at home. And he's been drinking this stuff off and on for twenty-five years and seems pretty healthy. Strange! I guess he figured the alcohol in the mash kills the bugs. Must be instant death for them, although that's hardly logical. No, I decided, it must be those lumps. I hate cottage cheese and they look just like cottage cheese lumps. That's it. I eye the lumps in the proffered bowl of chicha.

As if reading my mind, the Achuar woman plunged her right hand in the bowl and strained out some of the lumps with spaced fingers. She flung the offending pieces on the dirt floor of the tsupim jea (a house built at ground level) and held the bowl to my lips.

"God, there's no way out of this," I sighed. I barely sipped, making slurping sounds greatly out of proportion to what I was swallowing. I pushed the bowl back to her and smacked my lips in appreciation. "Uuuum, good," I said, hoping she will think me as gracious a guest as she is a host. She moved to my right, over to Wendy, and out of the corner of my eye I see her looking back at me. Then I knew what she was thinking: faker! Yes, I sighed, reflecting that deceit is probably part of the human condition.

Later that evening the dozen of us from the States spread our sleeping bags on the rough bamboo floor of an uncompleted lodge at the Kapawi Ecological Reserve in the heart of the one-million-acre Achuar lands. The lodge was built on stilts and extended out over the edge of a small fresh water lagoon. It had a thatched roof, but no sides. Our group abandoned all pretense of privacy and began our stint of communal living.

That night, as our group quieted and we lay about, too tired and too excited to sleep, I said in a little-child voice to John Perkins, "Tell us a story, Daddy John. Tell us the story of how you came here such a long time ago."

The howler monkeys, tree toads and a distant jaguar quieted so they, too, could hear the story. Wendy and I lay clothed in bare minimums sprawled on our sleeping bags under a canopy of white mosquito netting, waiting for the last of the day's heat to say good-by. I wished there was a breeze so the water in the lagoon would be stirred into the song of waves gently lapping at shore's edge.

"In the beginning," John's voice reached out to our band, "I took a bus from Cuenca, high in the Andes, down into the Amazon. It was a wooden bus, without windows, painted blue with wild stripes and curlicues in pink and yellow. It was named La Florita Bonita, the beautiful flower. It looked fantastic from the outside. But from the inside..." John paused, digging deep into his memories. "It was a fourteen-hour ride on a winding, pot-holed dirt road, and the passengers were Highland Indians dressed in wool who sweated buckets of water each as we descended into the lowlands. It was the first time I knew just how sour sweat could smell, and it mixed with the aroma of vomiting children and the random contributions of assorted pigs, goats and chickens that rode cheek by jowl with us.

"I was ecstatic to leave the bus and didn't mind stepping knee-deep into mud as I got out. Not even a five-hour horseback ride to El Milagro could dampen my youthful Peace Corps enthusiasm. I was there to help those people, and a hard trip just made my efforts that much more important!

"El Milagro was a settlers' outpost in the middle of Shuar territory, not much more than a few shacks and a school. When I dismounted, the school teacher came up with a big smile and asked me my name and my training. I said, 'I'm John Perkins from New Hampshire in the United States, and a business school graduate. I have been assigned here as a Credit and Savings Cooperative specialist.'

"His smile turned to a scowl. 'Credit and Savings? We asked for an agricultural specialist.' The teacher swore under his breath and shook his head. 'There's no money in this town. What need do we have for a credit and savings specialist? No money, do you understand? We don't use money here! If you want eggs for breakfast, you trade bananas that you've gathered. Can you understand how that works? It's called barter!'

"The teacher walked away disgusted, leaving me standing with the horse reins in my hand and a queasy feeling in the pit of my stomach. But my spirits improved during the next few days. I come from a Calvinist background and I've been taught that if you're sent out to do a job, by God, you do it!

"Every evening I stood at the edge of the jungle handing out comic books depicting the benefits of cooperatives to people as they returned from the fields. They were printed by USAID in Spanish, but I didn't know that few people in El Milagro could read. Every night I stood in front of the school house and talked about credit and savings and cooperatives. Lots of people came, night after night. I thought I was making progress.

"As it turned out, few people spoke Spanish, either, and of those who did, fewer still could understand my beginner's lingo. It was then that I discovered that I was entertainment, just entertainment. The Indians would come from miles around for amusement. I didn't want to disappoint anyone, so I kept it up. I can't say I did the people any real good during the time I was there, but I got a hell of an education, let me tell you."

"Dad, you've talked enough! Let's go to sleep." Jessica shushed up our storyteller.

It was just as well, I thought. The image of the gringo speaking into the wind of things the locals gave neither thought nor care for was a good one to consider. Like John, our group had to come with a full heart, but hopefully ready to empty our minds, so that we would be receptive to learning something. I drifted off to sleep, wondering if I would know where I was when I awoke.

But John didn't sleep for a long time. He kept thinking about why we were there, about the strange turns in his life.

After the Peace Corps, John joined an international consulting firm headquartered in Boston. He moved rapidly up the organizational ladder, soon had fifty management consultants reporting to him, and became a partner. It was a lucrative life, and he traveled all over the world supervising World Bank and United Nations development projects. Having been introduced to shamanism by the Shuar, he sought out similar learning opportunities in his business travels in places such as Indonesia, Egypt and Iran. It was a happy time for him.

Although his projects made sense from the macro-economic perspective of his business school training, he came to see that they weren't so good for the environment. The mega-developments, such as dams and highways, and the large scale economic projects like cattle grazing, ended up with seriously destructive consequences, even if they were unintentional. When he thought of his days at El Milagro and his learnings about nature, he was sad. Gradually his sadness turned to disillusionment and he quit in 1980 just as his career was reaching full-flower.

Over the next ten years he successfully developed and ran a $60 million non-polluting U.S. energy plant which used waste coal, and provided many environmentally beneficial innovations for the utility industry. When he sold it in 1991, he went back to Ecuador for a while to clear his head and decide on his next course of action.

El Milagro now had a road into and on through it, and when he stood in front of the old school house which had been in the middle of a magnificent rain forest twenty years ago, he could not see a single tree in any direction. And the Shuar families he had once known had moved on down river to the east. They were said to be a fifteen-day walk away.

John didn't walk there. His youthful jungle toughness had faded to a memory, but he had more money now, and the missionaries had built airstrips. So John chartered a plane and he flew east. He found the Shuar, and met with their elders and shamans. He kept telling them, "I'm here to help."

"Don't come here and try to change us," they said, as if in one voice. "We want no more languages, religions, cattle, agriculture, or economic development. We only want the Four Sacred Sisters saved. The earth, air, fire and water. All life depends on the Four Sisters, and they depend on trees. You in the North are destroying the forest and the Sisters. If you want to help us, go back home and get your people to change. For you are the ones causing all the destruction!"

Change? John thought. How in the world could he get people at home to change, and how will that help?

A shaman broke in. "It's a well known fact that the world is as you dream it. Your people dreamed of tall buildings, factories and as many cars as raindrops in this river. And your dream came true, but for us it's a nightmare. It's becoming that for your people, too. Your country is like this pebble." The old man picked up a rock and threw it into a still pool lying behind a submerged tree at river's edge. "See the ripples? Everything you do in the North ripples across Mother Earth, just like that."

An elder summed up. "You must change your people, not us. Do not bring us any more of your schemes. But, if you have people who really want to learn about changing the dream, bring them to us. We're experts in dream change, and we'll teach them."

And that's what John had been doing since 1991; writing books (*The World Is As You Dream It*, *Psychonavigation* and *The Stress Free Habit*) and bringing people to the rain forests of Ecuador. All this was done in working towards a new dream. John's ultimate dream was to marry the vision of the shamans and elders with the Katalysis partnership model as a new way for the industrialized North to interact with the indigenous South. He also wanted to introduce his daughter to the Achuar as a bridge to the next generation. During that night in Kapawi he could feel the dream beginning to materialize, and he drifted off to sleep.

•••••••••••

As I started to regain ordinary consciousness the next morning, I knew I was somewhere very different, perhaps India. The truth came hard and fast at Josh Mailman's scream. "Tarantula! Tarantula!"

We all scrambled from our slumbers to our elbows to see Josh trying to get out of his sleeping bag and shake a tarantula off at the same time, considerably handicapped by the collapsing mosquito netting he shared with Jim Gollin. Josh's jump-ups put Jim into action as well, and for a moment they looked like whirling dervishes doing a slam dance.

After a surprisingly good breakfast of bananas, yucca, and a sort of pancake made from a local variety of corn, we continued to sit in the cooking shack while John's Ecuadorian partners, Daniel Koupermann, Juan Gabriel Carrasco, and Arnaldo Rodriguez, gave us a briefing. Seems that we were stepping into the middle of a very complicated situation.

A week earlier, Arnaldo had made the rounds of a few Achuar villages to tell them of our visit. He explained that we would have to be on our best behavior. "You're the first outsiders to visit the Achuar in this part of the Amazon. The most common concern of the people is that you are white cannibals!"

This caused great bewilderment among our group. How could it be? Here we were, sort of afraid of them because we knew they had been fierce warriors, fighting to prevent their Shuar neighbors from shrinking their heads, fighting because, as the young men say in a song they still sing, "We were born to die killing our enemies"; and there they were, sort of afraid of us because they thought we might be cannibals!

"Look, this can all be worked out, but we're talking about two different worlds here, and we will have to be mindful of our actions and the sensibilities of the Achuar in the villages. We will be their guests," Daniel explained patiently. "Just don't be taking pictures without permission, or giving people money, or candy to the kids. Remember the males' jealousies. And, for those of you who speak Spanish, there will be one or two villagers who do also. But, don't be asking them what they need or promising them anything. We'll be there to listen and for them to observe us. In a few days if all goes well, we'll have a big meeting with their leaders and then you can ask all the questions you want."

Daniel continued, "Let me tell you a little bit about Kapawi and you'll get some information on the Achuar that way. We believe this to be a historical project. It is sponsored by CANODROS, a tour company headquartered in Guayaquil, and by the OINAE, the

Organization of Ecuadorian Achuar Nationalities. I have to admit that I talked CANODROS into this. When the project is completed, it'll combine eco-tourism and ecological preservation. It'll provide jobs and monthly rental payments to the Achuar community. We are on Achuar land and in fifteen years all of the facilities will belong entirely to the community.

"It's a million dollar project. We will be able to accommodate forty visitors, and it is being built in accordance to the Achuar concept of architecture. Not a single nail will be used. We've got solar energy, trash recycling—everything we can do to avoid leaving our footprints on this fragile area. Basically the rainforest works on an almost closed nutrient cycle. So foreign materials raise havoc with the diversity we need for survival. That diversity is shown by the fact that in less than three acres here you will find 300 tree species, and more than 400 species of birds!"

Daniel paused as we tried to digest the significance of that number of species and I asked, "How many Indian workers do you have, and what do you pay them?"

"Now it's about fifty workers. We pay the Ecuadorian minimum wage. That's about $30 a week for six days, 7 a.m. to 5 p.m., with an hour lunch and two, twenty-minute chicha breaks. Plus health insurance. It's hard to get workers, though, because the concept of working in this way, of doing the same task over and over, is contrary to the way Achuar live—they live very spontaneously, in rhythm with what's going on around them. And once we get them, we have turnover. $100 will provide the cash needs for a family here for a year, so the workers save and leave. But we persist."

I nodded and tried to picture what it would be like if Daniel allowed his employees to work spontaneously instead of from seven to five. After all, they got their houses built working without a time-clock. On the other hand, would such a place as Kapawi ever get built without following a regime? Doubtful. I looked at the master plan for what was becoming a world-class eco-tourist facility and wondered if it would really benefit the Achuar in the long term. A worthy experiment, but the concept was audacious in many ways and the challenges immense. But perseverance could go a long way, I thought, even in the rain forest. And Daniel Koupermann had perseverance in spades.

• • • • • • • • • • •

The man of the house, a young brave, wore a tri-color headdress of yellow, red and black toucan feathers, and sat at guard at the half-walled entrance to the ekent, or female side of the house. Part of the head-dress fell down over one shoulder, across his black Los Angeles Raiders tee-shirt and onto the musket-type shot gun he cradled. His electric blue pants gave an interesting contrast to the red, yellow and black feathers and the burnt-red cat whiskers painted on his face. He maintained a wary silence during the interminable speeches being exchanged by the village elders and our leadership trio of Daniel, Juan Gabriel and John.

Facing the man of the house and the many villagers fanned out on either side of the house, our group sat on low, make-shift benches and tried to look attentive. Given that most of us couldn't follow what was going on, that we had awakened prematurely due to Josh and his tarantula friend, and that our two-hour dugout canoe ride to Guayusensa had its share of mini-adventures, it was hard to do. At last there came a signal that we would eat. This produced certain anxieties in our band for, on the one hand we were hungry, but on the other, we didn't know what kind of jungle delicacy we might be offered.

Amid our speculations—what if they give us rat, or snake?— Achuar women began spreading large palm leaves on the ground before us. There was a happy buzz that we were being provided with unique picnic tables for our food. It was a bit sobering, though, when we saw that the leaves were not only our tables, they were our plates. A line of women followed with cooking pots of monkey meat and wild boar and the ubiquitous manioc, dipping their hands into the pots and splashing liberal portions of the food onto the leaves before us. We were also offered chicha and river water, but wisely stuck to the purified water we had bought with us. The food tasted surprising good, and I hoped it would be good to us, as well.

Later we explored the village and its surroundings. This meant walking up and down the riverside air-strip, circumspectly looking at the houses, and going to the bathing hole when no villagers were present, as we had been warned not to offend their modesty. Mostly we fussed with our gear, looking for soft sleeping spots in the earth at the Achuar houses we were assigned to, and waited for our visit to the uwishin, or shaman. We had been told we would all have a chance to receive a healing, a healing more exciting than any of us had experienced because it made use of the hallucinogenic ayuhuasca.

"Are you going to take ayuhuasca, Bob?" It was Dave Ellis.

"No," I answered. "Are you, Dave?"

"Yes." Then he shook his head, "I mean no, I'm not. I don't know. Why aren't you? Are you afraid of the vomiting and the diarrhea? They say that's just a cleansing, and once it's over you're Alice in wonderland. The plant world starts talking to you and you learn some of the secrets of the universe. Doesn't that appeal to you?"

"Yes, but...I hate to vomit, absolutely hate it. And maybe I have some fear of what might happen when I'm in wonderland. Get out of control or something. But those aren't the real reasons. I'm writing a book that includes my experiences of nonordinary reality, and they've all happened without the influence of any substance. I want to be able to say that in the book, so a reader doesn't slough them off as drug induced."

"Yeah, but how often do you get this chance? Couldn't you make just one exception?"

"No. It may be the easy way out, but I want to be able to make that statement. My point is, an experience of non-ordinary reality can happen to anyone at anytime. You don't have to be special and you don't need drugs. But I know that this could be a once in a lifetime experience, and I respect anyone who takes advantage of it. And if I'm down here after I've finished my book, well..."

That night we visited the shaman who worked on a large number of the locals and three of our group. Dave and I were among the "buddies" who kept an eye on our pals. Later our friends reported that they saw marvelous sights and learned wondrous things when the ayuhuasca opened the door to a different reality, although they had a hard time explaining in words just what they experienced.

Fortunately only one of them underwent "the cleansing." But the next day they received an unexpected levy for their once in a life-time adventure—a bill from the shaman for $1,000 each!

After Josh offered to put the whole thing on his American Express Gold Card, the situation got serious. On the one hand, the shaman was the most feared man in the community, and no one wanted to cross someone who regularly dealt with evil spirits, demons and the like. On the other hand, the amount was clearly outrageous, and, if paid, would spoil things for the future. Someone suggested that it was a matter of a misplaced decimal and the shaman really meant $100. But Daniel said no, that wasn't it. The problem was that the shaman had always been paid in food or labor and had no real concept of money.

Daniel, Juan Gabriel, and John left to talk with the shaman, leaving the rest of us to contemplate the problems that the Achuar would face in entering the cash economy. It was a sobering example of just how overwhelming the next decade would likely be for the tribe. Our negotiators returned in an hour with an elegant solution: the shaman's price was tied to the cost of a visit to a chiropractor's office in the U.S. In one case, one's external body was adjusted and, in the other, one's internal reality adjusted. When all was said and done, our "ayuhuascaed" trio felt they had a bargain, and the shaman probably had made a killing, so to speak.

● ● ● ● ● ● ● ● ● ● ● ●

Our group sat in a semi-circle with the six leaders of the OINAE (the Organization of Ecuadorian Achuar Nationalities) in their rent-ed office in the town of Puyo, just down the road from the Shell airport where all this started. There were many remembrances exchanged of our visit, pictures taken, the beginnings of friendships affirmed. I was especially taken with Pedro Anank, the President, and Luis Vargas, another officer. Their Spanish names weren't real, I thought, but their head-dresses certainly were. The colorful finery gave a festive air to the occasion.

The OINAE had a proposal to make to us. They wanted help in their efforts to have the government declare their lands a national ecological preserve, which would block any development in the future. Although the government had recognized the land as belonging to them, it held the subsurface rights under Ecuadorian law. This meant the government could lease out those rights to oil and mining companies. And history had shown over and over that once oil and mining came, any pretense of the land belonging to indigenous peoples was abandoned. Undeclared, but deadly, war was waged against the Indians with great vigor by foreign and local companies alike.

After a great amount of give and take, John announced that we would give serious consideration to their request. He stressed that any action that we would take would be guided by the ideas of partnership developed by Katalysis, that we would do our best to be good partners and would expect them to do the same, teaching us about ways to honor the earth and change our unsustainable lifestyles. It seemed a novel idea to the Achuar, being partners with people of the northern culture. Amazingly novel—and to us as well!

"Look out," Wendy screamed.

"What? What?" Our group continued to crane our necks up into the top of the rain forest canopy looking for what we couldn't see.

"Down here. Don't move!"

I looked down just in time to see a deadly poisonous black fer-de-lance squiggle amongst our black rain boots with one of our painted-face Achuar guides in pursuit with a stick. The snake was gone before any of us really knew what had happened. Then there was lots of nervous laughter.

"Close call," someone whistled. We all agreed. Close call indeed!

Later I asked Arnaldo about the significance of the painted faces of our guides.

"They paint their faces because you're here. It's to ward off any bad energy you bring. Once they really get to know you, it won't be necessary. But for now, there's no reason for them to take unnecessary chances."

The images of the snake and the precautionary-painted guides ran through my mind the morning after our meeting with the OINAE leaders. Our group of John and Jessica, Lynne and Bill, Dave and Trish Waldron, Jim, Ella Alford, Deb Imershein, Josh, Wendy and myself debated how we could constructively help the Achuar. We all acknowledged that they had already helped us to see the rainforest and its peoples through a new prism. Nor longer would the issues of the forest seem unrelated to our actions, and no longer its peoples unconnected to our lives.

A biblical passage came to mind, an admonition of Jesus to be "As wise as serpents." Appropriate, I thought. We needed to be cautious and wise in our actions. We were dealing with the possibility of creating unreasonable expectations and a dependency with the Achuar, and we were in unfamiliar terrain. At the same time, there was a great opportunity for a new model to save part of the very rain forest that processed our carbon dioxide and provided us with oxygen for life's breath.

Finally, our group was ready. A decision was taken. We would form an association, Friends of the Achuar Nation (FAN). We committed over $100,000 to fund OINAE and their development of a resource plan that could lead to the permanent preservation of the one million acres of rain forest and at least a good part of the Achuar culture. We would do this in partnership with the Achuar people, a partnership where all participants were equally valued. A more guileless way of doing things, I thought.

That's when I remembered the whole of Jesus' advise about going out in the world: "Be as wise as serpents and innocent as doves." A very good idea, indeed!

15

PRAYER, DREAMS AND MIRACLES

First light, and our golden retriever and I walk through fading shadows in the forested Pescadero Canyon near my home. Just like the other 3,000 mornings before this, I say my prayers, and sometimes Noelle cocks her head when she hears something sounding like her name.

I like to pray when I take my early morning walk. It's an important part of starting my day in a positive state of mind, a sort of morning "cleaning the temple." As I swing along the path, chanting my prayers for forty-five minutes, or "walking and talking with God," sometimes I achieve the alpha brain wave state. That's the state that athletes experience when they are "in the zone," when time slows way down and the eyes see with unusual clarity. That's when I get creative as well.

As always, my words this morning consist of prayers to God and various saints, and mantras and songs of various traditions. In the middle of this time comes my prayers for family, friends and people I've never met. There are usually sixty to seventy people who get prayed for in the particular style I've developed.

Sometimes the people I pray for seem to get worse, but I don't get discouraged. I know that in a small way I'm probably helping them. That's a scientifically established fact.

"What..." you say, "what on earth could possibly be scientific about prayer?"

Until recent years there has been a major fiction about prayer—that it can't be scientifically proven to work. But now there have been more than 130 controlled laboratory studies that show that prayer, or a prayer-like state of compassion, empathy and love, can bring about healthful changes in many types of living things, from humans to bacteria. This does not mean prayer always works, any more than drugs and surgery always work, but that, statistically speaking, prayer is effective.

Let's look at two experiments that have shown that prayer works. The implications of their results are immense, although both the medical and religious professions seem to be slow to catch on to them. You're doubtful? Even a hard-boiled professional skeptic like Dr. William Nolan, who has written a book debunking faith healing, said about the coronary care unit study at San Francisco General Hospital, "It sounds like this study will stand up to scrutiny...maybe we doctors ought to be writing on our order sheets, 'Pray three times a day.' If it works, it works."

Let's pause before reviewing the studies and look at where prayer fits in the cosmic communication system. There seems to be two commonly accepted states of active communication with God. One is meditation, or "listening to God." The other is prayer, or "talking to God."

Meditation can be a challenge to beginners and experts alike as it involves the difficult task of, at least to some extent, taming the "monkey mind." (The normal state of the mind as it flits from subject to subject, like a monkey ceaselessly flitting from tree to tree.) Basically meditation consists of slowing our brain waves from the beta range (that of normal waking consciousness characterized by external attention), to the alpha range (that of pre-sleep/pre-awaking and light meditation), and then on down to the theta brain wave state (that of dreaming sleep and deep meditation).

In alpha, and especially, theta, our thought stream slows enough to allow God Consciousness to occur in the gaps between thoughts, and for us to experience the "ah-ha's" of sudden creative connections. For most of us, mastering this meditative process takes years of practice and patience.

On the other hand, prayer is a snap. We usually do it in the beta brain wave state, or ordinary consciousness. Our normally-active mind state is not a hindrance to effective prayer, so long as we focus our attention and keep the mind's monkey on a relatively short leash. We can enter into the practice of prayer, or "talking with

God," with little preparation and great ease.

The 1988 San Francisco General Hospital study by cardiologist Randolph Byrd shows that doctors should be advising us that when we are ill, we should "pray three times a day and get our friends to do it for us, too."

It was a ten-month study at the coronary care unit. The double-blind experiment was designed according to the rigid criteria used in the best clinical studies in medicine. During that period a computer randomly assigned all of the 393 coronary admissions either to a group that was prayed for by home prayer groups, or to a control group that was not prayed for.

The prayer groups were scattered around the country. They were each given the names of a few patients and something of their condition. They were asked to pray each day, but were given no instructions on how to pray. Each patient in the experiment had between five and seven people praying for him or her. The positive results of prayer, if obtained from a new drug or surgical procedure, would have been heralded as a breakthrough! One of the telling findings of the study was that a prayer group around the corner from the hospital and one thousands of miles away had the same degree of effectiveness, a vivid demonstration that the mind can operate beyond space or time.

The prayed-for patients differed remarkably from the others in several areas:

- They were five times less likely to require antibiotics.
- They were three times less likely to develop pulmonary edema, a condition in which the lungs fill with fluid as a consequence of the failure of the heart to pump properly.
- None of the prayed-for group required an artificial airway inserted in their throat, while twelve of the others did.
- Fewer of the prayed-for died, although this was not a statistically significant correlation.

A second study gives us valuable information in determining how to make our prayers. This decade-long experiment at the Spindrift Institute in Oregon consisted of rigidly controlled experiments to determine if spiritual healing is real, if prayer works, if there is an effect that can be measured, and if the effect is reproducible.

The answers were yes, yes, yes and yes. In these experiments the subjects of prayer were seeds and plants of various kinds. The findings may be summarized as:

- The effect on prayed-for living organisms was significant, quantifiable and reproducible.
- Prayer was increasingly effective as the organism was subjected to increasing amounts of stress.
- Twice as much prayer yielded twice the effect.
- While directed prayer was successful, nondirected techniques were even more effective, frequently yielding results twice as great. (Directed prayer occurs when the petitioner has a specific goal, image or outcome in mind. Nondirected prayer involves an open-ended approach in which no specific outcome is held in the imagination.)

As a result of the findings about non-directed prayer, Spindrift recommends that when we pray we strive to be completely free of visualization of outcomes or of specific goals. We should exclude from our thoughts the hoped for changes in physical, emotional, and personality characteristics of the person we are praying for, while at the same time keeping our awareness of them strong.

How can we pray without an outcome in mind? For example, instead of praying that a person's cancerous tumor be healed into remission, one could pray that the person be in harmony with the universe. Instead of praying that a separated couple be reconciled, one might pray that the two people be blessed by God.

The two prayer studies raise several interesting questions. Just who, or what, is answering our prayers? Is it really God, a God that favors those who are prayed for but leaves those without prayerful friends to make it on their own? Or is it an underlying law of the universe, not understood by us, that says for every action there is a corresponding reaction? Or are these prayers going directly to the people or beings in question, via an invisible web of connection, and thereby stimulating the person's internal system of self-healing and self-guidance?

There are more questions. Since prayer is more effective when it's nondirective, the implication may be that we don't always understand what is best for us, or for others. Does this mean that other agendas exist for ourselves than our own? Could it be that we are here to do specific things, things that are not initiated by either our conscious selves or society?

And, just how is it that plants respond to prayers like humans? Could it be that nonhuman life forms have a much more elevated position in the "great scheme of things" than we give them credit for? If so, should we be treating the plant and animal kingdoms—for what animal owner doubts that they communicate nonverbally with their "best friends"—differently than we do, perhaps with reverence? Are humans, animals and plants linked mind to mind, thought to thought, feeling to feeling? If so, what does this do to the idea that you and I are separate, distinct, concrete and independent; and why should I give a damn what is happening to some poor soul in Bosnia or in the inner-city of Los Angeles?

I don't know the answers, possessing only beliefs and not facts, but these studies have certainly informed my prayer methodology. I ask that each of the few dozen people that I pray for "be in harmony with the universe," regardless of the amount or kind of physical and/or emotional stress they may be under. I don't pray for specific results. This approach of "Thy will be done," or "what's best" acknowledges that I have no way of knowing what the best outcome is for anyone. I pray for the "right thing" instead of "my thing."

Not a bad guide for life, really.

●●●●●●●●●●●

The dream was breath-taking, emotionally powerful. Tears were flowing down my cheeks when the earthquake hit. In bed at Chuck Blitz's Santa Barbara home, I was violently shaken. Later I learned that the quake, centered in the San Fernando Valley sixty miles away, had killed scores of people and caused twelve billion dollars worth of damage. My dream was quite a wake-up call for me as well, as it seemed to cry out for action. Within days I was writing letters about my dream to a dozen or so mentors that I'd had in my life, most of them businessmen. My dream involved John Baumgartner, an old friend, business client and highly-valued mentor. The last time I had seen John alive had been fifteen years prior at a funeral. John himself had died about ten years ago. The dream went this way:

I'm looking at a map of San Benito County ranches when my view changes and I see the hills, streams, and oak-studded pastures from an aerial position. It is earth that I love, much as John did. I am shown into John's office by a secretary. He is at his desk, rises and acknowledges me. Behind him is a long platform with a model train approximately two feet high, on tracks. He finishes loading his valuables onto the train: bank deposit books, stock certificates, deeds, jewelry, and gives the train a small push. It chugs off into a tunnel at the end of the platform. John watches it leave and tells me his things are being turned into the "King."

He turns to me and I know this is good-by. As we hug I notice his deeply-aged face and the cataracts clouding his eyes. Our embrace is heavy and tears come to me. He kisses me on the neck and says he loves me. I am surprised and overwhelmed by the depth of his actions. Gathering myself, I respond in the same way. Our tears flow. As I turn to leave I notice that his secretary has been joined by three other staff people who are standing in a row, heads bowed, as witnesses to the parting.

That dream prompted me to write several letters. Here is the letter I wrote to one mentor, Gordon Brooks, who counseled me many times when I was a young CPA.

January 18, 1994—Bob's 58th Birthday

Dear Gordon:
(First, I described my dream and the circumstances in which it occurred.)

Gordon, upon reflection, the first teaching I discerned from the dream of John was to never leave any important thought unsaid, or any strong emotion unconveyed. I never expressed to John during his lifetime the depth of gratitude I obviously felt toward him. Similarly, I never told you of my strong positive feelings for you. Seemingly, the right time never came. What folly to wait for the right time!

Secondly, I am thunderstruck by the depth of the mentor relationship that in many ways I have taken for granted. Not just with John, but with others as well. I was surprised that John loved me so much, and that I similarly loved him. Respect, trust, admiration, yes—but the love! And the dream was as real as the "reality" I am in as I write this! It seems to me that these deep mentorships may arise out of karmic fields of past lifetimes. Surely the principals have worked together in the past or lived together in the same family group or perhaps were strong adversaries with the actions of the current lifetime being the final healing of past conflicts.

I see this type of mentor relationship as being quite different from the traditional teacher, or guru-and-disciple field of play. In mentorship, we do not surrender our judgment or our position as co-creators. Instead, while the relationship proceeds on the basis of the surface attraction, i.e., the business or professional context, we find fundamental learning occurring by being included in the mentor's life. By that inclusion, and experiencing the ups and downs, the good and the bad, we receive knowledge from our mentor even as the mentor is receiving knowledge himself/herself.

And so I come to the purpose of this letter. I want to acknowledge you as one of the major mentors of my life, and to not only express my gratitude, but also my love for you and for your intentions in our relationship. The early years of my accounting career were guided by you in so many ways. Professionally, you taught me in both the technical aspects that I needed to learn, and in the ways to handle myself with clients and within the firm. Beyond that was your inclusion of me in your life and that of Pat and the kids. That bought a special richness to our relationship. We had so much fun together with jazz music and the general celebration of life!

It is with deep regret that I now recognize that I never initiated an effort to heal the break in our relationship caused by your departure from the firm. I can only guess at your pain during those times. I'll bet you felt that I let you down, that I chose Mac and Wayne over you. Frankly, I don't even remember my reasoning process at the time. I do remember being very ambitious and I'm sure that my evaluation of my career direction had a lot to do with it. In any event, what needed to happen was a healing and sense of clearing around our respective roles in the process. I wasn't wise enough then, so this is my effort to effect it now. I sense that your ability to see through all this to the deeper parts of both of us will allow us to go forward at peace with each other. For that I thank you.

Until we meet again, Bob.

I was excited to write letters to those who had been powerful mentors in my life. I had never before formally acknowledged those relationships, but there was no time like the present. Unfortunately, Gordon was dead and his wife also had passed, so that letter remains in my files, waiting perhaps for a future mailing to an unknown destination. But all my other letters were delivered.

The response that I received to those letters has been incredibly uplifting. "I'm reading it for the third time." "I'm going to frame this." "I have tears in my eyes." "This is going into a very thin file of things I have kept during the last fifteen years." "I am grateful to be part of your life and to have you say so."

I repeat these words not to feed my ego, but to indicate the happiness that the action has bought to my mentors as well as to myself. Although it is not considered manly in our society for me to express my deepest feelings, and many men, including myself, feel uncomfortable in receiving such feelings from other males, these letters facilitated a mutual suspension of our socialization that made our hearts feel big and free and soaring!

(A businessman and social-entrepreneur-par-excellence, friend of mine, Dave Brown, had the following experience. He sat down and put a sack over his head. Another person sat opposite, silently meditating in support of Dave's work. For two hours, Dave imagined that he was dying very soon and therefore proceeded to tell his loved ones good-by, one by one. What a powerful way to discover the things that are unsaid—and the things that may never be said, given that death is always looking over our shoulder!)

Time was running towards dawn, and once again I was dreaming. At first I wasn't aware that it was a dream, because I thought what I was experiencing was real.

I was looking at an oil painting, rendered primarily in the dark colors of the American School of Realism. The painting depicted a large number of men, women and children moving up a gently sloping, grassy field to the lighter side of the picture. There was a storm gathering behind them, and they were moving towards The Rapture. Some of the people were smiling radiantly, expectantly; others were sobbing joyfully as they plodded towards the end of time as they knew it.

Their faces were so expressive that their joy suffused me, and I felt the magnetic attraction of The End. Suddenly, I realized that I had joined the crowd and was moving eastward with it through rich earth smells towards a golden-white light coming up on the horizon like a never-before-seen dawn. Bliss welled within me and a thrill shook me to my core. Tears of gratitude streamed down my face and I eagerly increased my pace towards The Goal, towards the Divine.

Then the dream turned lucid and I realized I was dreaming. I stayed with the flow and was struck with the notion that I might well be dying right then as I lay asleep. Momentarily, I regretted not having finished my book, then felt that what lay ahead was so ecstatic that it transcended any need I had for its completion. I continued walking towards the brilliant white light, but it began to fade. I shrugged off my deep, coma-like sleep, understanding with neither joy nor regret that my time had not yet come.

It took a long time for me to fully awaken. When I did I lay there in the darkness, playing the dream over and over again in my mind. The next morning I found the dream still at the edge of my thoughts and let my morning meditation become a movie-house for reruns of the dream. Heavy, honey-like emotions clung to me, and the colors of the gathering storm, the field, the people, the sky and The Light reappeared at the closing of my eyes.

The movement in the dream felt promising, as if my life were similarly shifting from fixed line patterns, such as those used by the artist to draw and paint the picture, to the earthy, creative, ecstatic, sensual, even erotic experience I'd had when I entered into the painting. By spontaneously joining the picture I seemed to have gone with the current of life instead of fighting it. Did this portend that when my time came I would be ready, willing and able to meet my Creator? I knew what I needed to do next. I brought out my journal to take a closer look at some of the dreams in my life and reflect on what dreams are about.

Carl Jung called dreams "the royal road to the unconscious." That unconscious not only includes the great territory of self, it also includes the vast stretches of the collective unconscious, and the infinite reaches of the kingdom of Divinity as well. Exploring these largely uncharted territories is as exciting an adventure as we can possibly have!

What do we find when we enter the dream world? In the territory of self we discover golden nuggets of personal information. We also find entertainment, despair, fright, and love in living color, stereophonic sound, as fully emotional and fully physical—remember your last really good sexual dream?—as anything that happens when we're in an ordinary consciousness state.

It is in the lands of the collective that we discover a shared, transpersonal reservoir of experiences which are the source of images and symbols common to humankind. These images can give us guidance for the future or help us interpret the meaning of our lives in relationship to the rest of humanity. For example, the burning bush dream that I had has come to many people. What that says to me is that I'm connected by this dream, and its symbology, to all of the human stream down through the millennia; connected psychically and spiritually in ways that transcend the physical and genetic.

And the Divine comes to us through dreams, sometimes directly, sometimes through universal symbology, and sometimes obliquely. When this is all added up—the past, the present, the future, myself, humankind, the Divine—I paraphrase an old song, "Dreams, dreams; who could ask for anything more?"

Dreams are my most cherished spiritual practice. I find that the more I work with my dreams by recording them, thinking about them, sharing them with others and acting on them, the richer my dream life becomes. It's like paying attention to a teacher in class and then the teacher pays more attention to you. I especially love to create out of dreams, to bring them into my world. If I dream about a mentor, I write to him; if I dream about someone, I call them; if I dream about a bear, I read something about bears; and I guess if I dreamed about a cake, I'd bake one.

I found a dream in my journal similar to the rapture dream. As I recorded it the morning after:

Returning to San Jose, I drive to Alum Rock Park. As I enter the area, the road narrows and is full of people. I park and take a footpath to a series of pools surrounded by grassy banks and rock outcroppings. The water flows into great depths of clarity. I sit by the side of a pool and wonder why I never saw the transcendent beauty of this park when I was there in my college days.

I enter a state of rapture, marked by muffled sobbing, and feel my connection with Divinity. I plead with Jesus and God to take me, and almost leave my body. Distracted by people walking by, I follow them into a beautiful shrine at the edge of a grotto. Everyone is very mellow, lighting candles and saying prayers. Even in this peace I feel a need to find a secluded spot to say oms. As I gather myself to go outside, the rapturous feeling comes again, and I experience sobs of healing. A progressively louder noise—not quite the om signifying the creation of the universe, but more of an Ah—arises and people look to identify the source of the heavenly sound. Amazingly, it's coming from me. The sound gets louder, and I become more and more excited as I hurry out of the shrine and down a path that I know leads to Home.

Later, I was reflecting on the dream, on leaving this earth and going Home, and remembered what Emerson said when told that the end of the world was imminent. He calmly replied, "I can live without it."

I take great interest in dreams about my demise. The appearance of death signals the need for transformation of personality and character. Our conscious is being told that there are elements of our persona, old habits, old ways of thinking, that need to be set aside to make way for the new, the fresh, the more vital. And, if one is frightened by a death dream—if it's a nightmare—the more important the change is. It seems that the harder it is for our subconscious to get our attention, the greater the fear and intensity it injects into the next dream. Then the dream literally screams for us to listen up and act differently!

On August 29, 1995, I spent the day at my cabin writing about death and dying.

In the early hours of the next morning, I heard the phone ring and struggled to find it in the darkness.

"Hello..." My voice was groggy.

"Dad..." It was my daughter Sarah, bawling.

"What is it, Sarah? What is it?!"

"Agh...agh..." Gut-wrenching sobs came down the phone line, up the cord and into my ear as the dream ended.

I laid there, half-awake, feeling adrenaline's panic course through my veins. What bad news did Sarah have for me? I came more awake and listened for the phone for a long, long time, finally falling back asleep with a queasy stomach. When there was no phone call by the next morning, I decided the horrible event was yet to come, and resigned myself to it being part of the ways of life.

That evening Wendy told me that Charles Berolzheimer, grandfather of Carin, Laura and Michael, and someone that I greatly respected, had died the night before at age ninety-two. It wasn't a horrible event at all, rather a peaceful death at home. My dream had been exaggerated, but perhaps dreams have to be that way from time to time to obtain clear transmission space on the massively jumbled airwaves that service our brains.

Where did I come from? Along with "what are we doing here?" and "where are we going?" this is one of the truly profound questions in life for each of us. As fortune would have it, I also had a dream about that question.

I'm in a large crowd. A man draws everyone's attention by saying, "I discovered the most powerful words in my life when I opened the Bible and came upon these verses." I feel very skeptical about his claim, but listen closely. The man reads from notes: "And then I realized that I have come to earth from space, from the region of (unintelligible) stars, so far away. Elsewhere is my home, not here."

To my shock I burst into deep, wrenching sobs as the innate truth of this information hits me. Yes! I shout to myself, I am from else-where, a place of indescribable peace, beauty and shining love. Compared to that, this plane of existence is like a straight jacket, full of tears, constraints and illusions. This is not Home! How homesick I am!

Later, I leafed through the Bible to see if I could find a similar reference to humans originating from the stars, but found none. Perhaps I should have tried a computer search! I set aside the literalness of the dream and focused on how perfectly true the assertion of beauty of our origin, our Home felt. The dream became one of great inspiration for me.

Imagine my surprise when sometime later I was reading a scientific account titled "Creation," by physicist John Polkinghorne, and discovered a remarkable clue to my dream. Although my lack of a scientific background allowed me only superficial understanding of the article, a sentence jumped out at me. "Every atom of carbon in every living being was once inside a star, from whose dead ashes we have all arisen." So we did come from stars! Not every bit of us, but a good part, for carbon is a major component of our bodies.

Perhaps you're thinking this isn't very practical. But...

May, 1992. Over the weekend my sister and I talked about hiring a new attorney to handle her divorce. She was in great despair about the lack of progress and totally frustrated with her legal counsel. I decided to call John Hopkins, a business attorney friend, for a recommendation of a divorce specialist. But before I could call, I had a dream.

In the dream I was pondering Mary's divorce situation. A voice advises, "Call Bill Dok."

On Monday morning I told Mary about my dream. I explained that hearing Bill Dok's name was a total surprise to me because I last knew him socially in San Jose more than twenty-five years prior. I said I didn't know if he still lived there, and if he did, whether he practiced divorce work or if he ever had.

Using the telephone company information service, I found Bill. His first words were, "Is this the Bob Graham I knew more than twenty-five years ago?"

After renewing our acquaintance, I told him I'd had a dream advising that I call him. I asked, "Do you do divorce work?"

He responded emphatically, "Bob, that's all I do now!"

He agreed to take the case, and my sister credits him with breaking the logjam and achieving a reasonable settlement. I thought he did a great job. The dream had directed me to just where to go!

Interstate Five, Central Valley, California. Flat, monotonous. Not much traffic. Speed limit and beyond. Boring.

The motivational speaker hiding somewhere in my tape deck was pretty interesting, though. He was extolling the values of planning and said, "The future belongs to those who plan for it."

"Amen, brother," I replied. After all, I thought of myself as a world-class planner and capable of judging his pronouncements. I thought about my one-time extensive personal planning process and how I had to let it slip away. How had that happened? Probably got too busy, I told myself. The speaker seemed to be telling me to get back to it.

"Okay, it will be fun," I thought. It was time to dust off my neglected Picture Book of Life and update it.

I received contrary instructions that very night, in what had otherwise been a vacuum of dreamless sleep.

A commanding, distinct voice said in a dream:

"You are a receptacle for the creative energy of the Universal Life Force. You are no longer to exert your will. Instead, you are to respond to the flow of that creative energy and act it out. You are not to plan your life; the Universe has its own plans for you."

The voice was so forceful it woke me up and I lay there repeating the message, over and over. I had never heard words like that— "the Universal Life Force"— in a dream before. There was no doubt the voice had put them in capitals and expected me to act accordingly. I immediately dropped the idea of personal planning.

"Wow," I marveled the next morning. "The Universe is articulating Ram Dass' theme, BE HERE NOW!" Not planning my future, not reliving my past, but being fully present; that's what I was to do.

You might ask, "What do you mean, be here now? Where else would you be?" Well...I can be in a lot of places. As you speak, I can be in the future, projecting what I am going to say when it's my turn. I can be in the past, thinking about what happened the last time we talked. Or, I can be in fantasy land, thinking about drinking rum and Coca-Cola while sitting among red bougainvillea in Puerto Vallarta.

By not being here, by not being fully present for you in the moment, I miss a lot. If I'm thinking of something else, I could miss opportunities to dissolve current problems. For example, our words might create a small opening to bring a misunderstanding to light in a way that it's easily dissolved, but the subtlety of the opportunity requires my complete attention to see it. Or my preoccupation may cause me to miss the fact that you and I have something in common that I didn't realize before, something we could share together. And if I'm not fully present, you don't get all of me, an experience all of us remember from questioning our parents as small children!

When I realize I miss so much, I vow to keep trying this slippery concept of being consciously present. Unfortunately, I have been schooled to do that only when someone says, "Pay attention!" So I experience frustrating difficulties. Habits are hard to break. The mind is hard to control. But breakthroughs come. And when they do, I feel a deeper sense of the other person, and myself as well.

It's also in the present that I feel more attuned to my spiritual self. There is a saying that explains this, and tells why religious traditions put a premium on awareness: "All paths lie in the moment!"

For another example of "practical dreaming," let's turn to a recent article in the Los Angeles Times and read about Dan Gold, an ace product developer for Price Pfister, a plumbing fixture manufacturer. Gold says that his best designs and engineering solutions come in dreams. "I wake up in the middle of the night and say, 'That's the answer. That's how you do it.'"

Last year he ran into a roadblock. He needed a motor for a promising new invention. Time and time again he tried different motors on his prototype, only to discover that the motor was too big or too noisy. Then he had a dream. "I was out in the wheat fields some place and ran into this guy. We chitchatted and his final words were, 'What you're looking for is in Kansas.'

"I woke up and wrote it down. What did it mean? I didn't think a hell of a lot. But then I got to wondering if it had anything to do with motors because that was the only thing I was looking for. I had never been to Kansas, but I called a friend there and told him, "Look in your business-to-business phone book under 'motors.'

"He called me back and said there was one listing. I called it and they sent me a catalogue. I ordered a couple of samples and one was exactly what I was looking for! Right size. Right price. I was talking to the salesmen, and he wanted to know how I found out about them. They only supply auto makers and don't do any advertising. When I told him he just said, 'Wow!' "

Wow, indeed! Is nonordinary reality the real information super-highway? Should we call it the inner-net?

Would you like information on what is going to happen in the future? Sometimes dreams tell us, like this dream:

A doctor called from a hospital. "Mr. Graham, we have your mother here. She's receiving the treatment she needs and doing fine."

I tried to call Mother that morning, not knowing what I would say about the dream. But she wasn't home. That afternoon a San Jose hospital called and said, "Mr. Graham, your mother was bought in by ambulance an hour ago. She is doing well, everything is under control. You can come and visit her anytime."

I've heard that dreams of precognition are fairly common. Sometimes they are of extraordinary importance, revealing impending disasters of one sort or another. People have been known to avoid airplane or auto crashes by acting on their dreams. More often the dreams deal with events that we can't or don't wish to change. A wonderful example of this was reported in the newspapers in May, 1994. Dikembe Mutombo, star of the Denver Nuggets basketball team, reported to sports writers that he had dreamt that his team would win game four of their National Basketball Association play-off series with Seattle—which they proceeded to do.

Two days later, he told reporters that he had another dream—that game five would go into overtime. Denver's victory—in over-time—in the decisive fifth game of the playoffs gave them one of the most shocking upsets in pro basketball history! But to what end were the dreams? After all, the games still had to be played, and the superb efforts made. Were the dreams to inspire, to instill the sense of the possible in what otherwise seemed an absolutely impossible situation? I like to think so. I like to think that we should chase our dreams, and realize them in our everyday lives.

All of my life I've had fearsome snake dreams, usually every two or three months. I would thrash, moan and wake with a pounding heart and sweating body. Why these dreams? I wondered. The answer came during a past-lives regression session. Nadja Gusti, a Carmel psychologist and hypnotherapist, had put me into a dream-like reverie and turned on a tape recorder. I was coasting through black space when I suddenly saw the snake, just as if I were in a dark movie theater and a movie abruptly appeared on the screen.

"There's a snake! I'm in a small cave with a poisonous snake! I was thrown in here and the entrance blocked. I've been very bad and that's why I'm being punished in this way. I'm a thief who took other peoples' cattle—but my family had nothing to eat! There's a candle, and I can see a big, thick, black snake. It has horrible eyes, and it's coming toward me. I've been starved and I'm weak. The snake is really mad as it's trapped in the cave, too. The snake is coming up on my body, now it's on my chest! I try to fling it off, but it strikes me. I feel pain, but more terror. It's over, I give up. Why fight it? It's just a matter of time until I die! Now I've passed out from shock. No one dares to get me out because they know evil spirits are coming to get me. People are afraid of the spirits as well as the snake.

"Things are falling away and its getting harder to breath. Now I have a solid pain; it feels like I'm freezing. I'm going to leave my body soon. Now my spirit lifts up and I see my body. It's African, black, thin, tall, gaunt. Wait, there's no evil spirits here! All I had to do was leave my body. I'm free! There are some spirits, but they're friendly. I can't see them, but I understand what they are saying. It's fantastic: there're no evil spirits here!"

Nadja interrupts my joy and I listen carefully. "Bob, can you see the snake as an agent of liberation from that part of you that was terrified? You're free. Starvation would have been a longer death. See the snake as he strikes you. Two living creatures in fear of each other, but you were in this together. Can you see yourself touching the snake? Imagine yourself sleeping. A dream begins and a snake appears. See your response as one of trust and compassion, knowing the snake won't bite you. Your fearful snake dreams in this life have been a result of your previous experience, but now you see that the death was an illusion. That death was your freedom; that cave couldn't contain your spirit. You've nothing to fear."

Months later I was on an airplane to India. A film had been shown, "Indiana Jones' Last Crusade," a story of the search for the Holy Grail. In true Indiana Jones fashion, he'd been menaced more than once by wriggly, fast-moving snakes looking for human flesh. After the movie I fell asleep, and a dream began.

I know a large poisonous snake will come to me. I twist and moan in the expectation of being with it. But I hear a message: I'm not to fear; I'm to take a leap of faith. The snake appears, large and evil looking. It crawls up over my bare chest, it's skin dry rather than slimy as I imagined it would be. The snake looks into my eyes but I hold its gaze. I surrender to whatever might happen. The snake gradually draws away, leaving me unharmed.

I had gone to Nadja out of curiosity about past-life regression work, without any idea that it might help me with a problem. My inquisitiveness was rewarded in an amazing way. After that airplane-ride experience, I've not had any dreams in which I feared death by snake bite. In fact, snake dreams are rare for me now. The experience with Nadja suggested that my violent snake death in a life in Africa had carried over to this life. It had been a death not fully assimilated into my stream of consciousness. This makes the case that clues to unexplained problems in our lives sometimes can be found in prior lives via past-life work. Many therapists now are using past-life regression techniques in the same fashion as they do in looking into childhood experiences for explanations of current psychological problems.

On another level, my snakes may have been speaking to me in an archetypal way. According to experienced dream workers and ancient wisdom traditions, a snake often symbolizes awakening and rebirth. The analogy is that the snake sheds its skin to accommodate physical growth, and so must we shed old beliefs and behaviors to accommodate personal and spiritual growth. Struggling with the snake shows that we think we aren't ready, but we are called to surrender our fear of change. Dream snakes can also serve in another way, as part of a struggle with the shadow or dark-side parts of ourselves that we refuse to acknowledge. In every story of the hero's journey of personal transformation, there is a struggle with the dark-side, personified by evil in the form of dragons or monsters or such. They must always be confronted and overcome.

A good way to experience nonordinary reality, and obtain the information that can come with it, is to simply "get out of town." However, we can't go just anywhere, rather we must get as far from our ordinary reality as possible. This means other neighborhoods, other cultures, places where the material aspects of everyday life are distinctly different from ours. In such places we often find ourselves slightly disoriented, and this can yield an openness to what we wouldn't normally perceive. Dream life becomes more exciting!

In 1991, Wendy, Merede, Lara, Sarah, two nephews, Wes Graham and Jason Pollock, a niece, Denise Graham, Wendy's brother, John Pollock, Father Charlie and myself went to India for three weeks. It was my third trip, but the first for the others.

India is vastly different from our homeland. The sights, smells and sounds of a country of nine-hundred million people living in every imaginable condition alternately assaulted and soothed our senses. None of us had experienced before a country where religion, myth, legends, and spirituality were such an integral part of everyday life. In this fertile field our tribe of ten mostly-happy travelers experienced heretofore unmapped aspects of our inner worlds, especially through dreams. Merede immediately got into the mood with a dream on our first night in India, at the Kashmir Cottage in Dharamsala:

Our group was sitting in the living room of the Kashmir cottage at Christmas. Double French-doors were open to the patio, which was covered with bougainvillea. A black limousine pulled up with bright red fringe on its doors and a red and gold lantern on its roof. A young boy about six years-old with dirty blond hair stepped out. His ethnic look seemed to be a cross between Scandinavian and

Tibetan. He was wearing a red and gold outfit that included a skirt with lederhosen. He came in, stood next to my mom, and announced that he had come to receive his gifts. He told us that he was often disappointed in the presents visitors brought, because they were usually silly items with the name of an airline printed on them.

My mother went into the next room and returned with several boxes. The first few gifts were books. Then the boy unwrapped the largest item, a twelve-foot, papier-mâché snake representing a sign of wisdom in the Tibetan culture. The snake had a lever under its chin that made its tongue flick in and out. The young boy wrapped the snake around his neck and laughed with complete happiness. Our group was caught up in the laughter, and I woke up from the dream with a smile on my face.

The next morning Merede told us about the dream. She remembers, "My father thought the dream might have been about the reincarnation of a Lama Yeshe, a highly respected spiritual leader who had established a retreat center nearby. He went off to rummage in his suitcase and came back with a book he had just acquired. It was *The Boy Lama*. I had never seen it before, but in it was a picture of a boy who looked every bit like the boy in my dream. He was Lama Osel, born of Spanish parents in Spain, and believed to be the reincarnation of Lama Yeshe."

Toward the end of our trip during which several people had wonderful dreams, including one of an interview with the Dali Lama, Denise had an unsettling experience which she calls "my dream of terror."

We were meditating together in a circle. There were two other people besides our trip group. We were supposed to try to figure out an animal, but I didn't understand how to do it. I peeked at Wendy; she was making a biting gesture with her mouth. I thought she was making a lion, but then I knew it wasn't; it was a bear.

When I thought "bear" I was pulled up above one of the strangers in our group. It was as if he and the bear went with me. I looked at Bob and his eyes were very large. He looked confused, but I felt safe because he was there. I went through an archway so fast I hardly saw it. I was speeding towards a red and black wall bearing a Chinese design. Just before I hit the wall a very deep voice spoke to me. The voice said "A child..." and I finished the sentence, "...is born."

Recently Denise said, "My thoughts on the bear dream are very strange. The images are so real in my memory that it feels like it happened just the other night! It was the most terrifying moment of my life when I woke. My hands and head were full of energy, and I was disoriented and uncomfortable. I felt so alone. Even today when I think of it, I'm uneasy. There's something I should be learning, but I don't know what. I think I'm afraid to find out what it is, because the message could be life-altering, and that's scary. I feel if I try to figure it out, I won't be able to. I'm not going to realize what it means until the time is right."

•••••••••••

One afternoon I was idly leafing through the sports pages of the Chronicle when my eye was caught by a headline—"Reggie White's Miraculous' Recovery!" I sighed and said to myself, "Oh boy, here we go again. Miraculous? I wonder what this means."

"In a change described as 'nothing short of miraculous,'" the article read, "Reggie White returned to the practice field yesterday and showed the Green Bay Packers he doesn't need season-ending hamstring surgery after all. A day after the Packers said that White, the National Football League's all-time leader in sacking the opponent's quarterback, would be lost for the rest of the season, the team said that next week's surgery has been canceled—and he's listed as possible for tomorrow's game at New Orleans.

" 'The difference between Tuesday's workout and yesterday's is nothing short of miraculous,' said a statement from the team's medical staff. White said he was at home playing with his children Wednesday evening when he noticed that as he ran, the hamstring felt better. White, an ordained minister, credited his ability to pass all the medical tests on the injured leg to divine intervention."

As a child I had been taught that miracles were confined to the Bible, therefore its all encompassing power over people. The story of Reggie White and his miracle was provocative, but I didn't know just how far one could go in describing life's events as miraculous. So I found an old, worn *Webster's Collegiate Dictionary*. I flipped the pages and found the listing: "miracle: an event or effect in the physical world deviating from the known laws of nature, or transcending our knowledge of these laws."

I reflected that Reggie White's doctors had scheduled his operation one day and canceled it the next. They didn't know why there was such a sudden and profound change in Reggie's physical condition. It certainly sounded to me like the doctors witnessed a miracle, and I knew this book wouldn't be complete without mentioning a few that I'd seen as well.

Our extended family group of ten was at an orphanage outside Bangalore, India. The history of the orphanage is that a certain man was robbing travelers on the road from Mysore to Bangalore. Sai Baba appeared to him in a dream, pointing out the error of his ways. The robber had a major change of heart and reformed his life. Out of gratitude to Sai, he started the orphanage. He built a shrine on the site and filled it with numerous pictures of saints of the major religions, especially those of Sathya Sai Baba and his preceding incarnation, Shirdi Sai Baba. Vibhuti (sacred ash) spontaneously forms on the pictures—a phenomenon that is often reported around the world, and that I have personally seen in various places.

The reformed robber appeared from a side door and motioned us to come with him, perhaps thinking that we wealthy foreigners would make a nice donation. He lead us to a center alter on which rested a large vessel. Placing the vessel on the floor, he took a spoon from his pocket and fished in the syrupy contents. We gathered around, peering over his shoulder. Capturing something in the spoon, he brought it out and motioned me to open up my right hand. When I did, he turned the spoon over, dropping a medallion bearing Shirdi Baba's image onto my hand. As a honey-like substance ran from the medallion, the old man spooned it off and back into the container. Soon the medallion appeared dry, and my hand was dry as well.

I'd been to the orphanage before and knew what was going to happen. I called out, "Watch, everyone. The medallion will continue to give off the 'amrutha.' Think of it as 'the nectar of the gods.'"

And so it happened. Amritha flowed into the palm of my hand. The old man continued to spoon it into the container. He fished another medallion out of the vessel, one that bore Sathya Sai Baba's image, and placed it in Father Charlie's hand. Now he was scooping from both our palms, alternating, as if he were milking two cows at once. After several minutes our group was no longer content to "ouu" and "ahh" and demanded equal time. So the medallions were passed from person to person, and the amritha flowed and flowed.

The nectar has been streaming for years, a sign of Sai Baba's grace, it's said. Each week several large crocks are filled and visitors to the shrine are invited to bring containers and take some home. The story is that taking amritha when ill or in an emergency is a very good thing to do. (I can report that it has a strong orange blossom smell and has an orange-slightly-chocolate flavor. It crystallizes with exposure to the air much like honey does. Unfortunately I've never remembered to take it when I was sick, so I can't say anything about its healing powers.)

We were leaving the orphanage a half-hour later when Fr. Charlie said, "Can you believe it? I've cleaned my hand a dozen times!" He showed us the palm of his right hand. Amritha was still coming from somewhere, very slowly now, but surely. Later on the bus I saw him occasionally look at his palm. The flow had stopped but the memory lingered. Made a person stop and think, you know.

• • • • • • • • • • •

Thinking about this almost drove Busy Bob nuts the first time I was at the orphanage. "For God's sake, Robert! How can ash form on pictures and how can nectar keep flowing from an inanimate object?"

"Falls under the category of 'miracles,' Busy Bob."

"But what's actually going on? What is causing it?"

"One way to explain the mechanics of it is to talk about soul energy."

"What's that?"

"It's the idea that every living thing possesses a kind of spiritual, or psychic, energy that is unique to that individual. I'm sure you've heard of auras, Bob." This was another subject that Bob didn't cot-ton to due to an experience I'd had. I pressed on with my theory, "Well, they're real—they exist, even though most people can't see them. They're a manifestation of spiritual energy."

"Assuming, for the moment that that's so, Robert, what has it to do with ash spontaneously forming on a picture?"

"From what I've read, we leave something of our individual ener-gy on everything we touch, everything we contact. When I'm talk-ing with you, some of my energy rubs off onto you, and vice versa. Well, the same thing apparently happens when we touch inanimate objects. A bit of our individual energy is absorbed by the object. That's one way in which psychics can sometimes help police solve crimes—by touching an object of evidence and being able to identi-fy who that object belongs to."

"Okay, but these pictures and medallions of Sai Baba and his pre-decessor...?"

"Shirdi Baba."

"Yeah, these pictures and medallions of them...they've probably never seen or touched them. So what's the connection? How did their energy get to these objects and cause them to produce seeming miracles?"

"Maybe Sai Baba simply sends his energy to them, just as we send our prayers to another person?"

"Wait a minute, Robert. Haven't there been instances where statues of Jesus purportedly have 'bled' from the nail points on his hands and feet? Mind you, I'm not saying I believe that."

"There have, Bob, and now I'm inclined to believe them."

"Yeah, you would, but how can Jesus be sending energy to do that? He's dead, after all."

"Is he, Bob?"

• • • • • • • • • • •

Do you believe in miracles? If you do, you're in good company. According to a recent Gallup Poll, 83 percent of Americans believe in the possibility of miracles. Let's face it, we seem to be surrounded by them, don't we? It was a miracle that this person survived a car accident, or that person's cancerous tumor suddenly disappeared. There are miracles in sports, in business, in medicine, and in relationships. Life is truly full of unexpected, seemingly random miracles. With so many miracles going on, sometimes it's hard to tell just what is and what isn't miraculous. Maybe that's why Albert Einstein said: "There are only two ways to live your life. One is as though nothing is a miracle. The other is as though everything is."

I'm at the Esalen Institute on the Big Sur coast at a workshop. It's a beautiful sunny December afternoon, and I've spent two hours outside on the lawn in a six-foot circle as part of my "homework" on experiencing quietness. Suddenly hundreds of Monarch butterflies swarm overhead and I hope they're an auspicious sign. After more meditation, I do visioning work and adopt pledges for the new year:

- Wanting to experience the suffering and pain of others, I will to do more direct service work. (I later became an AIDS helper.)
- Wanting to experience more of The Divinity, I will build a meditation shrine. (This took two years to realize.)
- Wanting to experience Mother Earth, I will plant trees. (I planted only a few.)
- Wanting to experience more of who I really am, I will work one hour less per day and take steps towards voluntary simplicity in order to achieve greater freedom. (This is a continuing process that I don't have the hang of yet.)

I sit and chant, looking across the lawn to the ocean. The sun is lowering behind the trees. With the sun's rays shimmering on the ocean, it seems that I see the dancing image of the Indian god, Shiva. He perches on the water, one leg raised, and his multiple arms stroke the sea into long ripples destined to become waves upon the shore. One of the coastal pine trees becomes violet, then shows pink between periods of transparency.

A person walks to a house encased in a golden blaze, its human form is virtually indistinguishable. A person on my right stands, and the upper torso is a green rectangle, larger than the underlying body, legs still reaching the ground. Another person walks across my field of vision as a spire of royal blue. Behind me a cat's head is a swatch of yellow, but the yellow smear doesn't move as fast as the head, taking a second or two to catch up. Several times I close my eyes or focus on buildings or the sky in order to correct my vision, but when I look back the same appearances continue. In all I have about ten minutes of seeing some of the damnedest things I've ever seen.

Afterwards I sit in wonder. What have I been seeing? Was it some sort of miracle? I think back to a time a year earlier.

I was in a meeting with a half-dozen members of a family discussing ways in which they could bring about greater intergenerational participation in their foundation. We were using the experiences of my family foundation as examples. The younger generation was very enthusiastic about the possibilities, but their elders were concerned about breaking the traditional governance patterns of the sixty-year-old foundation and of losing control of the giving prerogatives.

At a pause in the discussion, when the process seemed stuck, the heretofore silent mother began to speak. She talked about her history in service organizations and her own personal service projects. At first these seemed mundane and dated. But as she talked, something else emerged. The activities she described had been undertaken outside the power structure of the foundation, without using the significant financial resources that it possessed. She had done them on her own.

She began to use her hands in slow, compact motions to help express herself, and her speech became rhythmic. Suddenly her hands and the immediate space around them turned golden. I stared in disbelief, then moved my chair a foot or so down the table to break what I assumed was a light pattern filtering through the window. Her hands remained golden. I moved again, but I saw that they were still golden. Only when she stopped talking did the wondrous color fade away.

I was still trying to understand my experiences in seeing those strange colors on people, trees and the cat at Esalen when I attended a lecture by a Monterey physician, Hector Prestera, MD. In addition to being an doctor of internal medicine, Dr. Prestera has received training in China in acupuncture, herbal medicine and an array of the healing arts. Thus he integrates Western medicine in curing symptoms of disease and treating trauma, and Eastern medicine in preventing and healing underlying causes of disease. In his talk he mentioned people as possessing colors and auras.

On my next visit to his office I asked him about what I'd seen. He described three kinds of nonordinary sight; that is, situations of seeing things in a different way. First he explained that seeing colors on a person, such as I did in my golden hands experience, is merely perceiving the full spectrum of normal wavelengths reflecting off people. It was quite interesting to learn from him that a person can be trained to do this. The reason this is a useful skill is that the reflections vary in color depending on the subject's current physical and emotional state. If a person is showing purple it means they are feeling a certain way, yellow, another, and so on. Thus a physician or nurse so trained can assess a patient as they enter the doctor's office.

The next kind of nonordinary sight Dr. Prestera described was that of seeing auras, which are energy fields surrounding our bodies. Apparently people can be trained to see auras as well as colors. Just to confuse things a bit, there are also colors in our auras and they perform the important function of indicating our basic or underlying mental and emotional condition. These colors disclose such elements as our spiritual, loving, compassionate, and intellectual natures.

There is another interesting aspect to working with auras. The length of an aura's radius is said to be indicative of cumulative spiritual growth. That is, the further the aura projects out from a person, the greater the growth to date. A trained aura reader can measure just how far one's aura extends. (I once had an Eastern trained metaphysician measure mine and mark it to the inch on the ground where I stood. Of course I had no way of judging his accuracy or even if he knew what he was doing.)

Lastly, Dr. Prestera described the nonordinary sight of seeing luminous beings or luminosity. He said that is what my Esalen experience was. It is the sighting of a radiation from a being that incorporates all the elements of the prior seeings—the colors of reflective

light (physical and emotional) and auras (mental and emotional)—
in a very refined and ethereal way. While a person can see either the
colors of reflective light or auras in ordinary consciousness, one must
be in a state of nonordinary reality to see luminosity.

As I left his office with my head spinning over these unfamiliar
concepts, I thought that the only thing I did understand about my
Esalen experience was that I was in nonordinary reality when it happened. But I still wasn't sure what I'd seen. So I turned my mind in
another direction, wondering if there were any messages for me in
these unusual sights.

In the golden hands incident, where the mother was explaining
her simple acts of service, I came to believe that her intentions and
actions were "golden." Especially sweet was the realization that she
not only hadn't needed the power of the family foundation to express
her intentions, she'd managed to do her work while staying away
from the negative ego involvement that can arise while giving away
large amounts of money. She'd shown her love for other humans in
simple, direct ways, and I believe that's why her remembrances were
transmitted as a golden light. For some unknown reason, I was lucky
enough to have picked up on it.

The message of the Esalen experience is more difficult for me to
grasp. Apparently I'd entered into a state of nonordinary reality in
my meditation, and saw people, trees and that cat in a way that was
different than ordinary, but no less real. Look at it this way. If we
could shift our eyes to a setting that had x-ray capabilities, we would
see people as basically bones surrounded by shadows. Shift to yet
another setting that was primarily water sensitive, and we would see
people as suspended water with a few impurities floating around.
Shift to yet another setting that was primarily sensitive to energy,
and we would see humans as dynamic energy fields.

I guess I could say I happened to see things in a different way that
day, and it was no big deal. Or I could say I gained an astounding
insight into the underlying nature of the construction of humans,
and that it was at least a minor miracle! But no matter, because, for
me, the message of miracles is the process by which they appear. It's
a process that can take many forms: divine intervention (God
appeared in a burning bush and told Moses how to lead his people to

freedom); human efforting (the woman, her back broken in a crash, climbed up a 2,000 ft. cliff the night of a 20° below-zero blizzard wearing jeans and a tee-shirt); coincidental (just as he was ready to drown, he was rescued by the only person within five miles of the beach); statistical (the golfer made a 525-yard hole-in-one, a billion-to-one shot); or it's anybody's guess (the cancer tumor disappeared overnight).

While I believe most miracles are the result of the operation of the laws of nature that are beyond our current perception, it's just a belief. What I know about miracles is two things: first, a miracle can happen to anybody at any time; and second, it's very important to be open to the possibility.

For me this means setting aside time each day for mediation and prayer to open myself to Divinity. It means attending a church where the focus is on God discovery and spirituality. It means associating with fellow seekers. It means going to spiritual seminars and retreats and reading spiritual books for encouragement and inspiration. It means devoting time to service to others. It means trying to see God in everyone. Above all, it means being optimistic about each new day—because I believe in miracles!

16

SIXTY APPROACHES

Echoes of conversations drifted into my mind and played against a backdrop of bird songs and lilac smells one sunny March morning as I sat on my cabin deck, taking stock of my life. I had recently shared some of my writing with friends, and this had prompted some interesting discussions. One of them began with Wendy and a friend—I'll call her Gloria—seated in an Italian restaurant, waiting in the pause between salad and pasta.

"Wendy told me you'll be sixty on your next birthday," Gloria looked at me closely as if she were thinking of asking me an embarrassing question about my experience of aging. A slight shake of her brown hair indicated a change in the question to come. "Say, what's it like for you when Wendy's gone?"

I glanced at my wife and said, "That's an interesting question! Why do you ask?"

"Well, I know that in the last five months, on four occasions Wendy has been gone for several days at a time and you only once. How do you feel when you're home alone?"

"The days are okay. I've got my writing, the phone, the fax, meetings and so on. It's the evenings that are lonely. Being home alone for dinner is a downer, and the same for eating alone in a restaurant. Why are you interested?"

Gloria paused and said, "Because Tom wants to stay at home just when I want to go more. I want to visit my children and grandchildren. I want to travel to places I've never been. I want to leave my nest now and then, and try my wings!"

Wendy interjected, "We're getting to be like eagles and our husbands more like.....mm.....like bears! Are you guys going into hibernation?"

I laughed and said to Gloria, "I certainly identify with your husband. A few years ago I was away from home 150, 160 nights a year.

It was too much, and I've cut back to less than half that. Of course, I've had to say no to lots of things I used to enjoy doing."

"You're no longer doing things you used to enjoy? Why?"

After some reflection, I said, "What comes to mind is life cycles. In India, life is said to be made up of four cycles, or stages. I know this isn't India, but perhaps there're some clues for us from their 6,000 year tradition. The first twenty-year cycle is youth and learning. The next is householder, about thirty years of that...marriage, children, jobs, acquiring material possessions. Then people turn over responsibilities to their grown children and enter the third stage. It's one of contemplation and spiritual practices, maybe in a small hut in the forest or by going to a monastery on retreats."

"Or going off to your meditation room," Wendy observed. "Are you in this third stage? And what's the fourth stage? Do you disappear all-together?"

"No, no I'm not going to desert you!" I reached for her hand and gave it a squeeze. "Actually the fourth stage is rarely used in India these days. But at one time people became renunciates; they abandoned their homes and wandered the countryside, begging. They were seeking unification with God here on earth."

"Well, I don't see why they couldn't find God right there at home," Gloria declared.

Wendy jumped on that. "I agree, there's no need to leave home. You're always saying God's inside us. So there's no need. And I don't feel like I need to sit in some meditation room for hours, either!" She shook her head to emphasize her feelings.

"Okay, okay. Forget the leaving home part," I said. "As to meditation and contemplation, you probably don't need that either. You know, I think women are more connected to their spiritual source than men, anyway. You're more in touch with your feelings, more nurturing. And, in general, you're probably more at home in the universe than we men."

"Well," Gloria said, "my kids sure gave me lots of opportunities to practice nurturing! I miss them now that they're gone, but I've got my horses, the two collies, and my garden. But Tom, who's worked twelve hours a day all his life, just wants to sit!"

"Maybe he just wants to see what a little peace and quiet feels like," I ventured. "If he's like me, he's been so busy that when he wasn't busy, he felt guilty. For years the clock has been my king and I measured how much I was getting done against its tick-tock."

"Is that why you're always looking at your watch while I'm getting ready to go out? Checking the tick-tocks?"

"Honey, you know I hate to be late. But now that I think about it, there's been a downside. What with watching that clock, I'd go to a meeting even if I hadn't completed what I was working on. And I'd mentally carry my unfinished business with me, which made it hard for me to be fully present for the next thing. Maybe that's why I've felt uneasy so much of the time." I smiled at the women, pleased with my new discovery.

"Now me," Gloria said, "I almost always finish what I'm doing. The clock has nothing to do with it. Of course I don't have all those meetings you men do. Do you really like it that way, or is it that you can't do anything about it? If I were in charge of a business, I know I sure wouldn't schedule so many meetings. Maybe I'd make a rule that we couldn't have a meeting until everybody was done with what they were doing!"

"Let me know when I can come to work for you, Gloria. In fact, you'd probably have a whole lot of men lining up for a job. Especially guys in their forties who are wondering whether their work really means anything, anyway."

"Does this have something to do with "male mess-o-pause?" You know, what you men call the mid-life crisis?"

Gloria laughed at Wendy's description of the common male ailment. "I think so," I said. "It's not just meetings or being out of touch with feelings. I think it's because of a weak connection to our spiritual source. After going though the same old stuff year after year, men start to wonder, 'Is this all there is?' Too often a man without a spiritual anchor mistakenly decides what's wrong are the externalities of his life. So he gets busy changing his car, wife, family, house, or job."

"Oh yes, we women are familiar with that," both women said, almost in unison.

I decided to forge on and take men right up to retirement. "Later, when men see the end of their careers looming, they ask a new question, 'What was my last twenty or thirty years of work about? What's life all about, anyway?' They see a lot of impermanence in what they have invested their lives in. They see that jobs, careers, businesses and relationships have come and gone. They see life as being basically unstable—sometimes even their favorite sports team is sold and moved to another city!

"Finally in their fifties, they start turning inward. They're approaching the third stage of life. It's time to ask a lot of questions, a time for searching and reflection. This takes space, quietness, relaxation, and absorption in nature. Moments of inner peace are discovered and valued. Comings and goings are curtailed. Our equivalent to the cycle of contemplation in India is probably this mysterious thing we call retirement. Maybe our retirement condo is like their forest hut. There's a problem, though, when our time to be quiet to get to know ourselves and God is misinterpreted as boredom, either by ourselves or by our social director!"

"Okay," Gloria said, "but things change for women, too, not just for men. There's menopause, gray hair, and the empty nest of the kids leaving home. There's that nest thing again. I nested in my twenties and my husband wants to nest in his fifties!"

"Yes, but the things you've invested your energy in are relatively more permanent. Take all those days spent with your children. One usually doesn't hear of a woman getting tired of relating to her children—and she's still got them when she's seventy. But for a man who has invested his days in a job...well, now he's losing his career, his identity, really. That's scary but also good, for it brings a man face to face with the meaning of his life...the fact that he's going to have to deal with his own death."

"What's so good about that?" Gloria exclaimed. "Besides, your interpretation is the charitable one. Maybe Tom's just being lazy in his golden years. How about desert?"

•••••••••••

And just what does it feel like for me to turn sixty? My mind drifts back to June, 1995, to a far, far away land...

Anxiously I shifted my gaze between a small fire with a heap of wild flowers alongside, and the shaman sitting quietly. Don Alberto Taxzo, the noted Ecuadorian cloud forest healer, was middle-aged and handsome in his long black hair and white shift. I felt quite comfortable with him—and the fire, wood, and flowers.

No, my problem wasn't him, it was that I didn't know what to ask for. Along with my dozen U.S. companions on our trip to the Andean Highlands and the Amazon Basin of Ecuador, here I was with an opportunity for a healing from Don Alberto. And right on his home turf, too, a round medicine house partially sunk into the ground, with a hole in its conical thatched roof to capture the smoke from the center fire ring. I was captivated by the medicine house. It included three concentric circles: the adobe walls making up the exterior; the ceremonial pit where we sat, dangling our legs from its edge; and, below, the fire ring. The stimulation of an open fire burning in the middle of an otherwise substantial building seemed to somehow pull me down, to ground me into a world of accumulated wisdom.

An image of having such a place at home came to me, a picture of being with all the generations of my family, of eyes peering into a fire and our voices passing experiences down from great-grandparents to grand-parents to parents to children and back up again...maybe not so much up and down as around, because we would all be listening. If we could only do that, I told myself, maybe somehow our four generations could together make sense of all of our lives.

Sighing, I dismissed the idea of such a life-enhancing structure. "Never get a building permit," I said under my breath, and turned back to my question. "What am I going to ask him for? I don't hurt anywhere."

Don Alberto began to talk softly in Spanish and our leader, John Perkins, translated. "When you come to the fire, pick up a stick and some flowers. Take a piece of wood that calls to you. And be sure to look at the flowers; smell them. That will clear your head. Reflect on what you need in your life at this time. What do you need healed, what do you want to change? Release those needs and wants into the fire along with your wood and flowers."

I held back and watched our group slowly and carefully do as he said. Six men and six women, clothes with earth and plant stains brought from the river and jungle, and faces fresh for the ceremony. My thoughts gave way to feelings. There came a deep longing, for what I didn't know. But it was a longing that I had often felt in the past year.

What was it about? The only other time that I remembered having such stirrings of deep longings was as an adolescent. Then the feelings revolved around females. Now, how could I so long for something I knew nothing of? I understood my early stirrings to be largely the urgings of testosterone hormones. I chuckled to myself and thought, "Do I have a spiritual hormone kicking in?"

Whatever it was, the longing was what I needed help with. Call it a healing, some advise, or a blessing—it was what I would ask from Don Alberto. I let a stick pick me. It was a long, sturdy, serious stick. The wild clovers I grasped were fragrant with freshly-picked smells, of dew, of the warmth of the sun, of bees droning in the air looking to make a pollen pickup in the meadow. I held the flowers next to my cheek, closed my eyes and saw billowy clouds against the thin blue Andean sky. How grand it would be to fall asleep into Mother Earth's arms in a field of that clover! But now was not the time to sleep.

Carefully I laid my stick into the fire, adding redness to the blaze. I smelled the richness of my bouquet once again and sacrificed it to return to the elements. I felt, and thought, "I'm releasing responsibility into the fire of creation. May I let go of it gracefully." I whispered that three times in all, and felt something shift in me.

My yearning was to harmonize into the next season of my life, a longing as natural as winter's sap quickening to the creativity of spring, and spring's exuberance craving the expansive growth of summer, and summer's pregnancy looking to the harvest of fall, and fall's desire for the slumber found in winter's stillness. It was time for me to harvest my abundant crops, sharing what I had acquired and learned, setting aside only what I would need for winter. For my life would not have another season of spring nor one of summer; I could only go back to those places in my memories...and I could not stay there.

As I sat at the edge of the fire pit and watched others receive healings for various afflictions, I thought about the first time I'd verbalized these stirrings. It was with Wendy at the Ventana Inn in Big Sur, on my fifty-ninth birthday.

• • • • • • • • • • •

Fifty-nine years old! Time to celebrate and to reflect. I threw in more oak to urge on the bright fire in our room at the Ventana Inn in Big Sur. Settling into a properly relaxing chair, I began to take stock of what I wanted to accomplish in my last year of being fifty-something. I sensed that the decade of my sixties would be much different than the last. It had the feel of a time when I might discover who I really was underneath all the roles of my life.

I picked up a yellow legal pad and listed each area of my life. Okay, now what? So I gave each area a molding, a massage. More of this and less of that. Add something new here and discard something old there. When I looked at the plan, it looked good. But then I realized it was a doing plan, just like all the other plans of my life. Wasn't something fundamental supposed to change? What if I had a being plan? What if I focused on being rather than doing? Would I experience a time of spontaneity? Would I begin to discover just who I really was? What if? But I didn't know how to write a plan that didn't call for me to do something and I lay the papers aside. I listened to the fire for guidance but hearing nothing, I fell into watching the patterns of flames advancing across logs, sucking out their life force but only momentarily possessing it.

The bedside clock informed me that quite a bit of time had passed and I had a "Eureka" understanding that I had been being rather than doing. I squirmed deeper into my chair to focus on the unusual experience. But now that I understood what was going on, being made me nervous. Things that I could be doing, or should be doing, raced into my mind. God, I couldn't just sit there.

"Wendy, I want to go for a hike. Want to come?" She didn't.

Looking southeast down the receding shore line from a bluff overlooking the Pacific, I felt the water asking that I please sit down so it could demonstrate the ceaselessness of its waves to me. Their repetition was hypnotic and a message was unfolded that I would not enter the field of spontaneity and deep personal self-discovery until I let go of my long list of responsibilities. I needed a break, maybe a sabbatical—anyway, some space. I became dreamy and excited at the prospect and wondered if this is what Joseph Campbell meant when he described "following one's own bliss."

Heading back to Ventana, I decided that beginning on my sixtieth birthday I would let go of most of my list of twenty responsibilities: the board of directorships, the affiliations, the investments, the projects, the trips. I knew I'd have to do it skillfully, because I didn't want to cause suffering to those who depended on me. But I sensed that as those responsibilities were set aside, one by one, they would be like costumes being removed. Then in the beauty of my nakedness, perhaps I would discover just who I really was. And, hopefully, I would discover my very own bliss and be able to follow it as well.

As I walked down the ridge line, my footsteps gave to me how I should think of myself in the meantime...Writer, Walker, Wisdom Seeker. Left, right, left, right. Writer...Walker...Wisdom...Seeker.

• • • • • • • • • • •

Writer...Walker...Wisdom...Seeker. Now it was my turn to walk over to the spot across from Don Alberto and seek some wisdom.

Making the bowing greeting of *namaste* to the shaman, I sat, closed my eyes, and prayed. Looking up, I fished a half-burned stick from the fire and picked up remnants of unburned red, yellow, and blue wildflowers. I looked through smoke wisps into Don Alberto's black eyes and there seemed to be a flicker of recognition. Could he see beyond my jungle tan, my bald head, my gringo clothes?

"I ask the shaman for his help and blessings. My wish is to gather assistance in a most important life transition. My next birthday will be my sixtieth. It will be a time of putting away some old things and picking up some new. Your request that we work with the stick and the flower at the beginning of this ceremony was very significant for me. First, I see the stick as the symbol of striving and leadership."

Suddenly Alberto picked up a handful of flowers from his side and reached forward on his knees to lay the stem of one in the fire, connecting to it a chain of two more flowers, the last of which he placed in a certain position on my bare left foot. I was startled and stopped talking. What did it mean to be connected to a fire by the stems of white and pink flowers? With quick, efficient movements, he resumed his position on my left and smilingly encouraged me to continue.

I nodded and held out the smoldering branch. "With the sharp end of a stick we can dig holes in the earth for planting corn and beans. The seeds will grow and feed our families. This is the striving that I speak of, that time of life when we must work hard to produce things for those who depend upon us. The stick is also good for guiding our animals, our sheep and cattle. This is the leadership aspect, something that I have strongly felt in my life, sometimes to the point of burden."

I paused, feeling a little uncomfortable. I was starting to sound like a shaman myself, a little too serious, I thought. I didn't want to look at my companions for fear of embarrassment. The surprisingly white teeth revealed by Don Alberto's smile said he was enjoying it, however, and he motioned for me to proceed. I thought, "Oh well, in for a penny, in for a pound," and plunged on.

"To me, the flower represents an entirely different phase of life. In our culture we have a saying, 'Don't forget to smell the flowers along the way!' But it's a fact that very little flower smelling goes on for anyone in the striving phase of life. On the other hand, we envision that retired people spend most of their time smelling the flowers. Whether people do or not, after a lifetime of not smelling, is questionable. My wish is to be able to smell the flowers while still being productive, but being productive for the needs of others in ways that further my personal growth. I have met my own material needs. Now I want to become a Spiritual Elder in the deepest way."

I glanced down at the stick and flowers in my hands. Looking up and straight into Don Alberto's eyes, I said with a low, passionate voice, "So now I lay down the stick," tossing it into the fire and causing the flame to rise, "and pick up the flower." I pressed blossoms to my cheek.

There was a long silence and I let out a sigh of relief. I was feeling better already. The shaman selected a half dozen large leaves from a nearby pile and vigorously rubbed them together. When he had created a sort of herbal mash he began a chant and was joined by three of his helpers. Their guttural voices echoed back from the adobe walls and they sounded strangely like Benedictine monks doing a Gregorian chant. When the rhythm was well established, Don Alberto approached me on his knees and pasted the mash onto my feet, careful not to disturb the flower chain leading from the fire across the toes of my left foot.

With my feet cooling from the herbal juices, Alberto reached over the fire and completely encircled a puff of smoke with his cupped hands. Moving quickly he bought his hands close by my forehead and slowly blew the smudge onto my head. I closed my eyes to avoid the smoke and felt the warmth of the fire's offering to me. The heat on my scalp settled down through me and met, at my gut, the coolness of the herbs traveling up from my feet. And there in my gut I felt unity and balance and joy and anticipation.

Don Alberto broke off the chanting and started talking in a voice full of loving strength, "When you reach the age of sixty, it's time to start letting go, time to begin entering a new stage of life.

"Now your stage is that of collecting flowers, yes, but it's also the time of giving and sharing. You've learned from your hard work and struggles, accumulated much wisdom. Now you've crossed over to the spiritual side of life. Stop, smell the aromas of the fruits and flowers of your efforts and see just what that wisdom is. Then spread it to others, sharing it open-handedly. Give freely, so you can benefit others.

"Your persona has chosen to go into the garden and take advantage of the fruits and flowers. Most people at this stage get to the garden, but they don't go in to enjoy it. Instead they think and worry about the activities of their other adult life stages. A 'second childhood' is a very precise definition of this stage. Children start out their childhood taking full advantage of it, with their play and focus on what's at hand. But then adults begin to interfere. They don't like the child's restlessness, and they want the child to be still. They say children should be responsible and that they should begin to worry about the same things that adults worry about. Soon society has stamped the childhood out of children."

The shaman stirred the fire, causing several pops and crackles, and looked up at me with a sly grin. "Don't let society do this to you in your new stage. Use your intelligence to fool them! Make them believe you're doing what they want, while at the same time you're doing only what you want! Don't continue to participate in the strivings and responsibilities of your past forty years. You now have new things to work for!

"This connection between the foot and the fire should never be lost by a person who has reached this stage," he said, pointing at my feet. "This part of the foot has an intimate connection with your head. There's a link that runs through the body. I'll strengthen the tie so that you don't fall into the dictates of society. Once more is the time of the heart, humor and happiness of childhood!"

I didn't understand the physical or spiritual basis of the foot-fire-head connection, but I was all for a second childhood! With that, Don Alberto half-sang, half-chanted a high pitched prayer and pressed the remaining herbs onto my feet, hands and face. It felt wonderful! When he finished I stood, bowed to him with gratefulness and said, "Namaste."

He smiled broadly, and then with the air of a physician saying in dismissal, "Go home, take two aspirin and get some rest," he said, "Go home, mix some honey and some bee pollen, keep it by your bed, and each morning when you wake, take a spoonful in your mouth. Let it dissolve before you get up. You're going to be just fine!"

What a beautiful picture of the next stage of my life: shedding responsibility, gaining spontaneity and tasting the sweetness of honey!

• • • • • • • • • • •

Some time after hearing the shaman's advice about letting go of old things, I realized that I was holding on to my disillusionment and anger toward my birth religion with altogether too much fondness. When I went back to church in my forties and began to study church dogma, I had found much that disturbed me. The more I read, the deeper I felt the betrayal of organized religion. For example, the multitude of contradictions found in the Bible and in the words of theologians and religious writers made it impossible for me to get a clear picture of Jesus, or God, or why the Christian religion deserved to be considered anything special.

Moreover, I saw Christianity's claim of divine supremacy over all other religions, over all people, for that matter, and its demand for unquestioning obedience from its followers as an abomination. The goal of organized religion seemed to be to seize and consolidate power over as many people as possible. My attitude become one of "Down with religion and up with God!"

Therefore I began seeing Father John Adams, an Episcopalian minister and psychotherapist, about my anger towards my cultural religion. I thought his unique perspective as a religious professional and as a trained psychologist could help me deal with my unwanted and unnecessary burden. Within a few weeks I began to see things a different way. One of the things that happened outside our sessions was that I was inspired by the fellowship of several Christians—highly successful businessmen—who were contributing to the welfare of our diverse society through social action. It was obvious that they were taking some of the hard teachings of Jesus to heart, and going straight-away to service of others without being hung up on the ups and downs, or the imperfections and foibles of organized religion.

I mentioned this to Father Adams, questioning how they could do that. After a thoughtful pause, he said, "Who did you trust when you were thirteen?"

"Umm...one or two teachers...and I had a couple of good friends."

"No one in your family?" he questioned.

Slightly embarrassed, I said, "Well...no, I guess not."

"That's all right; no one does at that age. Usually by then we've learned that we can't trust our family members to be perfect. So we're usually very critical of them. But we give outsiders the benefit of the doubt."

"I've got it!" I exclaimed. "That's why I'm so faultfinding of my religion. In effect it's my family, and I learned I couldn't trust it to be perfect, or even especially good. You know, I've certainly given other religions the benefit of the doubt—that is, until I learned about their shadow sides as well."

This was just what I was looking for. If I could forgive my birth family (and hopefully they've forgiven me) for imperfections, then why couldn't I forgive my birth religion? Surely I could. As I write this, I can report that my anger has greatly diminished. But it's still there, alive in pockets of resistance. It looks like it's going to take a while to completely eradicate. Sort of like crab-grass, it seems.

• • • • • • • • • • • •

My straight-ahead, left-brained, linear-thinking, practical and pragmatic side, my alter-ego known as Busy Bob, has something to say.

"Robert, I have the feeling that you're getting ready to close this book. Am I right?"

"You are, indeed."

"Since I don't get as much of a chance to speak out anymore, I want to grill you a bit. You know, ask you a bunch of questions."

"All right, I'll try. But no trick questions, please!"

"Fine, but one thing: you have to keep your answers short. So here's the first one...what have you learned in this lifetime, Robert?"

"Hah! In ten words or less?"

"All right, I'll be more specific. What is the purpose of life?"

"Okay, with a disclaimer that I don't know all the answers—I'm just speculating, like everyone else."

"Granted, Robert. Now, what's the purpose of life?"

"The purpose of life is to exercise creativity."

"Who or what wants to exercise creativity?"

"The Divine."

"Why does God want to create?"

"That's its nature."

"How does God create?"

"It divides itself and spreads its life force into innumerable forms."

"Hey, Robert, that's not bad. Okay, how do we perceive God?"

"By experiencing love."

"Why doesn't everyone experience God's love?"

"The element of free will gives everyone a choice of what they'll experience."

"Why did God give us free will?"

"That's the creative part; it makes the game more interesting."

"Okay, Robert, that's Round 1. You passed."

"Thanks, Bob. I was really worried."

"Ready for more?"

"Sure, go ahead."

"What's heaven?"

"It's a mythological place of happiness with a core of truth, but based on a misunderstanding of reality."

"What? That's not comprehensible. Put it another way: does something like heaven exist?"

"Only as we individually and collectively create it."

"With pretty clouds, golden angels, harps...?"

"If that's what you want."

"You mean we create it? It's not created by God for us?"

"We do it."

"And hell?"

"Same thing."

"Who would want to create their own hell?"

"An individual's conscience."

"Who sits in judgment on us after physical death?"

"We do."

"Are we able to judge ourselves accurately?"

"Yes, with the help of guides."

"Does everyone have guides?"

"I think so."

"While we are physically alive also?"

"Yes."

"Then how come only a few of us are aware of them?"

"Most don't take the time to find out."

"How can we find out?"

"By learning to be quiet and listen."

"Okay, okay, Robert. Now try this. Why is service to others beneficial for us?"

"It gets us past our personal ego state."

"Why do we need to get past it?"

"Because when we do we expand our perceptions."

"Why should we expand our perceptions?"

"Because until we do, we only experience a small slice of life—we're missing the best part."

"What's the best part?"

"Truth, love, and beauty, beyond anything available in our limited state."

"What if we're satisfied with our limited state?"

"Fine, stay there."

"No one forcing us to move on?"

"No one, except ourselves."

"So if I opt out of spiritual growth this lifetime, it's okay?"

"Bob, you can't opt out of spiritual growth. Everything you do causes spiritual growth."

"But if I choose not to follow so-called spiritual practices, if I choose not to learn from a spiritual teacher, if I choose to do whatever I damn please?"

"It's up to you—you're in charge."

"So, Robert, it's okay if I waste a lifetime?"

"Sure, it'll just take you longer to get where you're going."

"Where am I going?"

"Back to the Divine."

"Does God want me back?"

"If one of your fingers came loose and started dancing, would you want it back?"

"Yes, probably."

"But if your finger's dance was interesting, would you want to watch it for a while?"

"Robert, I'm asking the questions. So we're all dancing?"

"Yes."

"And God is watching us? Each of us?"

"I think so."

"And when do we want to go back to the hand?"

"When we get tired of dancing."

"And when does the dance become tiring?"

"For most of us, when we have exhausted all of the possibilities of experiencing life."

"And do we exhaust all the possibilities of life while here on earth?"

"No, not by a long shot."

"So there are other kinds of experiences beyond earth life?"

"I'm certain of it, Bob."

"So it will take a long time to experience all life possibilities?"

"Yes, a very long time."

"A moment ago, when I asked, 'When does the dance of life become tiring?' you answered, 'When we have exhausted all of life's possibilities.' What if some of us want to get back 'home' really badly, and we don't want to experience all of life's possibilities?"

"It depends on why you don't want to experience them."

"How do you mean?"

"If you're afraid of experiencing them, then you have to experience them until you learn not to be afraid of them. If you want to get back because of the intensity of your love for the Divine, I think you get to take a short cut back home."

"Whew, Robert, this is wearing me out."

"Running out of questions, Busy Bob? That's hard to believe."

"No, I'm not. What are miracles?"

"They're manifestations of laws of nature that we're currently unaware of."

"So they're really nothing special?"

"They're special so long as most of us don't understand how they work, and thus they remain relatively rare."

"What makes prayer work?"

"It opens up channels so that beneficial energy flows to us."

"How is the beneficial energy generated?"

"I think it exists all the time as an emanation from the Divine and through prayer we just tap into it."

"What about dreams? Why is it important to pay attention to our dreams?"

"Because they contain beneficial messages from our own deeper selves."

"Are dreams real?"

"I think dreams occur on many different levels. In one sense, everything our minds create is real, even if it does not manifest on the physical level."

"Okay, okay, Robert. My head is spinning from all this metaphysical stuff. Let's get practical."

"Okay, Bob, I'm feeling practical."

"Right, first question. Why should a businesswoman or businessman be interested in your experiences and your ideas?"

"Because success in business is not an end in itself, it's a milestone on the way to a larger goal of life. And if I can influence someone to use their business experience to further that larger life goal, then I'll have accomplished something."

"Robert, you've spoken of nonattachment in this book. How can a businessperson be both successful and nonattached?"

"Good question, my friend. Nonattachment doesn't suggest idleness, nor does it mean to stop trying to succeed; on the contrary, it means to try as hard as you can but not to be attached to the results."

"If I need to show a decent profit each quarter, how do I let go of the results?"

"Bob, you do your very best to meet your goals, give it your best shot, but you leave the results to a higher power. In fact, when you do that, you'll free up the energy you waste on worrying and use it to be more effective."

"All right, Robert, try this one: what's your reading on life's tragedies. Why do we have to have tragedies in our lives?"

"I believe they're wake-up calls, Busy Bob. We don't really pay attention to life until we've experienced tragedy."

"And why are you so interested in rituals of passage...for adolescents, for those becoming elders, and so on?"

"Because, Bob, different stages of life have different purposes and rituals of passage help remind us of those purposes."

"What have you learned about philanthropy?"

"Oh, Bob, I could spend a lot of time on this one. I've learned to listen to what people need and want before I assume that I know what to give them. I've learned that it's best when you get personally involved with the people you're helping rather than allowing giving to be an abstraction. I've learned that philanthropy is most effective when it goes two ways; that is, when the recipient gives something back to the giver. I've learned that a good way to expand your horizons is to stretch yourself by giving a bit more than you think you should. And, finally, I've learned that giving is an effective way to help a family learn to work together and become closer. So that's a short answer."

"Not short enough. Let's quit," Busy Bob replied.

Somehow the Robert and the Bob sides of me seemed to be in balance; about 50-50, one might say.

● ● ● ● ● ● ● ● ● ● ●

Life is all about being fully present in the moment, moment after moment. Here is my way of saying, "Be Here Now": a poem I composed as I walked along Carmel's beach, my eyes caressing the Pacific.

> The rolling rhythms of the water's waves set me to thinking about the constancy of life.
>
> It's like going to a baseball batting cage. You buy a block of time, and stand there swinging at pitch after pitch.
>
> There is no let up; the pitches just keep coming. It does no good to holler at the pitching machine for a break, a rest, or a better pitch to hit.
>
> You have a batting average. It consists of millions of swings at life's situations over hundreds of lifetimes.
>
> Your past actions and results have an effect on the present, for the pitching machine is extremely intelligent in determining how to pitch to you.
>
> The machine's goal is for you to become perfect. So it keeps throwing to your weakness and with each swing you have an occasion to improve.

And each action in turn influences the next pitch to you.

Still, even with the effect of the past, what is so immediate about life is the present, the now. For each pitch in life is perfect in its chance for right action.

Concentration on the moment is key. Forget the past, it never happened the way you remember it.

Forget the future, you can't possibly conceive of all the potential outcomes.

Focus, breathe into the moment, and blank out all externalities. There is an opportunity to hit the next pitch perfectly!

Here it comes...

AFTERWORD

Dear Grandchildren:

Do me and yourselves a favor now and then as you rush through life. Each of you ask yourself, "Am I doing anything about that 'Just Beyond' program old Grandpa Robert used to talk about? Remember, that Twelve-Step-Plus program for getting the most out of life?"

Locate yourself a comfortable chair in a quiet room and find something in these thirteen Just Beyonds that is ready to work for you, an action that is going to make you s t r e t c h.

1. *Just Beyond Authority:* Enhance the directions of your life by listening to what your dreams, intuition and feelings are trying to tell you. Write down what you're picking up and see if it settles in with a peaceful, knowing feeling. If it does, act! Don't take all your ideas from the outside, pursue some of your own heart-felt yearnings. Remember, you're the expert about yourself! You'll know you're stretching when you find yourself saying, "Other people may think I'm a little nuts, but..."

2. *Just Beyond Attachment:* Give up your fixation on things turning out the way you want them to. Continue to work just as hard as ever—perhaps even harder than you are now—for the desired result, but accept what comes with calmness and assent. Learn from your experiences and move on, letting go of any disappointments. You'll know you're stretching when you hear yourself saying, "Damn, I know I used to get angry in this situation, but..."

3. *Just Beyond Tomorrow:* What would you like to change about your life that will extend beyond tomorrow? What small step can you take today to demonstrate your commitment to realizing what you might become? Do you want to be a little more trusting or do a little more exercising or be a little more adventuresome? Whatever it is,

go far enough with your action so that you're saying, "I'm a little afraid of this kind of change, but..."

4. *Just Beyond the Normal Kind of Love:* Stretch away from conditional love by practicing with that spouse or child or special friend who sometimes acts in ways that closes down your heart. When that kind of trouble happens, tell them—and yourself—how much you unconditionally love them, before and after you bring up offending behavior. You'll know you're pushing your envelope when you choke back words of anger to make room for those first words of love that precede what would normally be a hostile discussion.

5. *Just Beyond You and Me:* Turn your special relationships into partnerships by giving the other person the benefit of the doubt, the bigger piece of the pie, or help that they didn't ask for. Soon they'll be doing the same thing for you, and you'll become partners in building a deeper and more rewarding relationship than you might have imagined possible. (If the other person responds negatively to your repeated efforts by continually taking advantage of you, you may want to terminate the relationship!) Your stretch will be confirmed when your critical voice says, "Why am I doing this? What have they done for me lately?"

6. *Just Beyond Yourself:* It's hard to grow when we see ourselves and the people just like us as the center of the universe. Allow your horizons to expand to include people with different ideas. Get yourself into situations with people whose economic, social and religious circumstances are different than yours. You may find that a poor person or someone with AIDS or a Muslim—and you're a Christian—can not only be a friend but a teacher! You'll be on track when you say to yourself, "It would be more comfortable to stay in my same old setting, but..."

7. *Just Beyond Your Front Door:* Get out into the community as a volunteer at Hospice, the hospital, the homeless shelter, anywhere! Our culture longs for a greater sense of community, and blames its loss on automobiles, moving every three years and the demise of the

extended family. But we can do something about that. Reach out, give a helping hand and receive in turn good feelings, love and a sense of belonging and contributing. Stretch away from the TV, newspapers and books and make sure you've inconvenienced yourself a bit!

8. *Just Beyond Madison Avenue:* Are we consumers or are we human beings? Lightening up our possessions and lessening our purchasing of nonessentials contributes to a sense of ease, contrary to advertising blandishments. In reality, possessions often possess us, and shopping has never yet made for lasting happiness. Give your infrequently-used stuff to someone who can really use it, and stop buying as if there were a world-wide shortage coming to your neighborhood tomorrow. Get past your thought that, "I may need this someday..." and you'll feel lighter and freer.

9. *Giving Just Beyond:* St. Francis said, "It is in giving that we receive." Try it—you'll like it! But give a little more than you're comfortable with. Not enough to make you broke for the rest of the month, but more than you previously gave. You can always cut back if you've gone too far. Or you may never discover that point because giving has become so important to you. There's nothing so powerful as discovering something that is more important than oneself. The feeling you're looking for as you write a check to your favorite charity is mild nervousness to go along with the excitement and pleasure that sharing most always brings.

10. *Just Beyond Religion:* Look for the spiritual, for those moments when you feel a deep sense of connection to nature, to others, to God as you know it. Where to look? Take a quiet walk in the woods or along the beach, share your deepest burdens and joys with a friend, sit silently in meditation and prayer. Look every place you are, as God and the world of spirit is always present in you and around you. Never suppress a tear, especially one of gratitude or compassion. Risk feeling a little foolish and childish as you go about this, as the universe is just waiting to play with you.

11. *Just Beyond The Fountain of Youth:* Forget about society's obsession with youth. You're aging, and that's great. Explore what life stages are about and see where you currently fit. Embrace your phase with passion and enthusiasm! Remember, each stage builds on what came before, so you're not losing anything when you gracefully move on. Celebrate your transitions and design exciting initiations as you sail through life like a majestic ship. You'll be doing fine when people say you're going against the grain! (Try not to note their envy.)

12. *Just Beyond Life:* Periodically reflect on death by visualizing what you would say to the people in your life if you were on your death bed. Write it down. Read about Near Death Experiences so you can become comfortable with what's likely to happen to you if you die tomorrow. Prepare your funeral instructions and your obituary. Share them with the person closest to you. Go deep enough in this process that you're saying to yourself, "This may be a little weird, but..."

13. *Just Beyond Science:* Don't limit what you believe to what you can see. Give possibilities like these a chance in your life:

- The universe is supported by an energy which is impartial.
- That energy is created from a field of love.
- Our needs are met when we make them known.
- Our needs are met when we don't make them known.
- We frequently don't understand what our real needs are.
- Life is a classroom and our personal lessons are influenced by our actions in this lifetime.
- Life is a classroom and our personal lessons are influenced by our actions in this, and prior, lifetimes.
- Life is a classroom and our actions in this lifetime will influence our personal lessons in our future lifetimes.
- Our consciousness is independent of our physical bodies.
- Our consciousness has a permanent existence.
- We experience reality on several simultaneous levels, but we are generally aware of only our ordinary reality.

And so on...
You get the picture. Go deep. Go far. Go Beyond!

Here's how to order additional copies of 50-50 at 50 by Robert E. Graham

Credit card telephone orders (toll free 24-hour service):
888-361-4667
Credit card fax orders (24 hours): 408-625-9447
Postal orders, please send check or credit card information to:

Pacific Rim Publishers
P.O. Box 1776
Carmel, CA 93921

$27.00 per copy + $4.00 shipping for 1st copy; $3.00 shipping and handling for each additional copy to same address. Books are shipped by Priority mail.
California orders: Please add 7.25% sales tax per book ($2.00) for all orders shipped to California addresses.

Credit card No. _____Exp. date _____

Your Signature _____

Your Name (please print) _____

Address to send book(s) _____

_____

No. of copies ordered _____

If check, amount enclosed _____

Please make checks payable to: Pacific Rim Publishers.

* BUY FOUR AND GET ONE FREE! *

For every fourth book ordered, the fifth is free.